Donna –

"You are an extraordinary person."

Sinha.
June 16, 1990

Other books by Dr. Shall Sinha

1. **Congratulations! You Have Problems.**
An entire book on the subject of our attitude to problems, why we see things the way we see them and what we can do to improve our attitude, perception and belief.
Soft cover. $14.95.

2. **The Management Team Anthology.**
An anthology of a wide variety of management topics such as People Management, Time Management, Communication and Relationships; written together with a number of authors, each specialized in his or her own field.
Hard cover. $19.95.

What others are saying about this book:

"I have enjoyed Dr. Sinha's newspaper columns for a number of years but it was only after reading this collection that I began to fully appreciate the tremendous depth and scope of his work. Full of wit, wisdom and common sense, these essays have something for everyone. Not only do they help us to make sense of our often confusing world and the people in it, they help us to understand ourselves. Anyone who reads this book will become a better person for the effort."

- Carl Carlson
Principal, Salisbury Composite High School.

"I found this book to be a treasure of valuable ideas and opinions on many aspects of our daily lives. As a Toastmaster I find it to be extremely valuable. If I had found this book ten years ago, I could have saved hundreds of hours preparing my own speeches."

- Majeed Mustapha
1988-89 District Governor,
District 42, Toastmasters International

"As one reads through the pages of this book, the passages definitely impact upon the way in which one thinks. In fact, I found that my attitude towards personalities and situations changed positively as I continued to read. I wish that this book had been available to me much earlier in my life."

- Christopher Harrison, Ph.D.
Dean, Continuing Education,
Alberta Vocational Centre

"This book is an important step toward recognizing that our present age is characterized by individuals striving to demonstrate their cleverness and efficiency rather than seeking for genuine wisdom, and perfecting goodness in their lives. The message is potentially therapeutic to those who would digest it. From these essays, everyone can truly learn how to enrich his own life as well as of those around him."

- Dr. David Skelton,
Specialist in Geriatric Medicine

"This is an inspirational text which should be placed on one's bedside table for regular reference. The bumps and pot-holes which we all experience in everyday living are easily

smoothed by Shall's direct writing style and motivational messages. This book should be considered as a required reading by those who aspire to greater personal well-being and success."

- F. Scott Montgomery, B. Comm., C.A.

"The essays are thought provoking. As I read them I started to reconsider my own approach to certain situations. I found the essays on leadership and team building to be of particular interest. I appreciated the synopsis, and the reference to other similar essays, at the beginning of each essay.

- Herb Martin,
Director of Personnel

"A source of insight into handling the events that happen to everyone of us in our daily lives."

-Ken G. Haywood,
President, Kentwood Ford Ltd.

"The essays are informative and very well presented. They are timely, interesting and easy to read. Everyone will find them to be valuable."

- Andy Watson, C.L.U., Ch. F. C.

"The essays are interesting and motivational. They are easy to read and are meaningful to both teens and adults."

-Ken Shearer,
Vice President and North Alberta Regional Manager,
Royal LePage

"I found the essays to be very valuable, well written, illustrated in an interesting way and altogether very helpful."

- Dr. Helen Hays,
Director Palliative Care Services

"An excellent series of essays. They show definite insight and offer inspired solutions. Definitely an asset to those who want to be more than ordinary."

-Ron Buffel,
Western District Manager, Johnson Controls Ltd.

From

Ordinary

To

Extraordinary

100
Selected Essays

b y

Dr. Shall Sinha

Published by SKS Publishing
7 Medhurst Crescent, Sherwood Park, Alberta, Canada T8A 3T5.
Tel. (403)- 467 8178

Cover design: Orest Andre

_____

Canadian Cataloguing in Publication Data

Sinha, Dr. Shall, 1942-
    "From Ordinary To Extraordinary"
    - 100 Selected Essays

Includes Index.
ISBN 0-9694381-0-9
158.1 SIN
Soft cover. 464 pages. $14.95.

1. Personal Development.   2. Goals   3. Leadership
4. Team Work   5. Communication.   6. Motivation.
7. Inspiration.

Printed in the United States of America

Acknowledgement

Many people have helped me in the publication of this book. I want to acknowledge, in particular, the following without whose help this book could not have been completed.

Brian   Alleyne

Larry   Anderson

Orest   Andre

Louise   Ball

Ron   Buffel

Carl   Carlson

Lorne   Clark

Max   Coderre

Al   Dodd

Hon.   Peter   Elzinga

Dr.   Helen   Hays

Ken   Haywood

Dr.   Christopher   Harrison

Ken   Jackson

Al   Jenkins

Ed   Ledieu

Majeed   Mustapha

Scott   Montgomery

Dr.   Harb   Sandhar

Ken   Shearer

Dr.   David   Skelton

Elmer   Stewart

Andy   Watson

Sherwood   Park   News

To

Shalini

Santwana and

Pramila

who have supported me throughout the writing of this book.

Table Of Contents

xii

Foreword

I have been reading Shall Sinha's writings for a long time. About two weeks ago, when Shall asked me to write a foreword for his book, I considered that to be a privilege and an honour.

Shall has a unique talent of putting any subject in a simple language embellished by illustrative examples, powerful metaphors and apt quotations.

I find this book to be very inspiring. It covers a wide variety of thought provoking subjects and develops the awareness that every one has many latent options for a richer living.

Each essay analyses some common problem and provides some recommended solution. It provides a different perspective for seeing the same problem from a different angle. It goads us to think and to act better, and thereby to enhance the quality of our life. In the very least every essay makes us realize that our particular problem is really not as huge as we have been believing it to be.

The format of the book is particularly appealing. Each essay can be read leisurely within ten minutes and one need not read them sequentially. One can start anywhere in the book and using the cross reference system, end up reading every essay.

The ideas presented in each essay are uplifting as well as a good topic of discussion among friends, colleagues or family members.

The book is replete with hundreds of examples of how some ordinary, or even below ordinary persons, such as

Abraham Lincoln, Thomas Edison, Glen Cunningham, Terry Fox and Mahatma Gandhi, struggled with their seemingly unconquerable hurdles and ended up reaching extraordinary status in their own field. There is no doubt in my mind that every one of us possesses the potential of accomplishing some extraordinary feat. As such, I find the title, "From Ordinary to Extraordinary" to be very appropriate.

I have found this book to be very beneficial for me and believe that every reader will benefit as well.

I extend my sincerest congratulations to Shall for publishing this stimulating book.

Peter Elzinga

Minister of Economic Development and Trade
Government of Alberta

Introduction

During the past five years, Dr. Sinha has published well over one hundred essays on Problem Solving, Leadership, Team Work, Communication, motivation and inspiration. Almost all his essays have received rave reviews. Many readers have requested copies of the essays that they did not have access to. This compilation is being produced mainly to satisfy such requests. It contains a revised edition of one hundred of his selected essays up to November, 1989, presented in the same chronological order as they had appeared earlier.

Although these essays were originally written for some selected readership, the message is applicable to everyone.

Every essay addresses and analyzes a common problem, and provides some practical tips for its solution. The ideas are supported by concrete, relevant examples. Every essay provides a good food for thought. As you read these essays, you will feel inspired and realize that your own problem or situation is but a trifle compared to that of many others.

Each essay includes a brief introduction to the content and lists other essays of similar nature. It is not necessary to read the collection from cover to cover. You can select and read only those essays that you find pertinent to your current situation. We suggest that you read two essays every week and allow time for the material to be digested.

An Index, for easy access or for cross reference, listing important names, events or other items of interest, is included at the end of the compilation.

The central philosophy of these essays is that no one is born as an extraordinary person and that every one, who reaches the status of "extraordinary", earns it in some way or the other. These essays search the récipe, the ingredients or the path that is required for the attainment of an extraordinary personality.

We trust that you will enjoy reading these essays and benefit from the numerous practical tips spread throughout the selection.

The Publisher

1

"Congratulations!
You Have Problems."

Problems have received a very negative connotation in our society. However, no life can survive without problems. If handled appropriately, every problem strengthens us. Every invention, and growth of our civilization, has its root in some problem. Your current problems are your current opportunities for unleashing your latent strengths.

Instead of letting your problems get you down, be thankful for them because they sustain your very life.

This essay shows you how you can change your current perception of the problems, almost instantly.

Read also essay numbers 67, 79 and 93.

1

D o you have problems? Would you like to get rid of them permanently? What would happen if you had a totally problem-free life?

Problems are the essence of our living. Life is virtually impossible in the absence of problems. The politician looks for an issue to champion. An engineer looks for a place where a bridge is required. The business executive looks for opportunities in his organization where he can apply his knowledge and skill. Each of these is an example where 'a problem' exists and needs to be solved.

Give a new puzzle to any child and he will enjoy the challenge of putting the pieces together. He may assemble the same puzzle two or three times, but after that it becomes simply boring. He doesn't find any more challenge in it. There is no 'problem' for him to solve. If the puzzle is too difficult for him, he may become frustrated. But he will still choose a 'too difficult' problem over a 'no problem'.

We maintain this characteristic throughout life. Every day, every hour, every minute, we keep looking for some new problem to solve. If we believe that we have the capability to solve the puzzle, we enjoy working at it. If we believed that it was beyond our capability, we would simply give it up and won't even try.

Unfortunately, the word 'problem' carries a very negative connotation in our society. The moment we say that John is facing a very difficult problem, everyone concludes that John is in deep waters. We forget that John's importance remains dormant till the instance that we face a problem that only John can handle.

Mahatma Gandhi became famous in South Africa for his fight against 'colour discrimination'. Had there been no colour discrimination when he arrived in South Africa, would the world have discovered his potential? Perhaps not.

One law of nature says that learning requires a stimulus. Another law says that strength can be developed only in the presence of resistance - the greater the resistance, the more strength can be developed. It is common knowledge that to build one's muscles, one needs to exercise those muscles. Trees that face the strongest wind yield the toughest wood which is used to build the most expensive furniture. Problems provide us with both 'stimulus' and 'resistance'. Thus they create an environment for the growth of our mental power.

Many years ago, a man faced a special problem. His wife could not hear him when he spoke to her. So he started looking for a hearing device for her and ended up inventing a special device that is called a 'telephone'. That man was Alexander Graham Bell.

Another man had a terrible accident. He was trying to start his car with a crank handle, a device which is now obsolete. The engine started all right, but he did not move fast enough. The result? He broke an arm. Undeterred by this mishap, he thought, there must be a better way of starting a car. Resolved to solve this problem, he invented the automatic starter which is a very common item today. His name was Charles Kettering.

A third man cut himself severely while shaving. He forthwith invented the safety razor. His name was Gillette.

In the South Pacific there is an eighteen hundred mile long reef known as the Great Barrier Reef., and there are coral polyps on both sides of the reef. Those on the quiet side of the reef are dull, pale and live for only a few days. But those on the side of the open sea are vibrant, green, and live for considerably longer periods. The explanation is simple. The polyps exposed to the open sea and the strong currents have something to fight for. They are fighting to live, and grow strong from the constant battle they must lodge with the sea.

A problem-free life is the same as a stress-free life. The only person who is really stress-free is the one who is lying six feet under ground.

The Chinese character for the word 'crisis' is a combination of the characters for the words 'danger' and 'opportunity'. According to the Chinese, every crisis contains some elements of both danger and opportunity. If we look for danger then that's what we see. But if we look at each crisis in a different light, we can find opportunity in every one.

Words have a very powerful influence on our actions and our capabilities. As pressure on the gas pedal can increase the speed of the car, and pressure on the brake pedal can reduce it, so the use of positive words lift our spirit, and that of negative words, put it down. Every time that you replace one negative word by some positive word, you experience a definite lift in your life.

'Problem' is a negative word. 'Opportunity' is the corresponding positive word. The word 'Situation' may be considered to lie mid way, or almost neutral, between the two extremes.

Next time you think you have a problem, try thinking of it not as a problem but as a situation. This will be similar to lifting your foot off both the gas and the brake pedals, or of putting your drive in neutral. You may need to do this to gain control over your car. Once in control, you can press the gas. Remember, to go somewhere, you must first lift your foot off the brake pedal. You will notice a definite improvement   in your capacity to look for a solution to your situation.

We are creatures of habit and therefore perform most of our activities unconsciously. To bring any change, we must practice the new activity consciously. In other words, we must exercise it consciously for a while.

After you have gained some experience in this exercise, try considering each 'problem' as an 'opportunity'. You may laugh at this suggestion but you will be amazed to note that every problem, or every hurdle, may easily be converted into a stepping stone. Napolean Hill used to say, "Every adversity carries in itself seeds of equal or better opportunity." The challenge lies in discovering these seeds.

Every business problem should be a welcome sign because if there were no problems in your particular business then the number of competitors would grow because   everyone would start a business in your line. 'Problems' work as screens that restrict the number of business rivals. You should think of your problems as 'opportunities' for you to stay in business.

When you face a problem (or a challenge) there are three things that you can do. You can bewail your misfortune; you can accept the problem as a challenge and look for ways to overcome it; or you can think of it as an opportunity to exercise your mental acumen and prove your worth.

What you do is entirely up to you. But once you get into the habit of accepting problems as real opportunities, you will want to grab not only your problems but also those of your friends, neighbours and everybody else. Then when someone comes to you with his problem, your immediate reply will be, "Congratulations! You have problems."

> "The man who has no more problems to solve, is out of the game."
>
> - Elbert Hubbard

2

Watch Out

For Those Golden Trinkets

Life is like an exhibition where we find ourselves surrounded by too many attractions. As a result, often we find it difficult to concentrate on one task sufficiently long to see a significant result. Failing to see the result we conclude that we lacked the necessary skill.

This essay draws our attention to the presence of the numerous attractions, or the golden trinkets, around us and suggests some techniques of guarding ourselves against their influence. This can enable us to pursue our important projects to their successful completion, and thereby, build our confidence and self esteem.

Read also essay numbers 43 and 87.

During my childhood I read a story that had a profound effect on me. Every time that I think of it, I seem to discover an even deeper meaning.

Once there was a very beautiful and intelligent princess. She was very fond of running and in fact was known to be the fastest runner in the country. No one could even come close to beating her in any race.

When she turned sixteen, her father started looking for a suitable mate for her. (In those days, in Indian culture, it used to be the parent's responsibility to find suitable mates for their children.) She was the only child and the king loved her more than anything. After a great deal of thought , he came up with an idea. He declared that whoever could outrun her in a race could marry her and become heir to the kingdom.

Many ambitious boys tried but they were no match at all. Finally a very clever boy came to try his luck. First he invested some time researching her likes and dislikes. He found out that she loved dolls and jewellery. So he bought a bag full of golden trinkets for the race. As soon as the race started, he threw one of the golden trinkets in her direction. She immediately noticed the glitter and could not resist her temptation. She slowed down and picked it up. She rejoined the race and soon took the lead again. The boy kept on throwing those golden trinkets, one by one, in her direction and she kept picking them up. Finally she lost the race.

This story relates to many of our everyday experiences. Life is a race. We set some goals for ourselves. But life keeps throwing golden trinkets (or temptations) in our path and very soon we get off track. The result is that we do not reach our goal, experience failure, and conclude that we did not have the necessary strength. Next time, we try another goal and experience another failure. We do not realize that the main cause of the failure was not the lack of strength but the temptations of some golden trinkets.

The other day I bought a very interesting book. I decided to finish reading it that evening. I had hardly read ten pages when my neighbour called me. He had rented an excellent movie. I could join him and see the movie for free. I was tempted but immediately recognized it as one of my life's golden trinkets. I declined the offer and finished reading the book.

Have you not been distracted by some golden trinkets? How about the television? Do you remember the time when you decided to watch just one program and got hooked for the entire evening? On many occasions I have resolved to watch just the first fifteen minutes of a hockey game - to relax after supper - but found myself listening to every commentary for the next three hours. The T.V networks hire experts who keep creating "ever-charming" and "ever-glittering" trinkets for the viewers.

Let's see how we can guard ourselves against those golden trinkets. The first step, of course, is to recognize them. Remember that a problem recognized is a problem partly solved, because when you become aware of a problem, you start taking some action to solve it. The trouble is that in most cases we do not even suspect that we have a problem.

One way of guarding ourselves against these 'golden trinkets' is to keep our eyes focused on our main goal. Let me share with you another interesting story from Indian mythology.

A certain prince had gambled all his possessions. He was required to perform an almost impossible task - to shoot at the eye of a fish, hanging from the ceiling. And he had to shoot it by seeing its reflection in a bowl of water. When he was about to release his arrow, his guru asked, "What do you see?" "I see the fish", replied the prince. "Oh! no. Your target is not the fish but its eye. Focus your attention on the fish eye and when you see nothing but the fish eye, only then should you release the arrow". It took the prince a while to focus only on the fish eye.

But when he did, he released the arrow and shot the fish right in its eye.

Unless you focus your attention on your goal and nothing but your goal, you are likely to be distracted by extraneous objects or activities.

Instead of seeing only the fish eye (our main goal), we generally see the entire fish, and sometimes a great deal of the ceiling. In most cases we miss the fish eye, hit a certain portion of the ceiling, and wonder why!

It is a known fact that our mind is ever fleeting, moving constantly from one subject to another. In order to focus it on one subject (or one object), we need to keep bringing it back to the main goal. A technique that has been found useful in this regard is to keep reminding ourselves of the benefits that we will receive when we reach our goal.

As a child, I enjoyed doing a certain experiment. I would collect some pieces of paper and use a lens to focus the sunlight on them. In less than thirty seconds the pieces would catch fire. From this simple experiment I learned that although ordinary sunlight does not burn a piece of paper, when a magnifying lens is used to focus it and to keep it focussed for a length of time, it acquires the power to burn almost anything. The same is true with our mind. If we can focus it and hold it focussed on one task (or challenge), for a certain duration of time, we will succeed in completing the task or challenge. Sometimes we lack the required patience. We want too many things, all at the same time. It's like the farmer who took a bunch of seeds and planted them at the same time and at the same location, hoping that he would cultivate everything simultaneously. He was really shocked when he discovered that only weeds grew in that location.

You can literally fulfil any desire if you hold on to one desire at a time. Keep your mind focussed on one desire until it is realized. Only then should you concentrate on your next desire. Think of your particular desire as the eye of the fish. Refuse to see the entire fish. See just its eye. And recognize and watch out for the golden trinkets that nature will throw in your path to test your ability to concentrate on one desire at a time. The moment life is convinced of your concentration, it will grant the fulfilment of your desire.

"Strength does not come from physical capacities. It comes from an indomitable will."
                                            - Mahatma Gandhi

3

A Simple Formula for

Growth

Using "GROWTH" as an acronym, this essay provides a simple six element formula for growth. The elements are: Guidance, Relaxation, Obsession, Writing Thankfulness and Humour.

This essay points out that every one of these elements were present in Mahatma Gandhi's personality, and they were definite contributors in transforming him from an ordinary to an extraordinary man.

Any person can cultivate these skills, and thereby become a super achiever.

Read also essay numbers 45, 85 and 95.

M ohandas K. Gandhi was born as the last child of an ordinary family. During his childhood he did not display any special talent except honesty and devotion to his parents. With borrowed money, he went to England to study law. During his three years stay he showed no sign of greatness. In fact he proved himself to be a 'clown' on numerous occasions. He returned to India as a qualified barrister but had some handicaps. When it came to pleading the only case he had received in eighteen months, he was dumbfounded. Consequently, he surrendered the case to another lawyer. By chance, he received an offer to go to South Africa to do some clerical work for a lawyer and to act as an interpreter between the lawyer and his Indian clients.

This proved to be a turning point in his life. Within a month 'the dumbfounded boy' changed into a great public speaker and the leader of thousands of people - not only of the illiterate Indians but also of many educated Europeans. He became so valuable that his one year assignment was extended to twenty-one years. He would never have left South Africa if the Indian leaders had not forced him to return to India. During those twenty-one years in South Africa he transformed himself from 'Gandhi who?' to 'Gandhi, the great soul'. After returning to India he kept growing. Everyone called him 'Bapu' which means 'Dear father'. He united the more than three hundred million people of India, who spoke six hundred different dialects, and liberated them from six hundred years of foreign rule.

How did Gandhi grow so much in such a short time?

After a great deal of study of Gandhi's work, I find some key characteristics that helped him in this growth. Interestingly enough, these characteristics can be identified with each letter of the word **GROWTH**

The first letter 'G' stands for **Guidance.**

Gandhi always looked for new and better sources of receiving guidance. He listened to people. He observed nature for ideas. He read books. During his first year in South Africa he read over 100 books on religion alone. He believed that God gave us two ears and one mouth so that we would listen twice as much as we talk. Poor listening is the main cause of most of our communication problems. To develop his listening skills he observed twenty-four hours of silence each week. When he returned to India, in 1915, he undertook a one year tour of the country, listening to the people, without making any comment. In 1935, when he was the most important political figure in India, he undertook one year of total silence on political matters.

According to him, God is within every one of us and He talks to us whenever we are willing to listen to Him. If you relax your body, close your eyes and try not to worry about any problem, you will experience an inner dialogue. This is your inner voice. It will provide you the best guidance. Gandhi received most of his guidance from his inner voice.

To receive guidance for your business, build your listening skill. Listen to your customers, your suppliers, your employees. But most of all, listen to your inner voice, and your problems will be taken care of.

The second letter 'R' stands for **Relaxation.**

To strengthen a muscle we need to exercise it. But the creative mind works in exactly the opposite way. The more you force it, the less efficient it becomes. And the more you allow it to relax, the more ideas it generates for you. All important inventions were made by minds that were totally relaxed.

Gandhi used to spin two hundred yards of thread every day. This helped him to relax his mind. He received most of his ideas while spinning. He also took time to work in the garden, to play with children, to care for animals and to try experiments that would keep his mind off his main problem. Whenever you face a serious problem, do the best that you can do and then put it aside and do something completely different. There is a good chance that you will receive the right idea for solving your particular problem.

The third letter 'O' stands for **Obsession**.

The key to success is obsession. You must be totally obsessed with your project. You must like it so much that every single thinking minute, you think of no other project but this one. There is a law of nature: "Whatever you pay attention to, grows." The corollary is that whatever you neglect (or ignore), dies. You have heard the saying that "Many have eyes but they don't see". The fact is that we see only those things that are somehow related to the thoughts we carry in our mind at that particular time. That is why we miss many opportunities. The only way you will notice all opportunities related to your project is if you keep the thoughts of that project in your mind at all times.

Gandhi was obsessed with 'improving the living conditions of fellow human beings'. More than half of his life, he believed that the British Empire was good for everyone. So he did not think of independence. But when he realized that the living conditions of the Indians could not improve under the British rule, then he advocated independence for India. But independence or not, he never got distracted from his main obsession, 'improved living conditions for everyone'.

Nature tests our steadfastness to one one goal by luring us with various distractions. The moment she is convinced of our 'sole-interest', she grants us that goal. For a fruitful completion of your project, be obsessed with that project till its completion. Let nothing distract you.

The fourth letter 'W' stands for **Writing**.

Since Gandhi's family had borrowed money for his studies abroad, he felt obliged to keep account of every penny that he spent. He reviewed his records weekly and discovered some expenses that he could have avoided. He extended this habit to keeping track of his time. He wrote down the foolish things that he did. Analysis of these records helped him to avoid making the same mistake again. He found this habit to be so valuable that he maintained it throughout his life.

There is a simple formula for success: "Find out what works for you and do more of it. Find out what doesn't work for you and avoid doing it the second time." If you make one less mistake every day, you are bound to be on your way to success. Writing a diary helps you recognize your strengths and weakness.

Writing promotes thinking. You do not write anything without indulging in some thinking. According to Dr. Kenneth McFarland, only two per cent of the people really think. By cultivating the habit of writing a diary you can soon join the top two per cent of most successful people. Think of that!

Writing keeps us on track. When Columbus left Europe in search of land, he maintained a diary. After writing his daily experiences he always wrote, "Today we sailed west because that was our destination." Some historians claim that Columbus might not have discovered North America if he had not maintained his habit of writing this statement day after day.

The fifth letter 'T' stands for **Thankfulness**.

We often become frustrated because events do not work out as per our plan. But we should remember that nature wants us to grow all the time. Occasionally it trips us to teach a lesson. Therefore, whenever you feel tripped ask yourself, "What lesson am I supposed to learn from this?" Unless you look for the lesson, you will not see it. Remember, nature will keep tripping you until you do learn the intended lesson.

Every situation has positive and negative aspects. If we curse the situation, we see only its negative aspect. But if we approach it with a feeling of thankfulness, we start observing its positive aspect. Napolean Hill said, "Every adversity carries in itself seeds of equal or better opportunity." We cannot recognize this seed unless we develop the habit of being thankful for every situation.

Gandhi spent seven years of his life in jail but never cursed any imprisonment. On the contrary, he welcomed it. Once he remarked, "Now I will catch up with my sleep." During another imprisonment he wrote his biography. He used his prison time for reading and planning. The days of isolation provided him with tremendous opportunity to listen to his inner voice.

The last letter **'H'** stands for a sense of **Humour.**

Gandhi once said, "If I had not maintained my sense of humour, I would have gone insane a long time ago." No matter how well you plan, some things will definitely go wrong. Being serious in every situation may make the matter worse. It pays to take things lightly. Learn to laugh at yourself and your situation. This is actually an extension of 'being thankful'. When you laugh, everyone shares your laughter. But when you cry, everyone deserts you. Therefore learn to develop a sense of humour.

Briefly, this is Gandhi's formula for growth. Listen to your inner voice for guidance. Learn to relax. Become obsessed with your main goal. Develop the habit of writing a daily diary. Be thankful for every situation. And develop a sense of humour. By following this simple, six point formula, you can ensure personal and business growth.

"Lord, grant me that I may always desire more than I can accomplish."
- Buonarroti Michelangelo

4

Thinking

Is Our Highest Function

Thinking is our highest function. Every other function can be delegated to machines or to other animals, but thinking remains to be our sole responsibility.

Unfortunately, we seem to have lost this skill, mostly because of the lack of use. This essay draws our attention to the importance of thinking and provides several simple exercises for reviving or improving this skill.

Read also essay numbers 45 and 91.

Some years ago, Dr. Kenneth MacFarland conducted a study and concluded that only two per cent of the people really think. Another three per cent think that they think. And the remaining ninety-five per cent would rather die than think.

Isn't it amazing that nearly ninety-eight per cent of us do not really think? If there is one faculty in which human beings outperform all other living beings, it is their supreme ability to think. It is said that God created man in His own image. God gave us full freedom in the area of creating, planning, and thinking. You have heard that an average person uses less than five per cent of his or her potential. The main cause for this, in my opinion, is the fact that we do not take time to think.

A common characteristic of all great men and women - philosophers, inventors, scholars etc. - is that they are all great thinkers. There is a direct correlation between your ability to think and your degree of success, no matter what your endeavour.

If thinking is that important, why is it that nearly ninety-eight per cent of us avoid it? The answer is simple. It takes effort to think.

Although we know that physical exercise is good for our health, most of us postpone it until 'tomorrow'. Why? Because it takes effort. It is much easier to relax on the sofa, drink a coke, munch some snacks and watch television.

It's the same story with our thinking. It's much easier 'not-to-think' or 'to postpone thinking until tomorrow'.

When you listen to the radio, you have to exercise some imagination. But the television puts everything on a silver platter. It deprives you of the opportunity to exercise your imagination.

There is a universal law that says, "If you do not use a skill, you lose it." Those of you who have ever worn a cast will testify that the muscles under the cast felt very weak when the cast was removed and that it took several weeks of regular exercise to bring full strength back to those muscles. If this is the result of 'lack of use for six weeks', what do you think will happen if you did not use those muscles for several months or even several years?

Like all other skills, you can cultivate your thinking skill if you make some regular effort.

If you have never jogged in your life, would you have any knowledge of the pleasures of jogging? Most likely not. You need to experience it in order to really feel the pleasure (or the pain).   Would you be able to jog a mile the very first day? Perhaps not. But experts claim that anyone can train himself or herself for a marathon race, if one follows a planned six-month program.

As you need physical push-ups to strengthen your physical muscles, you need mental push-ups to strengthen your mental muscles. No matter what state your mental muscles are in, you can prepare them for a mental marathon race in six months if you pledge to exercise them regularly by following a definite plan.

You may or may not realize that you have two sets of eyes - physical and mental. With your physical eyes you see the world that exists around you. With your mental eyes you imagine a world that does not exist immediately around you. When you sleep, both the physical and the mental eyes are put 'out of use'. During your waking hours you use one or the other. At any given moment you may use both of them partially. But the use of the mental eyes is greatly enhanced when you keep the physical eyes closed. Remember that everything that has happened to you has come about because you first saw it happening, with your mental eyes.

There are several exercises to stimulate your mental eyes. Here are a few.

1. Sit comfortably in a chair. Relax for a few seconds. Look at the objects around you. Now close your eyes. With your eyes closed, try to recall as many objects from the room as you can. You will be surprised how many objects you will fail to recall. Continue this exercise as often as you can. As you recall an

object, try to recall its colour, shape, texture, size etc.. The key is to recall the object by its picture and not by its name. Try to recreate the picture of the object, in your mind, in as much detail as possible.

2. Close your eyes and hold an object in your hand. Try to feel the object by moving it from one hand to another. Try to describe the object. The more you try, the more you will stretch the muscles of your mind.

3. Borrow a drama record from the public library. Sit comfortably, and with your eyes closed, listen to the sound very attentively. As you listen, try to create the mental picture of the drama. Imagine the gesture, the costume, the facial expressions, body movements, the setting etc. Don't worry if your imagination runs wild. The purpose of mental push-ups is to stretch the muscles of your mind. You can also do this exercise while listening to a radio drama or a story narrated on the radio. CBC has some good programs.

4. Try watching a television program with your eyes closed. It may sound silly, but it is very effective for exercising the mind. You may not be able to resist the temptation to look at the screen. As a start you may keep your eyes alternately open and closed, for some fixed duration (say a minute).

It is my personal experience that writing fosters thinking. You cannot write anything without thinking. The more you write, the more you are bound to think. Like any habit, you can cultivate the habit of writing by consciously forcing yourself to write every day for at least a month. It doesn't matter if you write only two lines but do write every day. I take notes whenever I am reading something. I find that I have a better retention of the material, even if I do not read my notes even once. As a matter of fact, I do not read anything, not even a newspaper, without a pen in my hand. Writing activates the muscles of my mind. I start thinking.

If you are the average person, you will not find time for these exercises. You may find yourself already so busy that you may not have time for any new activity. At the same time, it is equally true that you always find time for something that you really like to do.

Psychologists say that the only way that one human being can properly attempt to influence another is by encouraging him to think for himself.

With some effort you can cultivate the forgotten skill of thinking, and place yourself among the top two per cent of the most successful persons in the world, or you may stay with the vast majority who would rather die than think. The choice is entirely yours!

"If I have done the public any service,
it is due to patient thought."
                                    - Sir Issac Newton

5

Only You Can Decide Your

Life's Purpose

Are you working towards some specific life goals, or are you just trying to stay busy? Have you thought of some overall purpose of your life? This may be a tough question, but it needs to be answered, and only you can answer it for your life.

Working without a clear purpose may be compared to the non-stop march of a number of processionary caterpillars that starved to death, although food had been available to them within a distance of three inches.

This essay draws our attention to the importance of life goals, and provides a number of ways of selecting them.

Read also essay numbers 10 and 13.

S ometime ago, my wife and I were having a lively discussion. According to her I was not devoting adequate time to my family. I, on the other hand, maintained that I was doing everything in the best interest of the family. No matter how long we talked, we could not see each other's point of view. Since we were getting late for our respective appointments, we cut the discussion short and agreed to continue it in the evening.

Throughout that day I kept thinking about the subject. Perhaps I was looking for some strong arguments to support my case and get ready for the show down.

Suddenly a question flashed into my mind, and it kept haunting me for hours. "If I die tonight, what would my family and friends remember me for?" Finally, I sat down to think of the answer to that question. I made a list of some of my contributions and accomplishments, including some souvenirs (such as a book, the papers published in magazines, tapings of television appearances etc.). I felt that those who truly loved me would remember me through these.

I found this exercise to be a great revelation of my purpose in life. I then asked myself another question, "What would my family and friends have remembered me for, had I died a year ago?" I listed as many of my contributions as possible. I compared the two lists to see my growth in the past year. Without any doubt, I saw that I had accomplished more, and had shared more time with them than I had done before.

By this time, I felt so excited that I decided to ask myself one more question, "What would my family and friends remember me for, should I die exactly one year from today?" In answering this question I listed the projects that I planned to complete during the next year. When I compared this list with the other two lists, I felt that my family would be very proud of me should I live for just one more year and work on those projects.

How about you? What would your family and friends remember you for, should you die tonight? This may not be a friendly question, but the answer will help you clarify your purpose in life.

Have a Clear Purpose

Every single person believes that he or she is working to his or her full capacity. But then why is it that very few of us make a significant contribution to our society? The answer is simple. Only those who work with a definite purpose in their mind, accomplish anything significant. Let me illustrate my point.

Some psychologists conducted an experiment with Processionary Caterpillars, a special variety of caterpillars that are characterised by the fact that whenever they move, they touch each other's head or tail; thus they form a line and appear to be marching in a procession, hence the name Processionary. The psychologists put enough of these caterpillars on the rim of a flower pot to form an endless chain. They put some pine needles, the ideal food for these caterpillars, in the centre of the flower pot and let them march. The caterpillars marched round and round on that rim without breaking the chain. They marched non-stop, day and night, for several days. After about seven or eight days they all died of exhaustion and starvation. They had walked for several miles and yet they had found no food, although food had been available to them at all times at a distance of only three inches. This is a classic example of working to your fullest capacity but achieving nothing. Unless you have a clear purpose in mind, you will achieve little.

The Last Day of Your Life

You have heard the saying, "Today is the first day of the rest of my life". This is a good philosophy. It advises us that we should not dwell on yesterday's mistakes, We should forget them completely and concentrate on building a new life, starting today. I totally agree with this philosophy. But may I suggest something different? May I ask you to imagine that today could be the last day of your life? If you were given only twenty-four more hours to live, what would you like to accomplish in those precious hours? Please do not misunderstand me. I hope that you live forever. But asking this question will bring new awareness to your life. It may awaken you from your slumber. It may stop you from going round and round like the processionary caterpillars.

It is tragic that most people do not know where they are going. No, they are not lazy. They are working as hard as they can. But they have nothing to show for their work at the end of the day. In some respects they stop growing around the age of twenty and live in a mummified state for the rest of their lives.

Having a Purpose Brings a New Life

The moment you have a clear purpose, you experience a new life. It is a known fact that most people live to see their next anniversary, birthday, Christmas day or some special occasion. They look forward to enjoying that special day. By some miraculous means they acquire the strength to live until that day. Mahatma Gandhi lived just long enough to see an independent India! Let me tell you a true story.

During World War I, a certain town was sieged by its enemies. Some residents of the town decided to escape. In their group they had an old man, some ladies and their children. After some discussion, they agreed to take every one with them. The men agreed to carry the children by turns. After two days of exhaustive walking, the old man collapsed. When he regained his consciousness, he looked at the others and told them that he was unable to go any farther and he requested them to leave him behind. Seeing no alternative, everyone proceeded without the old man. At this instant, one lady grabbed her child, ran to the dying old man, put the child in his lap and said, "Get up! Now it's your turn to carry my child". She left the child there and walked away. They had scarcely gone another hundred yards when they noticed the old man following them. He was carrying not only his own load, but also that of the child. He experienced a new life, because now he had a purpose - he was living to save the life of the child.

Keep Checking Where You Are Going

Whatever your business, take time to review your past year. Ask yourself, "Should I die tonight, what will my customers remember me for? What special service did I provide? How did I improve the living conditions of mankind? What did I mean to my family?" These are tough questions and only you can answer them. Believe me, they will increase your awareness of your world.

"Life is real! Life is earnest!
And death is not its goal.
Dust thou art, to dust returneth,
Was not spoken of the soul."
                    - Henry W. Longfellow

6

"People":

The Most Important Resource

Do you feel limited by your resources? What do you think to be your most important resource?

This essay points out that our people - our employees, customers, suppliers, etc. - are our most important resource.

Mahatma Gandhi considered people and time to be the only important resource. By focusing on the proper utilization of these two resources, he was able to command all other necessary resources.

This essay describes nine techniques that Gandhi used to develop his most important resource - people.

Read also essay numbers 30, 37 and 48.

M ahatma Gandhi never held any important official position. He never directly handled or controlled any resource except the human resource. He was mostly the unelected leader of the masses, the uncrowned king of the nation. Anyone who ever met him became his lifetime disciple. What was his secret? How did he charm everyone?

He was a natural inspirer. He always tried to exalt everyone. Thousands of people experienced a significant development of their personalities as a result of just one interview with him. In fact, Gandhi is believed to have touched more human lives than any other leader in the past several centuries.

How did he cultivate this extraordinary power?

He generally mesmerized people. Dr. Rajendra Prasad, the first President of India once said, "Being associated with the Mahatma took my mind off my asthma." Thousands of others had similar experiences. Wherever he sat, became the head table. Wherever he settled down, became the headquarter of the party. The government had to open a post office and a telegraph office wherever he went because his correspondence dictated the need for such offices. One is really amazed how he commanded the willing devotion of the masses.

There is no definite or scientific answer to these questions. Different experts will give you different answers. The following are my findings, based on twenty years of my research on his work.

1. He Communicated at the Right Level

He had trained himself to be able to communicate at the level of the person with whom he was dealing. With farmers he talked like a farmer. But with lawyers and magistrates he would talk adroitly in legal terms. Within seconds he could change himself from a politician to a religious person or even to a businessman.

Although most of us believe that we do the same, generally we do not. We tend to see and interpret the world from our own level. It takes rigourous training to walk in someone else's shoes.

2. He Let People Feel Comfortable

Although Gandhi never settled for anything less than what he wanted, he never appeared as a threat to anyone. He made everyone feel at ease immediately and maintained that atmosphere at all times. He never did anything to harm his opponent. On the contrary, he elected to assume all suffering himself. In this way, he tried to melt the heart of the people with whom he was communicating. People do their best when they don't feel threatened.

One way to do this is to accept people as they are - to recognize and appreciate their strengths and to play down their weakness. Remember that every weakness is an indication of strength in some other area. For example, everyone who speaks with an accent, speaks more than one language. Thus the weakness - the 'accent' - indicates the strength - 'multilingualism'.

The law of attention says that whatever you pay attention to grows. And whatever you don't pay attention to, starts dying. Gandhi never paid attention to an individual's weakness but to his or her strengths.

3. He Always Taught by Example.

It is interesting to note that everyone has the need to learn something, but no one likes to be taught. We resent the person who tries to teach us. All great teachers are known to have taught indirectly or by using third person illustrations.

Gandhi believed that action created much greater impact than words ever could. If he had an idea, he first practised it on himself. He wanted to experience the feeling. Later, others saw the merit of the idea and followed it as much as they could. He never forced anyone to use something which was not in the best interest of the person concerned. Gandhi used them in such a way as to draw out and develop the best in them. Consequently they grew in strength and stature from day to day.

Once a lady came to him and said, "Bapu, my son eats a lot of sweets. Please tell him to cut down because it is bad for his teeth." Gandhi looked at the boy, smiled and asked the lady to come back a week later. The lady left confused. A week later she came back with the same request. This time Gandhi touched the boy and said, "Please do not eat sweets. They are bad for your teeth." He then looked at the lady with his unusual smile. She was more confused than ever. So she asked, "Bapu, I had to walk several miles to come to see you. Why did you not say the same thing a week ago?" Very coolly Gandhi replied, "Because a week ago I myself ate some sweets."

4. He Was Consistent in His Ideas and Approaches.

He always thought of the overall good of other people. He believed in experiments. He first tried an idea on himself. If it did not suit him, it was not a good idea. If it suited him then he would let others have the benefits. Since his major purpose never changed, all his ideas were consistent and congruent.

During the Round Table Conference in London, September, 1930, reporters asked him what relationship he saw between Great Britain and India after independence, if it was granted right away. Gandhi described his vision, which appeared to be ridiculous to many. Seventeen years later, when India did receive her independence, the nature of the relationship happened to be precisely the same. Let's not forget that in the meantime there had been a World War which had significantly impacted on the relationship between many countries. This is a classic example of the consistency in his ideas.

5. He Expressed Love Every Single Moment.

His heart was full of love. He forgave anyone and every one. Even when someone did not follow his advice, and ran into some trouble, he did not say, "I told you so". He took responsibility for the consequences. He always assumed the risk himself when he tried something that would endanger him or the community. It was his caring nature that won the hearts of everyone.

6. He Abhored Inaction.

He did not believe in sitting and pondering until every step was fully described. He trusted God and did his best, without any delay. He expected the same from his followers. However, he had a strict code of conduct for himself but a lenient one for the others. He did not mind if others disagreed with his viewpoint. In fact he believed that dissent was a hallmark of manhood. He encouraged rebellion and non-conformity. Disloyalty to him never disturbed him.

7. He Believed in Selfish Personal Growth.

This may appear strange but he believed that a person must first grow individually before he or she could help the community. Look at the apple tree. In spring it starts growing leaves and flowers. It often grows at the cost of neighbouring plants. In some respect it behaves very selfishly. It does not think of giving anything to anybody. Then it bears the fruits and when they ripen, it is ready to share them with others. Gandhi believed that no one grew or fell down individually. When you grow, you elevate the entire mankind to some extent. When you fall, everybody falls with you a little bit.

8. He Was a Great Listener.

The greatest compliment that you can pay to anyone is to demonstrate that you listen to that person. Everyone is craving for an audience. When you listen, you increase the self-esteem of the person. Then he or she will listen to you, will work harder and produce more. Tom Peters, in his book, 'In Search of Excellence', talks about 'Management By Wandering Around'. The main purpose there is to listen to people.

9. He Believed in Being One of Them.

People like to do business with people of similar background. Gandhi always tried to mould himself to be one of those he wanted to serve. That is why he adopted the dress, the meals and the living standard of the poorest people. He could not have won the hearts of the poorest if he continued to live in the luxury of a successful lawyer.

These are some of my observations related to Gandhi's success in developing human resources. It is relatively easy to replace one machine with another but extremely difficult to replace one person with another. When a person leaves your company, he or she creates a void. And remember that nothing stays neutral in this world. You are either moving up or down. Your people are either growing or decaying. There is no middle road. Therefore, occasionally take a few moments to review how you are doing with your people. Make a conscious effort to develop your most important resource - your people. Try the Gandhi way.

"You get the best out of others,
when you give the best of yourself."
- Harvey Firestone

7

Symbols

Help Focus Our Mind

Do you sometimes find it difficult to get a group of people working harmoniously on one selected project? If you were able to improve that harmony, could you expect better results, less stress or more peace of mind?

You can easily achieve this if you care to design an appropriate symbol for each project. Every symbol generates some kind of binding force and prevents people from getting off the track.

It is believed that the main reason of Mahatma Gandhi's extraordinary success was his genius of coming up with effective symbols and his perseverance in holding on to that symbol until the satisfactory completion of the project.

Read also essay numbers 8 and 62.

Y es, it is true that 'A picture is worth a thousand words'. But, we should also remember that a picture is merely a symbol of something much larger and broader in scope.

Our mind is ever fleeting, moving from one thought to another. Consequently, we are unable to focus it long enough on any one thought for it to take a strong root.

Picture an elephant. Notice its trunk swinging continuously. Now imagine the same elephant holding a stick in its trunk. As long as the stick is there, the trunk stays steady. A symbol plays the same role. It helps steady our mind on one thought.

As a lens can focus and convert ordinary sunlight into an extraordinary beam capable of burning almost anything, so a symbol can focus our seemingly ordinary mental power and convert it into some powerful force capable of moving mountains.

In the absence of some effective symbol, our mental power remains scattered and powerless. A symbol focuses our thinking and makes us creative.

All highly successful people use some form of a symbol, logo or phrase. 'Quality goes in before the name goes on', 'Family of fine cars', 'Your neighbourhood realtor' are some examples. They do not have their symbols because they are very successful. They are very successful because they designed a suitable symbol and used it to focus their attention on their overall objective.

Every country uses some national symbol - a national flag, a national language, a national costume, a national anthem and so on. These symbols help unite the otherwise diverse people of the country.

Mahatma Gandhi, the great spiritual leader of India, was a firm believer in symbols. Let me give you some examples.

For his struggle in South Africa, he was looking for an appropriate symbol. When he could not think of any, he advertised in his newspaper and offered a prize for the best symbol suggested. Many entries were received. The best suggestion happened to be the word, 'SADAGRAHA'. This is a Sanskrit word meaning, 'insistence on truth'. Gandhi accepted it but modified it to, 'SATYAGRAHA', which is the corresponding Hindi word. This is how the word 'SATYAGRAHA' was born. For the rest of his life, he used this word as a symbol for his search for truth. It was this symbol that united over three hundred million people of India, who spoke six hundred different dialects.

To revive the basic industries of India, he adopted another symbol - the spinning wheel. Although it appeared to have no bearing on the independence struggle of India, Gandhi claimed that the day every Indian would adopt it, India would win independence. No one could understand his logic, but as more and more Indians adopted it, India did come closer to her independence. In 1942, while interviewing Gandhi, Louis Fisher asked him, "Do you mean that because of this interview the independence has been delayed?" "Certainly", replied Gandhi, "you have delayed our independence by ten yards." He believed so much in this symbol that never for a day did he part with it. He took it with him even to the Round Table Conference in London. The spinning wheel became the main force to awaken the people of India.

The loin cloth was another symbol. It constantly reminded him that he represented millions of starving and half-naked people. Even when he visited the King of England, he wore nothing but his loin cloth and a homespun shawl.

The Salt March was purely symbolic. He used it to prove that even the most ordinary person had the power and duty to defy an unjust law.

When he was released from jail in 1931, he asked permission to take his jail dishes with him. The government allowed it. From that day he never used any other dish. At every meal those dishes reminded him of his main objective. Because of that symbol, nothing could lure him off his chosen track.

Just before undertaking the Salt March, he vowed not to return to his ashram (cottage) until India won independence. This again was nothing but symbolic.

The main reason of Gandhi's extraordinary success was his genius of coming up with some powerful symbol for each project and his tenacity to that symbol until he achieved his goal.

Traditionally, every Canadian graduate engineer wears an 'Engineering' ring. This is a simple, stainless steel ring, worth about a dollar. But it serves as a constant reminder of his or her professional obligations. I wore this ring for over fifteen years. Two years ago I decided to change my career. As a gesture of my commitment, I replaced my "engineering" ring with another ring that has the word "GANDHI" engraved on it. It helps focus my thoughts of becoming commonly known as, 'The Mahatma Gandhi Keynote Speaker'. Without any doubt, this ring has played the most important role in my success in the new career.

Charles Kettering once bet one of his friends five thousand dollars that, if the friend hung an empty bird cage in his living room, soon he would have a bird in that cage. The friend accepted the bet. Everyone started talking about the bird cage and asking about the bird. He kept explaining that he wanted only the bird cage and not the bird. But, after a while, he got sick of the discussions and put a bird in it. Be careful of the kind of bird cage you hang in your mental living room, for soon you will find the appropriate bird in it. The bird cage is nothing but a symbol.

These, and thousands of similar examples illustrate the amazing power of symbols. No matter what your goal may be, you can achieve it if you find an appropriate symbol and keep it in sight twenty-four hours a day. This will stimulate your subconscious mind which, in turn, will come up with the right ideas for you. You may have a series of symbols, as long as they are consistent and convey the same central theme. Your symbol(s) will soon attract the resources and the environment that you require for the achievement of your goal.

I am an aerodynamic engineer. I can talk for hours on how an aircraft flies. But I am still amazed to see it lift off, as if by magic. Similarly, from what I have described, I am sure you understand the role of symbols. However, it is only when you

apply them to your particular situation that you can really
appreciate the amazing power of symbols.

"The opportunities of man are limited only by
his imagination. But so few have imagination
that there are ten thousand fiddlers to one
composer."
                              - Charles F. Kettering

8

Words

Mold Our Beliefs

Words have tremendous influence on our lives. In fact, our potential is limited by our beliefs which are formed by the words that we are subjected to.

There is some emotion associated with each word. The greater the degree of that emotion, the more potent that word becomes. We have the power to alter the associated emotion and thereby to alter the potency of any word. By using a mental umbrella we can protect ourselves against harmful words.

By developing an awareness of the words that we use, and with some conscious effort, we can learn to use the right words and thereby alter our lives.

Read also essay numbers 7 and 15.

W hat we are today is the result of the sum total of the influence of every word that we have ever heard or used.

We are totally controlled by our belief and the latter is formed by nothing but the influence of words. During our childhood we were influenced by the words of our parents. Then it was the words of our teachers. Much later it was the words of our employer, colleagues or friends. Throughout our lives, we continue to be moulded by words.

Words in themselves are purely neutral. Our interpretation of the words creates the influence on us. We associate a certain value to each word. For example, a baby believes in every word of his parents, but does not believe any of a stranger. Thus, the words of those we trust have a stronger influence on us. That is why it is sometimes said that those who love us, can hurt us most.

Our subconscious mind stores every experience in our memory bank. Along with the word that we are subjected to, it stores the associated emotion. Try to recall a song that you enjoy. You will notice that with the song you also immediately recall the feelings that you experienced when you first heard that song.

Every time that we hear (or use) a word, we recall the associated emotion and that makes some additional (positive or negative) influence on us. Thus, even a seemingly innocent word may have a deep influence if we use (or hear) it repeatedly.

Yes, words affect us. But words mixed with emotions have a profound influence on us. Jim Rohn illustrates this with the analogy of a pin. If I throw a pin at you, it may prick you wherever it hits you. But if I tie the same pin at the end of an iron bar and then press it against your chest, it may damage your heart and may even kill you. Words are like that pin. They affect us if they touch us. Depending upon their nature and the associated emotion, they may hurt us, wake us up from our slumber or spur us to action. Words, with emotions, are like the pin at the end of the iron bar. They may go straight to our hearts.

Every word that touches us has either a positive or negative influence upon us. If a certain word, that at present you are hearing or using, is not helping you to increase your self-esteem or your self-confidence, then it is definitely hurting you. Make note of such words and try to replace them by some that could influence you positively.

Any word that can hurt you is a poison word. Now, remember that a poison hurts everyone alike. Be aware of these words and avoid their contact. The container that holds poison retains some trace of the poison, even when all the poison has been disposed of. Similarly, when you use a poison word on somebody else, you yourself feel some influence of that poison. If you use one such word once on ten different people, each of them will experience a slight influence of that poison, but you yourself will be subjected to that influence ten times!

An Indian proverb says that the hand that gives away roses retains the rose fragrance. Then why not practice giving away roses - handing out helpful, encouraging words?

Life is full of echoes. What you send out, comes back to you, generally multiplied many times. If you send out one piece of hate, sooner or later, you will receive ten pieces of hate. But if you send out one word of encouragement, you will receive ten words of encouragement, especially when you are in need.

Zig Ziglar uses a very powerful analogy to illustrate the influence of poison words in our society. What would you do if someone walked into your living room with a garbage bag and dumped the garbage there? If you are a normal person, you will ask him to clean up the mess right away. You may call the police. You may even file a court case against him. But what do you do to a person who dumps a load of garbage into your mental living room? Saying "You are stupid" is equivalent to unloading a garbage bag entitled, "Stupid", into your mental living room. Again, if you are a normal person, you will not say a word. You will not even bother to clean up the mess after the person has left. You will allow the garbage to stay there and be seen by everybody who would happen to visit you!

To tell someone that he or she is stupid is a crime. We see the world through our own glasses. To us it may appear stupid but that does not mean that it really is stupid. Similarly, we have no right to say that a certain person cannot perform a given task. Just because it has not been done before, it does not mean that it cannot be done.

Then what are we to do?

We must become conscious of the role that words play in deciding our limits. We should pay attention to the words that we use. We should examine whether a word is harmful or helpful and we should consciously try to substitute every harmful word by a helpful one. When a harmful word is directed at us, we should prevent it from touching us. Suppose you are outside and it starts raining, what should you do? You should carry an umbrella and the moment it starts raining, you should pull it up. The rain drops will simply slide off your umbrella without touching you. Similarly, the moment you recognize a harmful word coming toward you, you should pull out your mental umbrella and the words won't be able to harm you.

As you increase your awareness of the influence of words and become selective in their use, you will experience a definite improvement in your self-esteem, self-confidence and peace of mind. You will be able to communicate more effectively with others. They will have more respect for you. They will like you more and help you succeed in your own endeavours.

We are highly vulnerable to suggestions. We need to be careful of the company that we keep. If we want to improve our lives, we must make a definite improvement in the quality of people that surround us. Words decide the quality of our lives, because they mold our beliefs.

9

The Main Objectives
Are Often Hidden

This essay was addressed to teachers, but applies to almost anyone.

Even though teachers are hired to teach some definite subject, they should remember that their ultimate objective is to inculcate sound character in their students. They should not forget that they "teach" as much, and perhaps more, outside their class room, than inside. This is because we teach more by example and less by preaching.

This essay makes reference to Gandhi's extraordinary ability of teaching huge masses.

Read also essay number 65.

S ome years ago, a reporter asked John Ziegler, the President of the National Hockey League (NHL), "Mr. Ziegler, what would you say is the NHL's main objective?" To this Mr. Ziegler replied, "The NHL is a business. Its main objective is to make a profit by selling entertainment through exciting and entertaining hockey games."

Let's ponder Mr. Ziegler's statement for a moment. On the surface, an NHL game appears to be a sport in which the objective of each team is to put the puck into the net of the opposing team and to prevent it from entering their own. But dig a little deeper and imagine the weekly company meeting where the employer is telling his employees, "Remember folks, we are selling entertainment. The more entertainment our team can provide, the more customers (fans) we will have and the more money we will receive. If, as a team, you fail to provide enough entertainment, we will lose fans and we will have to lay you off."

Mr. Ziegler's comment became an eye-opener for me. I realized that the true objective may be totally different from what we see on the surface. To discover and understand the true objectives, we must take a deeper look.

What would you say is the main objective of a teacher? 'To teach a particular subject within a prescribed curriculum?' Well, that may not be the whole truth. To teach a subject, and thereby to enable the student to earn a living, is only a secondary objective. I believe that the higher objective is to help the student become the kind of person who can weather the storms of life and follow a chosen course. The challenge, therefore, is to cultivate the student's ability to analyze facts and decide what to do in a particular situation. Life requires making some decisions every moment. Those who are able to make more of the right, and less of the wrong decisions, eventually succeed in life. And those who make more wrong decisions either fail or barely manage to get by. Education enables them to see a situation from a higher perspective. An educated person is likely to make more right decisions.

During the process of teaching a particular subject, you teach your students how to think, analyze, see the bigger picture, gather the needed information, maintain composure even in unfamiliar circumstances, express their views, organize different activities, share and manage resources, set norms, discipline themselves to obey those norms etc., etc..

No matter what subject you teach, I believe that besides helping your students acquire knowledge, it is your responsibility to help them become better people. The latter relates to character building and is definitely far more important than the former.

You may say that neither your contract, nor the curriculum, says a word about your responsibility for the student's character building. That's the paradox of life. Have you ever seen a union contract stipulating that the employer shall ensure that the work place shall provide enough air for the employees to breathe comfortably for the total duration of their work? I have never seen or heard of such a ridiculous demand! Is an adequate air supply less important than adequate pay? Of course not. The availability of an adequate air supply is considered to be obvious. And so is the building of the student's character.

When and how do you teach your students character building? You teach them mostly through your examples.

I believe that 'being a better person' is taught more outside the classroom than inside. Let's remember that, on a voluntary basis, we accept the words of only those whom we trust and respect. The greater the trust and respect, the greater the teacher's effectiveness.

It is interesting to note that neither the teaching contract nor the curriculum stipulates that you do anything toward earning the trust and respect of your students. If you think that this is a minor issue, I ask you to ignore it for a week and notice the change in the effectiveness of your teaching.

Mahatma Gandhi believed in teaching by example. Repeatedly he said, "My life is my message." He claimed that an ounce of practice is superior to tons of lectures. Whenever someone honoured him, by giving him a gift or erecting a monument, he commented, "You would honour me much more if you do what I stand for."

Ralph Waldo Emerson once said, "What you are, speaks so loudly that I can't hear a word you are saying."

I believe that this statement should be framed and displayed in the staff room of every school.

What you are speaks loudly of you. The more trust and respect you show others, the more trust and respect they will show you, and the more your students will accept what you teach. Without this trust and respect, your students will not hear a word you say. They may even go to the extent of hearing the exact opposite of what you say. Also, remember that you are being assessed on a daily basis. You are only as trusting and caring as your last act (or behaviour).

Yes, you were hired to teach a particular subject effectively. You must not fail to meet that objective. But you also have to meet another, more important objective, which is to teach your students to be better people. You do this by practising exemplary behaviour. We learn what we see, and we learn continuously, both in and out of the classroom. When you respect your students, they respect you. The more you trust them, the more they trust you. Your actions convey the message that you are concerned about them and their future. They will love you for it. They will become superior people who enjoy learning. And it's all because of your hidden objectives.

"We sure shook that bridge."
    - The mouse said to the elephant

10

Goals Enhance

Longevity

This essay suggests that there is a direct relationship between goals and longevity, and that we can literally prolong our life by getting involved in the pursuit of some meaningful goals.

Life may be compared to the building of a house. As long as we remain interested in it, we can keep modifying, or making it more interesting, and therefore stay alive. But the moment we lose interest, we find nothing to do.

The essay points out that we generally have dual responsibility - to shape our own lives and to help others shape theirs.

Read also essay numbers 5, 18 and 78.

R ecently, I read the story of a man who was building a house. He was getting old and was worried that he would not be able to finish his house in his lifetime. One day, he had a dream in which an angel visited him and said, "The day you finish building your house, you will die." When the man woke up, he looked at his unfinished house. Figuring that as long as he kept working on his house he would live, he decided to make some changes - add a room, change some fixtures, replace the carpets and so on. In the meantime, St. Peter was kept waiting.

This story has a profound message: We are given life so that we may do something with it - similar to designing and building a house. God left it to us to decide what kind of a house we would like to build. As long as we are making good use of our gift, the life that He granted us, He lets us use it (live our life). But the moment we stop making proper use of this gift, He takes the gift away. You can have your life only as long as there is a use, a purpose for it.

It is estimated that only three per cent of the people are really clear as to what they want to do in their lives. Another fifteen per cent have some vague idea, but they never take the time to clarify their goals. The remaining eighty-two per cent allow themselves to drift - to be tossed about - without striving to reach any destination. The reason most often given is that the task of making a plan for life seems overwhelming, especially since we have never received any training.

Just as you can eat a whole water melon, if you eat it one piece at a time, so you can handle, and solve, your problem, if you break it into small, manageable, pieces. Instead of worrying about planning your entire life, think of planning for a relatively short period. Focus on today, this week, this month and, finally, this year.

Imagine that one of the local media reporters has come to interview you. He asks, "What was your most important accomplishment this year?" Remember that only 'important accomplishments' endure as memories. Everything else is quickly forgotten.

The answer to this question will help you set some personal goals. Most likely this goal will be over and above, and very different from, the goals set by your company. You may recall the famous quote by John F. Kennedy, "Ask not what your country can do for you. Ask what you can do for your country." You may modify this quote to say, "Ask not what your employer can do for you. Ask what you can do for your employer."

Deciding what to do is the most important step. Once you have decided that, you will be able to work out a plan, identify the obstacles in the way and the resources that you require. To keep the overall goal in mind, you may like to design a symbol. Our mind acts much more readily on pictures and symbols than on word commands. Keep the symbol in sight until you accomplish your goal. You will be surprised to see how easily the pieces of the puzzle start falling in places.

The other day a friend of mine was discussing some problems he was having with his teenaged son. He asked me how he could help him. I suggested that the best way to do this was for him to become a better father. This idea came in a flash, but I later realized that it could be generalized. For example, the best way to help your spouse would be to become a better spouse. The best way to help your subordinates would be to become a better boss.

We can learn a lot from a salesperson. In one respect every person is a salesperson. In selling, we find that a buyer first must accept the seller as a person. Otherwise he is not going to even look at the product. First, the buyer must accept the salesperson, then the product, and finally the company that produces the product. Therefore, in order to be more effective, the first area to focus on is becoming a better person. What would you do this year to demonstrate your integrity and your love for your customers? Are you sold on the value of acquiring more knowledge? What additional skills are you planning to acquire this year? These are personal questions and only you can answer them. You, and only you, should be involved in setting your personal goals. Once you set some personal goals for the year, you can break them into monthly and weekly activities that could lead you to accomplishing them.

Not too long ago, I read a book entitled, "The 100 Most Influential Persons In History". I noticed that until the age of six years every one of these persons had had a very innocent life. But then they started showing some unique characteristics. By the age of eighteen, each one had acquired a remarkable personality. Reflect for a moment on the tremendous transformation occurring during those twelve years. Our future statesmen, lawyers, mechanics, doctors, and school board members are sitting in your class. One school year means approximately one-twelfth of the transformation time! In fact, a teacher is dealing with the most valuable resource available.

We do not know how long we are going to live, but we can live longer if we set some definite goals - some definite purpose - for our life. The more excited we feel about our purpose in life, the longer we will live. Goals not only add more years to our life, but also more life to each remaining year.

"Beware what you set your heart upon.
For it shall surely be yours."
                    - Ralph Waldo Emerson

11

Don't Join
An Easy Crowd

While searching for the road to happiness and wealth, most people seem to be influenced by big crowds. They are under the illusion that whatever the vast majority is doing must be right.

This essay suggests that reality is just the opposite. Without any exception, the vast majority are governed by some kind of sheep mentality. To rise above the crowd one must dare to be different from the crowd. Every leader has been noted for being a non-conformist.

The essay points out that although joining a crowd involves less risk, it rarely leads to any worthwhile accomplishment.

Read also essay numbers 28 and 92.

You have heard people say, "It's lonely at the top." What does this expression mean to you? Does it excite you? Or does it frighten you? Does it incite you to discover for yourself what it means to be at the top? Or do you feel like staying at the bottom where you know you will have lots of company? The answers to these questions may decide what you get out of your life.

I am assuming that you strive for success, that you want to accomplish something worthwhile; otherwise you wouldn't be reading this book. If I am right, then you are one of the few who dream of reaching the top. Why is it that only a small fraction of those who have such a dream, successfully achieve it?

Blunt as it may sound, let me tell you that you cannot reach the top unless you refuse to join the easy crowd.

By nature we are lazy. We like to avoid too much risk. We prefer to follow the path that has been well trampled and which is not known to have surprises. Naturally, this is the path that carries the big crowd.

Anything that is easy, or that can be found in large quantities is not worth much. There is only one lion in a given territory, but thousands of sheep in the same area. Notice that the sheep always move in a crowd, whereas it is rare to find two lions walking together. Let me ask you a question, "Which one is more valuable - the lion or the sheep?"

Statistics suggests that one per cent of people make things happen, ten per cent watch things happen, and the remaining eighty-nine per cent, the vast majority, wonder what happens. The easiest crowd is obviously the eighty-nine per cent group. They do not have to do anything. They don't even have to watch what happens. To which group would you like to belong?

Some years ago, I started speaking on Stress Management. The choice was natural. I have a Ph.D. in Stress Analysis. I am an expert on the Stress Analysis of aircraft components and I can compare the stress of the human body to that of an aircraft. The analogy is powerful and I could discuss a complex subject in a language that anyone could follow easily. I marvelled at my own brilliance. However, there was one problem. There was little demand for my talk. I soon discovered that in North America there were over one hundred speakers who claimed to be experts on Stress Management. This definitely was a big crowd. If I joined them, I would be struggling all my life trying to catch up with them.

Then I happened to meet Joel Weldon of Phoenix, Arizona. He gave me a simple piece of advice. He said, "Find out what everybody else is doing and then don't do it." This may sound a bit absurd, but it has a profound meaning. Perhaps it should say, "Find out what everybody else does and then do something different." In other words, don't join any crowd. Be one of a kind.

The more I ruminated over the idea, the more sense it made to me. In order to implement this idea, I had to devote some time to exploring and understanding the products and the services already available in the market. I had to research my market.

As soon as I started my research, I ruled out the idea of speaking on Stress Management. The market was deluged by 'Stress Experts', and I had a problem offering something unique.

While I was researching the market, I met a number of speakers who role play famous characters such as Ben Franklin, Abraham Lincoln, Mark Twain etc. I thought that I could play the role of Mahatma Gandhi. No one to my knowledge was doing that. This meant that I wouldn't be joining a crowd. Needless to say, the demand for my talks have been ever increasing.

To be successful in any business, you need to have a unique selling proposition - you must have something unique to offer. You cannot survive very long, in any business, if you join the easy crowd. The reason is obvious. If it is easy then it has two inherent weakness. First, it is not worth much, and second, anyone can start that kind of business and easily compete with you.

No matter what business you are involved in, you are selling one of three things: a product, a service or an idea. If you sell a product, you know that many people can easily (and definitely will) get into competition. Unless you keep developing your product, those people will soon catch up with you. As a result, you will always find yourself being chased by a crowd. And I can guarantee, your profit margin will be small. But if you sell a service such as accounting, engineering, medical diagnosis etc., only a select group of people can try to compete with the special service that you offer. It should be relatively easy for you to offer some unique (specialized) service that you, and only you, can provide. Your profit margin in this case will be much greater than that for selling a product. So you see, the smaller the size of the crowd to which you belong, the greater the profit margin and, therefore, the better chance of succeeding in your business.

Let's go one step further. Suppose you are in the business of selling ideas (such as business strategies, new techniques of target marketing, some innovative tax planning, unique port-folio management). If you do so, there is a good chance that you may find yourself alone. You can literally set your own price because you will have no competition. Sure, it is not easy to be able to specialize as an idea person. But you can do it if you decide that that is what you want and you channel all your efforts in developing your skill in that direction.

Every leader is noted for doing something different from that of the crowd. Society creates a norm and expects everyone to abide by it. The vast majority does abide, but a few disregard part of the norm. They have some unique idea and they are so obsessed with it that they simply don't care to fol-low the norm. In time they influence a handful of persons. Slowly the number of 'influenced' persons grows and the person who initiated the violation of the existing norm, forms a new, somewhat modified norm, and assumes the leadership of the group. Those who first looked at the person with disdain, jump quickly to join the bandwagon. This process applies to the evolution of every leader.

By definition, there can be only one leader to a group. This means that the leader must be willing to be different from the group in some respect. You can't be a leader unless you are willing to get out of the easy crowd. Trees that grow in isolation, grow strong. When you take the challenge to "do it alone", you definitely grow strong.

For decades, thousands of Indian leaders had been struggling for India's independence. Then came Gandhi. Instead of joining the crowd and following the age-old struggle techniques, he went it alone. He came up with a completely new strategy, 'Non-violent, non-cooperation'. The British Government knew how to suppress violence but had no idea how to suppress non-violence.

But what should a business person do?

If you are already in a business, you should devote some time to studying the market. Look for other products or services that are similar to yours. Is your product or service unique? If not, by some addition or modification, can you bring some uniqueness to it? This may appear costly and painful but will pay off handsomely. Keep looking for ways of making your product or service a unique entity in the market. This is one of the important keys to business success.

If you have not started a business, but are contemplating one, you are in a better position. Your strategy should be to find out what everybody else is doing and then to come up with something different in which you will have a unique edge.

It is true that there is always a great risk when you travel in uncharted waters. But remember, where there is no risk there can be no meaningful gain. Every success comes to you as a gift wrapped in a packaging of risks. The bigger the package, the bigger the enclosed gift. Similarly, the bigger the risk, the greater the possibility of accomplishing something extraordinary.

Success always lies on the upstream. To achieve it you must make the needed effort. But if you do not want to make the effort, if you want to go the easy route, you have to depend upon the flow and let it take you where it might. You know that all normal flows go downstream. You cannot go upstream without fighting the flow. You need to make a choice. Where do you want to go - down the stream with the easy crowd, or up the stream as a lone fighter?

I remember our first trip through the rockies. We were excited to see the first mountain. The subsequent mountains also excited us but not to that extent. After a few hours of driving we got used to the mountains. They appeared like crowds. We even started ignoring them. Only unique things draw anyone's attention. Do you wish to make an impact in your community or your nation? If 'yes' then you must become unique in some respect. You must not join an easy crowd.

> "Two roads diverged into a wood,
> And I took the one less traveled by;
> And that has made all the difference."
> - Robert Frost

12

A Quick Way Of
Overcoming Problems

Although we often complain about our problems, we forget that those very problems provide our livelihood. In the absence of "all problems" we would find ourselves to be unemployed, and perhaps disinterested with life.

Our activities may be divided into enjoyable and boring. The difference often lies in our perception of the particular activity. The locus of control, whether it is internal or external, can also change the nature of an activity, from enjoyable to boring or vice versa.

This essay suggests that by developing awareness, we can discover opportunity in the very problem that we have been dreading .

Read also essay numbers 17, 61 and 64.

The Bible says, "There are some people who have eyes but who can't see or who have ears but can't hear." This means that although we may be surrounded by opportunities, we could not notice them if our awareness was very low.

The radio is a good example. At this very moment, several radio signals are present in the air but, unless you tune in to one of those stations, we won't notice any of them. Even with a radio on, we can only pick up the station to which we are tuned.

For every station we tune in, there may be hundreds of other stations transmitting messages at the same time, but we do not notice them!

This also applies to opportunities. We may be surrounded by sought after opportunities, but we may fail to seize them, unless we tune ourselves into them by enhancing our level of awareness. Remember, when a ship misses the harbour, it is seldom the fault of the harbour.

A lady once remarked, "Dr. Sinha, the theory is good, but what do you do when you are overwhelmed by problems?" I asked her to describe her situation.

She said, "Well, I am a supervisor for Revenue Canada and I am literally overwhelmed by problems every day. I really get frustrated." I asked her, "Do you wish that your position had no problem at all?" Her immediate reaction was, "Oh, I certainly do."

Then I asked, "What do you think would happen to your position if it entailed no problems?" Her ears suddenly perked up. She was beginning to realize that her position, and therefore her job, would be jeopardized.

We continued the conversation for a while: suppose the position required her to handle only half as many problems; or suppose the position did not require her education and experience to be able to handle those problems.

The longer we talked, the more she realized that her job depended upon the existence of those problems.

The more complicated the problems, the more and the better the skills required to handle them - and therefore, the better the reward. That is why the Chief Executive Officer of a company receives the top remuneration.

What about you? Do you feel that you are overwhelmed with problems? Would you like to live your life with fewer or almost no problems? Think over this question with a cool mind.

It is human nature to look for and solve problems. You just cannot sit around for long and do absolutely nothing. Very soon you will start complaining, "I am bored. I have nothing to do."

Recall the instances when you had to wait for someone. Even during those few minutes you wanted to do 'something'. If there was absolutely nothing for you to do then you would look for some reading material or a cup of coffee. Right?

Why is it then, that we keep complaining about 'having too much to do'? And how can we decide upon the right amount of work (or activities) that would keep us occupied so that we would not get bored?

The answer lies in understanding the difference between 'enjoyable' and 'boring' activities.

It has been found that a person may be totally exhausted doing four hours of dull activity, but would not feel even half the exhaustion doing eight hours of enjoyable activity.

The difference therefore lies in the degree of enjoyment that you find in the activity that you are involved in. So, let's have a quick look at the factor that makes an activity enjoyable or boring.

You can divide all your activities into two main categories: the ones that you feel you have to do and those that you feel you want to do.

I used the term 'feel' because the difference between 'have to' and 'want to' is often very subtle. Any activity you feel

you have to do, you consider as a burden on you, and therefore you will resent or detest doing.

On the other hand, any activity that you feel you want to do,
you treat as your own desire and therefore you enjoy doing.

That same activity could be either a burden or a game for
you. Any burden is dreadful. Every game is a joy. The real
difference lies in the way that you perceive it.

Psychologists use the phrase, 'Locus of Control'. Whenever
you are doing something that you feel you have to do, you are
being governed by some external force. But when you do
something that you want to, you experience being controlled
by some internal force.

The more you are controlled by external forces, the more
stressful you become. Happy is the person who can exercise a
great deal of 'Internal Control'.

The lady interrupted, "Well, I understand the philosophy.
But what can I do? Can I get rid of of the external forces?"

To this I replied, "Since we live in a society, we must comply
with certain norms and standards and, therefore, we will always experience some external locus of control. However, we
have the power to convert some of the 'have to's' into 'want
to's'. Let me illustrate my point. Tell me one of your activities
that you feel you have to do."

She said, "I have to be at work at 7:30 each morning."

"All right," I said, "Instead of thinking that you have to be
at work at 7:30 each morning, tell yourself (and convince
yourself) that you want to be at work each morning at 7:30."

The two statements have the same end-result but will have
a dramatically different influence on her reaction to the same
activity. In the first case, she will hate doing it. In the second,
she will welcome it as a challenge.

You can try this technique in your daily life. Try replacing
some of your have to's with your want to's and see the difference. You will experience new excitement in an otherwise dull
day.

Are you overwhelmed with your problems?   A quick way of overcoming many of them is to look at them as challenges. Learn to replace some of your "have to" activities by some corresponding "want to" activities.

"The chains of habit are generally too weak to
   be   felt, until they become too strong to be
broken."

- Samuel Johnson

13

Live With A Purpose

"Living" means selecting some Major Definite Purpose for life and then putting our best effort towards the attainment of that purpose. There is an incredible potential lying within every one of us. The only way to tap it is to have some definite purpose for life.

This essay advises us not to be afraid of using up our skills. We cannot deplete them by using them. On the contrary, the more we use them, the more they grow. Great men, such as George Bernard Shaw, Oliver Wendell Holmes, Ralph Waldo Emerson and Will Rogers agreed that deciding on a definite purpose for life is the starting step for learning to live.

Read also essay numbers 10 and 27.

Just before his death, Will Rogers prayed, "Lord, let me live until I die."

What did Will Rogers mean? Do we not live until our last breath? The answer is, "Maybe?" There is a difference between living a life and just going through life.

The single essential sign of life is growth. Therefore, if you are not growing, you are not living. The greater the extent of your growth, the more fully you are living.

The dictionary meaning of "to live" is "to be able to regulate one's life", "to remain effective", "to exhibit force", "to remain in control" etc..

Will Rogers was not speaking of living in the biological sense. Doctors can keep patients alive by artificial means, but that is not real living. Real living means exercising some control on your life, being able to choose where you want to go, and then working towards getting there.

Are you growing (mentally and spiritually)?

Every child has great ambitions. As he grows, he is bombarded by negative suggestions - you can't do this; you can't do that; be careful; look for security, and so on. Year by year, he experiences the "realities" of life, and his ambitions fade away. Figuratively speaking, most children die by the time they reach their adulthood.

Proverb 29:18 says, "Where there is no vision, the people perish." To stay alive we need to have a vision.

A purpose gives us a reason to live. The moment we find no real purpose to live, we stop living. That is why the average life of a person after retirement is five years - unless that person picks up a second job, or finds a hobby or a new purpose in life.

Do you find your normal day too long? If so, then perhaps you are not living, but dragging your life.

A man in his eighties, who had been very successful in his life, was asked the secret of his longevity. He replied, "Just let the years slip by." That's the key. When you are so absorbed in your work that you do not notice the passage of time then you are living your best.

When you are involved in an enjoyable activity, time passes quickly and you experience more "life". Anything that you want to do, you enjoy doing. Anything that you have to do you find boring.

What can you do to ensure that you keep growing?

Invest some time every day in thinking what you would like to accomplish in your lifetime. What do you enjoy doing? Where do you find your thrills?

These questions will help you decide the Major Definite Purpose of your life. If you continue this exercise, you will discover that your Major Definite Purpose will keep evolving. This is natural. Do not get discouraged. Yesterday's challenges may not be today's challenges.

After having decided your Major Definite Purpose, set yourself some goals for each day, each week, each month and so on. Make sure that each goal is consistent with your Major Definite Purpose. If it is not, then either drop that goal or modify it so as to align it with your Major Definite Purpose.

Less than five per cent of the populace set some definite goals for their lives. Among the five per cent who have a clear idea what they want, most set their goals for acquiring material possessions. But money is simply a by-product of your accomplishment. You do not accomplish something because you have a lot of money. Rather, you acquire a lot of money as a result of an accomplishment.

Every single moment of your life you must choose from a number of alternatives. What you choose determines where you will end up.

If you don't have a definite plan, you will end up nowhere. Make a definite choice and then keep that selected destination in the forefront of your mind all the time.

Others may try to discourage you. Listen to them. Analyse the situation but follow only what your conscience recommends.   Recognize the negatives and guard yourself against them.

The great philosopher Ralph Waldo Emerson said, "What lies behind you, and what lies in front of you, pales in comparison to what lies inside of you."

Trust your own skills and abilities.   What you do with what you have is what counts.   There is no use saving your skills and abilities for tomorrow.   We deplete our natural resources by using them, but we multiply our skills and abilities by using them.   The more you use them the more you will be blessed with.   Put all your life in your today.   Take care of today and tomorrow will take care of itself.

Oliver Wendell Holmes once said, "The greatest tragedy in America is not the destruction of our natural resources, though that tragedy is great.   The truly great tragedy is the destruction of our human resources by our failure to fully utilize our abilities, which means that most men and women go to their graves with their music still in them."

George Bernard Shaw's philosophy was, "I want to be all used up when I die."

Learn from these great men.   Think of some project and try to use up all your skills, abilities and resources.   Put all your life into it.   The more life you put into it, the more life you will be blessed with.   When one project is over, take up another. Keep repeating the process, and then you will be really able to live until the moment that you die.

"Those who bring sunshine to the lives of others cannot keep it from themselves."
- Sir James Barrie

14

Don't Live Like

A Conditioned Elephant

Do you feel handicapped by some of your handicaps? This essay suggests that every person is handicapped in one way or another. There are some whose handicap is apparent, and who are attempting to alleviate the limitation, but there are others whose handicap is latent, and who continue to suffer from it all their lives.

This essay suggests that the so-called blind people may be "seeing" better than the normal people with two healthy eyes.

The essay also suggests some exercises for alleviating this limitation.

Read also essay numbers 30 and 33.

While speaking to the Alberta Association of Rehabilitation Centres on the problems related to serving disabled people, I realized that in some respect everyone is handicapped. There are some who have apparent handicaps, the ones that you can notice and do something about, and there are those who are suffering from self-imposed handicaps, which you cannot easily detect.

Since that convention I have been thinking about the influence of imaginary limitation.

Last week, the experience of speaking to a group of blind people turned out to be a revelation to me. I had learned that approximately fifty-five per cent of our message is conveyed through visuals. Here I had an audience that could not see a thing! I tried to convey my message through word pictures.

Fortunately they were able to 'see' what I was trying to convey. I asked myself, "Are our imaginary limitations not more serious and worthy of our attention?"

I used to be concerned about my height. (I am only four feet fourteen inches tall!) Then one day I met John and Greg Rice. They are two feet eleven inches tall. I had to literally bend on my knees to be able to talk to them. Did I have a genuine reason to complain?

Houdini, the master magician, once challenged his friend that in less than fifteen minutes he could open any lock. His friend accepted the challenge and put Houdini in a prison cell.

Houdini entered the cell empty handed. Within seconds, he pulled out a six inch steel plate that he had concealed in his belt and went to work. After two minutes of vigorous trying he started to perspire.

There was something wrong. He was unable to open that lock. But he had confidence in his skill. He kept working. After ten minutes he was almost exhausted. But he did not give up. After thirty minutes of non-stop work, he literally collapsed.

As he slid towards the floor, his body leaned against the door and the door opened. Perhaps you guessed it. The door had never been locked.

It is extremely difficult to open a door that has been locked in your imagination. That's why we need to be very wary of our imaginary obstacles.

You may say, "Well, that doesn't apply to me." Let me tell you, there may be surprises in store for you.

In my childhood, I read the story of a man who was walking with a big rock in his right hand. In his left hand he was carrying some bricks. On his head he was trying to balance a huge pumpkin and his whole body was wrapped by vines. Needless to say he was walking with great difficulty.

Many people noticed his awkwardness but everyone hesitated to mention it.

Finally one little boy asked him, "Sir, why are you carrying that big rock? If you throw it away, you will be able to walk much better." He looked at his right hand and said, "Oh, I wasn't aware I was carrying this rock. Thank you for pointing it out." He immediately tossed that rock away. One by one, the boy pointed out the bricks, the pumpkin and the vines. The man tossed them away and was able to walk with ease.

This story appears to be silly but it reflects our everyday behaviour. We are so used to our habits that we fail to notice them.

We create our own imaginary prison, live in that prison all our life and since we do not even suspect living in a prison, we make no attempt to get out of it.

We need to recognize this dreadful prison and work towards breaking out of it. This prison is created solely by the limitations of our beliefs.

As children we believed we could do anything. Then slowly, and repeatedly, we were told, "You can't do that. A normal person doesn't behave that way. That does not look nice." etc. etc..

These little suggestions worked like flimsy spider webs but with time they turned into powerful shackles and imprisoned us. It has been said that the man makes the habit and then the habit makes the man. More than ninety-five per cent of your behaviour is nothing but conditioned response.

You may know that a baby elephant is tied to a strong pole with a steel chain. The baby pulls and pulls and pulls that chain but is not able to break it. After a while it stops trying. Then it is tied to a tiny peg with a light rope. Just the feeling of that rope on the leg makes the grown up elephant think and believe that it does not have the power to run away.

The tragedy is that most of us are living the life of the grown up, conditioned elephants.

The first step in overcoming any habit is developing the awareness of that habit. You can do this by breaking your normal patterns. Deliberately try to do something differently.

Going to work, or while returning home, take a different route. Practise some role playing. Occasionally play the game, "just suppose". Just suppose you had all the money that you ever wished, what would you do? Just suppose you were a free bird, free of all limitations, what would you like to do in your life?

Exercise your imagination. Repeated playing of the "just suppose" game will slowly make you believe that what you previously considered to be impossible for you, may just be possible. You will be tempted to act. When you act, you get results and then some of your disbeliefs will be shattered. Your shackles will start losing some of their strengths.

Yes, it is sad to have inborn handicaps. We must accept them as God-given and then do the best that we can do. But the real tragedy lies in creating the prison of our own imaginary limitations and continuing to live without even realizing that we are living in the most dreadful prison.

15

"Good" Or "Bad",
Is A Matter Of Perception

Are you wishing for a good time?
This essay suggests that almost any time can be
converted into a good time. In fact, "good" and "bad"
are mostly a matter of perception.

It also suggests that some words generate negative,
while some others generate positive emotions. By
paying attention to the choice of words, we can gain
some control over our perceptions.

Even situations like a tornado carry some benefits.
We can see those benefits only if we look for them.

Read also essay numbers 53, 69 and 70.

R ecently I heard a person quote the Chinese proverb, "May you live in good times." Since that time this statement has been ringing in my ears. What does it mean ? What is the underlying message?

The word 'may' literally means 'to give permission to'. Does anyone have the authority to give you (or me) the permission to live in good times? It made little sense to me.

Is it possible that they meant to say, "Wish you lived in good times?" Personally I doubt it, because "wish" is a negative word. "Wish I lived in good times", actually means, "I find myself living in bad times and I regret it". It is difficult for me to believe that any wise person would suggest a negative phi-losophy like that. Moreover, we must remember that only good, positive and encouraging proverbs pass through the filters of time.

Since that luncheon, I have been thinking about the role that perception plays in determining the type of life we live. You must have heard of the two prisoners who looked out of their prison cell - one noticed the mud, the other saw the stars. Or, of the two persons having dinner and looking at the half bottle of wine - one said, "The bottle is half empty" while the other remarked, "The bottle is half full". In each case the two persons were faced with an identical situation, but they perceived it very differently.

Life necessitates making decisions. Every single moment of your life you make a decision of some sort. And every decision is governed by your prevailing emotions which, in turn, depend upon your perception of the situation. You make the decision based on your emotion and then look for some logical reasons to justify it. Your creative mind provides you a list of suitable, logical reasons.

Both "wish" and "desire" are emotions. One is negative and the other is positive. The moment you say, "I wish I were rich", your creative mind goes to work to prove why you can't be rich.

Desire lies on the other end of the scale. It is considered to be the most positive emotion. Whereas "wish" looks for reasons why you cannot have what you wish to have, 'desire' looks for every way that you may have what you desire to have. It liberates you from most of your inhibitions. It attracts everything that you may need to get what you desire to get. It brings you a feeling of control. It puts you in the driver's seat. You become the captain of your soul.

You experience the world from your perception. You see everything through your "rose-coloured" glasses. What you see may or may not be the truth, because it is coloured and distorted by the colour and type of the glasses with which you are equipped. Your perception and related emotions create your unique glasses. You generally see only that which harmonizes with your perception and your interest. Everything else goes unnoticed by you although it exists in reality. Your outer world is simply a reflection of your inner world.

You may argue that not everything depends upon your perception and that there are some realities of life that you must consider. The truth is that you still remain in full control of your thoughts. It is not what happens to you that counts, but how you react to what happens to you.

Starting from a penniless position, W. Clement Stone built a multimillion dollar insurance company. What was his uniqueness? He had a habit of saying, "That's good" to no matter what happened to him. He claimed that this habit enabled him to observe and capture many opportunities that he would otherwise have missed.

But what about situations that appear to be totally beyond one's control? Let's consider the Edmonton tornado in July of 1987. It caused huge damage and loss of lives. But if you review it in the light of "that's good", you will notice several blessings. For example, it united many diverse group of people. It taught us, in a hurry, how to cope with a serious crisis. It put the name of Sherwood Park on the front page of most newspapers in North America. And, of course, it brought tremendous business to the roofers and auto-body mechanics.

Can you change your perception?

Yes, you can, if you make a conscious effort. First of all recognize that there is always more than one way of looking at any situation. Look for the other angles. Like any skill, you develop this skill only through conscious and repeated exercise. By default you lose this skill.

You can even control how others treat you. In fact, through every act, no matter how innocent it may appear, you teach others how you want them to treat you. Then they treat you in exactly the same way. If someone teases you and you tolerate being teased, you teach that person that you like being teased. If someone calls you, starts chatting with you and you immediately interrupt by saying, 'What can I do for you today?', you teach that person to value your time and to get to the business right away. If you do not like the way that someone is treating you, simply review what you have been teaching him or her.

Take control of your perceptions. Do not wish for its change. Wishing paralyses you. It drains you of all your potentials. It cripples you. The moment you stop wishing, you start assuming control of your life. Always look for the positive. Think how you can make lemonade out of the lemon that you may have.

Treat "every time" as the "good time". When you look for the good, you will find the good.

Yes, now I feel that I can join the Chinese in saying, "May you live in good time", because I realize that we have the power to convert "any time" into "good time". Recognize and exercise this power. The more you use it, the more pleasure you will find in your life.

16

A Road Map

For Better Writing

This essay suggests that writing requires a fair use of the right brain. For this, we should slow down, at least temporarily, the activities of the left brain, which normally plays a strong dominant role in our lives.

This essay presents an easy three-stage process for creating a comprehensive report on any given topic or subject.

Writing may be compared to the building of a house. You must have a clear idea of the type of the house that you would like to build. You must have plenty of bricks and other necessary materials and you must know how to put them together, in a nice smooth manner.

Read also essay numbers 60 and 77.

I receive many compliments on the style and flow of my essays. Most of my readers find it difficult to believe that very few of my essays have taken me more than twenty-four hours to write. In this essay, I am going to describe the approach that I take. I hope that the ideas expressed here will enable you to write better and quicker and that you will have fun at the same time.

The normal practice in writing is to start with an outline. Experts advise that you should have an attention grabbing introduction, a reasonably good body and a strong conclusion. Although there is nothing wrong with this approach, I feel that we often ignore an essential ingredient.

To build a brick wall, you need a stockpile of bricks and a plan describing where you will place each brick. It is the same with writing. You need a stockpile of ideas and a good plan. Imagine for a moment that you start building your wall with only a few bricks. You say, "Well, I will start with whatever I have and then, as I go along, I will look for additional bricks." With that approach, your finished wall - if you are able to finish it at all - will be very unpredictable. On the other hand, imagine that you start building your wall with more bricks than you need. You can then spend some time thinking and planning how you would make the best use of those bricks, which brick would serve best where, and which bricks you could discard. With this approach your finished wall will definitely look much more attractive, won't it?

Ideas are to an essay as bricks are to a wall. Therefore, we must start with lots of ideas. This can be achieved by a 'brainstorming' process. It is interesting to note that 'idea generation' is a 'right-brain process' whereas 'outlining' is a 'left-brain process'. The more you try to outline, the more you exercise your left brain and, therefore, the more you inhibit the use of your right brain.

Brain-storming requires that you devote a certain amount of time solely for the purpose of generating ideas, that you keep noting down the ideas as they come to you, and refrain from evaluating them as they come to mind. In addition, I suggest that you deliberately break your normal pattern of writing your essay.

For writing an essay, or a report, I use a three stage process which I call

Pre-writing,
Free-writing and
Rewriting.

Let me elaborate a little.

Pre-writing

In the centre of a clean sheet of paper, I write the topic, the heading or some key phrase that would describe the essay that I am about to write. Then I jot down every idea I can think of related to the topic I have in mind. I write them haphazardly, and I deliberately keep crisscrossing the sheet so as to break any logical pattern and to free my right brain for generating ideas. I try to think of an incident - a personal experience - that relates to the subject matter. Once I am able to think of an incident, ideas start flowing very rapidly. When did it happen? What happened? How did I feel at the moment? Who else was involved? What did I learn from it? If I were in the same situation again, what would I do differently? The task is to relive the incident and describe it in as much detail as possible. Narrative or conversational style adds spice to any essay. When I feel that I am out of ideas, I take a five to ten minute break and come back to to the essay for one more try. I review the ideas that are on the sheet and add a few more ideas here and there. This is the end of my pre-writing stage.

Free-writing

Now that I have sufficient ideas, I start to plan, organize and put them carefully into the proper places. I try to group ideas that can be presented together. Then I put a number to each group describing its sequence in the essay. I transfer the group of ideas on to another sheet of paper, this time writing them in sequential order. When I have transferred all the ideas, I review them to see if they require something to bridge them. Then I spend a few minutes 'rehearsing' my entire essay. I imagine that I am talking to someone and describing everything. The imaginary person occasionally interrupts me, asks me questions, and I answer those questions. Sometimes I read his non-verbal signals expressing "So what?" or "What do I have to do with that?" I give my explanations and try to satisfy him. By this process, I have my whole essay organized in my mind.

Then I go to my word processor and write down everything - using these ideas. At this stage I do not worry about the length of the essay or its grammatical accuracy. I just keep writing until I have exhausted every idea that I have collected. I pay extra attention to the conclusion in which I try to give some how-to tips for self-improvement. I then print it out and am ready for the final stage.

Rewriting

I read the whole essay aloud and try to feel how it sounds. I ask myself, "What is the valuable message here?" I specially check for smoothness in the development of the idea or the story. I check for the length of the essay. Where needed, I may add some bridging material. I throw away all redundant material and check for grammar and spelling, and try to replace some phrases with simple words. The aim is to make the piece as crisp as possible. I believe that it is much better to be 'too short' than to be 'too long'. By this time, I find the essay rather messy. So I make the necessary changes, print it out and read it aloud one or two times. If I notice some area that may need improvement, I make a note of it at once. However, I do not rush into making the changes, prefering to sleep on it for a while (preferably four to six hours).

After having slept on it for a while, I read it aloud a few times and note any changes that are required. I make the changes, print it out and read it aloud again. After my second draft, I find that my essay is ninety-five per cent finished. I must make a decision at some point and print it out as my 'masterpiece'.

This approach has worked wonderfully for me and I believe that it can work for you. Just remember that creative writing is a right brain process. Refrain from using your left brain (the outlining process) until the moment that you have exercised - to a reasonable degree - your right brain, in the form of brain-storming for ideas.

"The writer does the most good who gives his reader the most knowledge and takes from him the least time."

- Sidney Smith

17

Get Control Over
Your "Have To" Activities

Our activities may be divided into two major groups, namely the have to's and the want to's. Most people feel swamped by their have to type activities.

One common characteristic of all great achievers has been their ability to get control over their have to type activities. In fact, there is a definite inverse relationship between the percentage of your have to activities and the degree of your achievement in life.

This essays presents several practical techniques of converting some of your have to activities into want to activities.

Read also essays numbers 8, 41, 74 and 89.

B ill woke up with the sound of the alarm. It was seven o'clock. He had to get up. He dressed in a hurry and had no time for a decent breakfast He grabbed a cup of coffee that his wife had prepared, and he rushed over to his car to begin his daily fight with the traffic. He had to be at the school by eight o'clock.

It was a normal day at school. He had to cover the modules prescribed by the school board. He had to maintain a certain level of discipline in the classroom. He had to project enthusiasm and energy right up to the final bell. During the lunch break, he visited the staff room. While munching a sandwich - which his wife had packed - he read some bulletins and browsed through a few magazines. Some he flipped through to pass the time. Others he scanned because he felt he had to keep himself up to date with information. Then it was back to the classroom, to do more of what he did in the morning.

Somehow the day was over, and after fighting some more of that traffic, he returned home with a sigh of relief. He joined the family at the supper table but did not really know who was around, or what the supper was, because his mind was preoccupied with the events of the day and the reports that he had to mark that evening. He sat briefly in front of the television because he felt he had to catch up with the news. Then he started marking the reports. "What a drag!", he thought. It was getting late but he had to finish them. On top of that, he had to prepare for the next day's class. Finally, when he hit the bed, he felt totally exhausted.

"How long am I going to be able to keep up this pace?", he asked himself. But, of course, there was no answer.

Is Bill's problem unique? How did he get into that trap? Can he get out of it? If he continues acting the same way, where will he end?

Bill's daily life may be a bit over-stretched but is not unique. Many of us follow similar patterns. We are constantly involved in doing what I call, "the have to type activities" - I have to get up, I have to be on time, I have to do this, I have to follow that order, I have to buy him a gift etc. Often, we are driven by some sense of duty, obligation, norm, etiquette, custom and so on. In that process we create a certain norm, and those who follow us feel that they must follow the same norm. We seldom question why we are doing some of the things we do.

You can put all your activities into two main categories :

(1) the have to and (2) the want to.

Every have to activity is a pressure on you and drains you. Every want to activity is fun and generally revitalizes you. After working for three or four hours on a have to activity, you experience some fatigue, and to recover from that, you require some recreational activity. The latter is an activity that involves you both physically and mentally, but, without draining you, it revitalizes you because this is something you want to do. The more you participate in the want to activities, the less additional recreation your body and mind requires. Mahatma Gandhi worked for sixteen to eighteen hours every day. Once a reporter asked, "Mr. Gandhi, you have worked so hard for so many years, don't you think you should take a vacation?" To this Gandhi replied, "Why? I have always been on vacation." Thomas Edison once made a similar remark, "Young man, I have never worked in my life. I do these experiments only because I love them."

Anything that you feel you have to do is work. Anything that you want to do is play. We can't sit idle. We must do something. Gandhi and Edison found themselves the ideal solution - doing what they wanted to do. But what can an ordinary person like you and I do?

Let's analyze how one gets into that trap.

A while ago, Paul needed some money to meet some of his basic needs. So he accepted a small job that would fetch him just enough money to cover those needs. He did not care for the job - it was going to be really temporary. Somehow, his basic needs kept growing and he kept accepting jobs that would provide him the needed money. He never bothered checking if he liked the jobs. Slowly, he found himself in a tight spot. He had a family to support, bills to pay and a certain lifestyle to maintain. He kept doing what he was doing, even though he did not like it. Now he is looking forward to his retirement - then he will be able to do what he really wants to do.

The have to activities burn you out very rapidly. You feel you are being controlled by external forces. The want to activities provide you with a feeling of control. You find yourself in the driver's seat. You work your hardest and you develop most of your natural potential. The pleasure of having accomplished something that you want to do is far more rewarding than any monetary reward. If you keep on doing what you want to do, then, in the long run, you receive far more monetary rewards than you would ever receive by doing things you do not sincerely like. A common characteristic of all great achievers is that they did what they loved doing.

You may argue that the great achievers were lucky to be in those fortunate circumstances. This is not true. Most of them found themselves in tighter spots than you and I are in. Space does not allow me to discuss how they broke out of their confinements, but I believe that the following ideas will enable you to deal effectively with your have to activities.

1. Make a list of all the activities that you presently consider to be of the have to category.

Do not worry if you find most (or all) activities to fall into this category. You can easily learn to control them. Making this list and developing the awareness is vital. No prisoner will make any attempt to get out of the prison until he discovers (and realizes) that he is imprisoned.

2. Voluntarily cut down on your minimum financial needs.   Refuse to work to death simply to meet your minimum requirements. You need not compete with the Joneses. Take a short break to regain some control of your life.

3. Every day do something that you want to do.

Even one such activity each day will suffice. The idea is to realize that you have the power to assume the control of your life.

4. Change your attitude toward your work.

See some of your have to's as your want to's. Tell yourself that the external forces do not have as much control on you as they had before.

5. Convert some of your have to's into your want to's.

For example, suppose you have been asked to do "X" amount of work. This is the minimum requirement set by some external power. As your personal goal, you can add another twenty-five to fifty per cent to that task. Even a ten per cent self-imposed addition will work miracles, but I recommend twenty-five to fifty per cent. Now, forget about the goal set by the external power. Simply focus on the new goal you have set for yourself. You will experience tremendous inner strength, and there is a high probability that you will far exceed the goal of the "X" amount of work.

6. Eliminate the expression "have to" from your vocabulary by substituting, "I choose to".

Words have far more influence on your physical, mental and emotional strengths than you realize.

Suppose you are getting late for an appointment. You have two options. You can say, "I have to leave now" or "According to my plan, I must attend to another activity at this moment." In the first statement you imply that someone else is controlling you. But the second statement clearly indicates that you are in control, specially if you emphasize the word "my". Just try it a few times and notice the difference in their psychological influence on you.

7. Whenever some one appears to impose a have to activity on you, mentally refuse to accept it as a have to activity.

Look for your personal benefits in performing that activity and then accept it as an activity that you want to do.

You have heard about the two persons who looked out of the prison bars - one saw the mud, the other saw the stars. Consider yourself a prisoner of "life". Stop looking at the nearby mud and focus on the distant stars. As you convert some of your have to activities into want to activities, you will find yourself having more time and energy for doing some additional want to activities. Once the ball starts rolling, it won't stop and you will become one of the great achievers.

> "The world is full of willing people;
> Some willing to work, the rest willing to let them.
>
> - Robert Frost

18

You Are Never Too Old
To Have Goals

Age is relative. It depends upon your will to live. Meaningful goals whet our desire to live. Thus, one is never too old to have goals.

This essay cites many examples where people have accomplished extraordinary feats in their late sixties, seventies, eighties and even nineties! "Old age" lies more in one's thoughts and beliefs, than in reality.

No matter what your age, this essay will instil some new vigour in your life. It will convince you that a man's most important years are generally past the age of 40.

Read also essay numbers 10 and 22.

R ecently someone asked me, "I am fifty-four years old, do you think that I can still have goals?"

How about you? How old do you think you are? Do you consider yourself to be too old to set some new exciting goals?

Our society seems to have set some guidelines for us. For example, consider the fact that the retirement age for most government jobs is sixty-five years.

My brother-in-law, who is a colonel in the Indian Army, told me that unless he is promoted to a Brigadier's position, he will have to retire at the age of fifty-five. Moreover, he has the option of retiring any time after the age of fifty-two.

Another word for "retire" is "superannuated", the dictionary meaning of which is "too old for work". In other words, our government thinks that the moment you reach the age of sixty-five, you are too old for work. What an irony! Someone who possesses such a huge wealth (experience of over thirty years), finds himself overnight, "too old to work" or even "good for nothing".

Where then, does the fifty-four year old man stand?

I sincerely believe that there is no direct correlation between one's age and one's ability to provide meaningful service to society.

One study suggests that our most productive years lie anywhere between the ages of forty and sixty. In fact, when you find yourself focussed on one mission, you are able to contribute (provide meaningful service to the society) more in a matter of three to five years than what you would do during a lifetime of unfocussed work. It is interesting to note that this "focussing" rarely happens before the age of forty. In other words, until you reach the age of forty, you have not entered the real game!

If you still think that you are too old to start something new, let me give you a few examples of what so-called old people have done.

At the age sixty-six, while on welfare, Colonel Sanders thought of the chicken business. But, for over two years not one restaurant in his home state of Kentucky, paid attention to him. Then, he went to Salt Lake City and sold the idea to one store. On his eightieth birthday, he sold his chain of Kentucky Fried Chicken outlets for two hundred million dollars!

At the age of fifty-five, while selling milkshake machines, Ray Kroc happened to approach the MacDonald brothers, who had a hamburger stand in San Bernardino, California. He was successful in selling six units of his machine, but was more struck by the idea of a chain of hamburger outlets. First he joined the MacDonald brothers and then, in less than five years, bought them out. The rest is history. It is estimated that if MacDonald's had been a separate country, it would be the fifth largest consumer of sugar in the world.

At the treaty of Versailles (attended by the world's most important and powerful men), the most powerful and dynamic person was the seventy-five-year-old Clemanceau. One of America's greatest financiers, Andrew Mellon, retained vigour, endurance and extraordinary energy up to the age of eighty-three. Vanderbilt planned and built most of his railroads when he was over seventy.

At the age of seventy-five, Walter Damrosch wrote and conducted one of the finest operas of our time. Kant wrote some of his greatest philosophical works after he was seventy. The French artist Monet was still painting his magnificent pictures when he was eighty-six.

Von Humbolt began his work on "Cosmos" when he was eighty-six and completed it when he was ninety. Goethe wrote the second part of "Faust" when he was eighty. Titian painted his incomparable "Battle of Lepanto" when he was ninety.

We can literally fill page after page with similar examples. We need not go too far back in history. Just look at what Bob Hope is doing at the age of 84. George Burns recently commented, "I can't die, I am booked for the next 25 years."

We become bored by everyday chores. We need some new challenge. Being unique, we find those challenges in our own particular ways. Only you can discover what really excites you. Let me share with you some ideas that will help you discover your unique interest.

If money was no consideration at all, with what kind of activities would you like to pass your time?

Recall some situations or events that really thrilled you. Where and, in what form, did you experience a feeling of great pride in yourself?

Is there an activity in which you lose all sense of time?

These, and similar questions, will help you uncover your true interest. It is only by getting involved in a project related to your true interest that you can develop your God-given potential.

Stop thinking about your age. You can make a start at any time. Discover your niche and you will start experiencing a new life. Have some dreams, some meaningful goals.

No, you are never too old to have goals. In fact, there can be no meaningful life without goals. Proverb 29:18 says, "Where there is no vision, the people perish". I think that we should extend it to say, "The moment men start losing their visions, they start to die."

You are alive only because of your goals. The more excitement you can experience in your goals, the more vigour you will find in your life.

Let me conclude by asking you one more question.

Imagine that you were involved in a traffic accident and thereby lost your memory. If no one told you your age, how old do you think you would consider yourself to be?

I do not deny the relationship of body-physiology and age. But I believe that "the feeling of life" is more in our mental make-up.

According to a particular experiment, the average gripping strength of three men was one hundred and one pounds. They were then told to believe that they were very strong. Their average gripping strength rose to one hundred and forty-two pounds. Just a few minutes later, they were asked to imagine that they were very weak. Their average gripping strength fell down to twenty-nine pounds.

Would you say that their body physiology had changed during that experiment? Certainly not. The most important factor is belief. How strong do you think you are? How old do you think you are?

"Old age is 15 years older than I am."
- Bernard M. Baruch

19

Get A Grip
On The Drip Of Your Time

Do you sometimes lose a minute here or a minute there?

If you are an average person, you lose many minutes during a normal day. If you could save all those little minutes, you could gain over two hours of time every day!

Your time is essentially a piece of your life. By saving a few minutes here and there, and by employing them in more productive activities, you can increase your productivity by a significant amount.

This essay provides several practical tips for saving a few minutes which you otherwise lose in waiting or commuting, on the telephone, at appointments or even due to poor memory.

Read also essay number 21.

D o you have a faucet that drips just a little bit? If you do then you may have realized that over time it leaks a substantial amount of water. Does that bother you? Well, it's a minor problem that may be fixed with a few cents.

But what about the leakage of the most important reservoir, your time? Without realizing, you may be losing many 'few minutes' here and there. The tragedy is that we seem to neglect the loss of a few minutes.

But let some minutes accumulate and they turn into hours. The hours can turn into days, days into weeks, weeks into months, months into years and, finally, years into a large part of your life. Alan Lakein, the author of "How to Get Control of Your Time and Your Life" says that time is life. I totally agree with him. An hour lost today is an hour of your life lost forever.

We need to recognize the value of every minute of our life. We need to be aware of situations wherein we lose those few minutes. And we need to learn some effective techniques for saving them.

Based on my experience, I am going to share with you some situations in which I recognize the loss of precious minutes and the techniques that I use to plug the corresponding leakage.

Minutes lost in waiting

It is estimated that an average person loses up to three hours every day in waiting for someone or something. Most persons waste these minutes browsing through old magazines. I have seen people reading **News Week, Time** or **Alberta Report** magazines that were up to six months old. Any news which is that old is generally useless. Why waste a portion of your life reading such junk?

I carry my own reading material that I want to read, a book that I am interested in, some clippings I have collected for my projects and so on. Sometimes, I even carry a scratch pad on which I scribble ideas as they come to me.

When you carry your own reading material (or knitting, or something that you want to do), you become in charge of your time. Buy some pocket books that interest you, and carry one with you at all times. The mere mechanics of carrying it will make you more aware of your minutes.

If you feel that it is too much to carry a pocket book, consider ripping the book apart, and carrying twenty pages. When you have read those twenty pages, carry the next twenty pages. In this way you could read about one book every week. That translates into fifty books a year! Do you know that the average adult Canadian reads less than two personal development or business related books per year?

The reading will soon start showing results in your business or career. The average cost of a paperback is under five dollars. You cannot have a better investment of those two hundred and fifty dollars a year.

Luckily, I don't have to wait often for buses, but when I do, I practise deep breathing during those minutes.

Minutes lost in commuting

Most of us lose about one hour every day commuting. In a year this amounts to over 365 hours, or over nine 40-hour weeks! A saving of one-fourth of that time would mean a gain of over two full weeks. Can we recover this loss?

One way is to use this time in listening to some pre-selected cassette tapes while commuting. You can find cassette tapes on almost any subject. Most public libraries contain a good selection of audiotapes. The annual membership fee is either free, or so nominal that anyone can afford it. I consider my library card to be more valuable than my credit card.

Consider buying some cassettes and exchanging them with other people with whom you share interests.

Minutes lost on the telephone

Have you noticed that the opening statement in a telephone conversation generally decides the duration of the call? If you want to keep it short, and to the point, just pay attention to your opening words, irrespective of whether you are initiating or receiving the call.

You may lose a few minutes looking for the right number. Or having found the number you want in the directory, dial it, and hear a busy signal. In the meantime you lose the page in the directory, and have to look up the number again, at the cost of more precious minutes.

The solution is to jot down the number when you have looked it up in the phone book. I group all my outgoing calls at one time. I jot down every number that I need, and beside the number, make a short note of the points that I intend to cover. If I do not reach the party I am calling; I make a note beside the name as to when I should call again. In this way I have a record of my calls and know the intention of the call.

Often, you may lose a few minutes because you are put on hold. I have designed a **Minute Basket** in which I collect tasks that require just a few minutes to finish - such as signing cheques for bill payments, writing addresses on some envelopes. I dig into this basket and pull out one piece of paper and work on it while I am waiting.

By the way, when someone asks me, "Can you hold?", I say, "Yes, I can, provided it is not more than a minute or two." In this way, that person feels obliged to check back with me soon, or else he or she knows that I would soon be off the line.

I also use my **Minute Basket** to use the commercial times when I am watching a television program.

Minutes lost on missed appointments

Have you ever arrived at an appointment and learned that the party had forgotten, had gone out of town, or had been diverted by some emergency? If not, then you must be very lucky. It pays to re-confirm an appointment just before you leave for it. The time saved may sometimes be well over an hour!

Minutes lost because of poor memory

We all forget something at some time or the other. To counter this, I carry some three by five cards and jot down an idea or a piece of information about which I may need to remind myself. I use one card for each item and discard it as soon as its usefulness is over. This has saved many, many minutes of my time.

Get a grip

Recognize that many a drop may fill the bucket. Your time is your life. Don't let it slip away. Keep looking for the leakage and get a grip on the drip of your time.

> "A man who dares to waste one hour of his life has not discovered the value of life."
> - Charles Darwin

20

Be Selective In Listening

We are often criticized for being poor listeners. But how beneficial is it to listen extensively?

It is impossible to please every one. Abraham Lincoln often said that if he cared to listen to everyone, he would have to close his office right away. If you want to make any decision, or to take some action, you must be selective in listening. You must also recognize that even "experts" can be wrong. Our civilization has progressed only because some men or women stopped listening to the experts of their time.

This essay suggests that you should be careful in choosing whom to listen to, and it is extremely important that you listen regularly to your own inner voice, and follow its advice sincerely.

Read also essay numbers 29 and 40.

In March 1966, while I was working in India, I was suddenly gripped by the desire to go to some foreign country. I sent some letters to West Germany and within weeks I received a job offer. In my excitement, I wrote to sixteen elderly persons asking for their advice. Fifteen of them congratulated me, but one opposed it very strongly. He specially advised against leaving India until I was married. Having sought his advice, I just could not ignore it. My dream of going to Germany was shattered.

With my desire still burning, I started exploring other possibilities. McMaster University offered me admission and a scholarship for post graduate studies. This time, I quietly prepared my papers, made a reservation and announced my plan just one week before my departure. It was too late for any one to stop me. I left India for Canada.

In this particular case, "listening to too many people" created an unnecessary hurdle for me. Does it then mean that it is better not to listen to others?

There is a lot of talk about the importance of listening. It is said that when God designed us, He gave us two ears and one tongue so we could hear twice as much as we speak. It is estimated that more than half of everyday problems are caused by poor listening. Should we, therefore, keep on listening and listening and listening? After all, how much can we listen? To make a decision, we must draw a line some-where! And at what stage of the game should we listen more? These are some of the important questions that we should address.

Yes, there is a danger in too much listening. By nature, everyone longs for an audience. The more we listen, the more we encourage that person to keep on giving advice. It is interesting to note that the less a person "knows", the more he or she seems to enjoy giving advice.

It is foolish to listen to everyone. We must be selective.

Salespersons use a term called, "Qualifying", which means to ensure that you are speaking to the right prospect. Similarly, I feel that we should qualify our advisers. We should find out if the person that we are listening to is qualified and competent to give us useful advice.

But how can we do that?

According to statistics, only a handful, less than five per cent of people, are truly successful. One of your goals should be to discover the successful persons in your line, to listen to them and then to discipline yourself not to listen to anybody else.

But the trouble is that even the advice of so-called "experts" is often wrong. Let me quote some of the "authorities", as published in official documents, newspapers and magazines, which were widely read during their day.

1840: "Anyone travelling at the speed of thirty miles an hour would surely suffocate."

1878: "Electric lights are unworthy of serious consideration."

1901: "No possible combination can be united into a practical machine by which men shall fly."

1926: (from a scientist) "This foolish idea of shooting at the moon is basically impossible."

1930: (another scientist) "To harness the energy locked up in matter is impossible."

Yes, even the experts have been wrong. But the real tragedy is that ninety-nine per cent of the people believed them. Those who refused to believe - or took it as a challenge - have been responsible for all the progress in our civilization.

Roger Bannister refused to listen to the hundreds of scientific publications which proved why physiologically it was impossible for a man to run a mile in four minutes. The Wright brothers refused to believe that a chunk of cast iron and some steel ropes could not be put together to fly into the air. Mahatma Gandhi refused to accept that non-violence was the weapon of the weak.

The solution is to listen to your own inner voice. If you take a few minutes to be completely still and free your mind from all distractions, you will feel as if someone is trying to talk to you. This is your inner voice, your best guide. This voice is never wrong and will never deceive you.

No matter what you do, you will not be able to please everybody anyway? So why bother too much?

There is a story of an old man and his grandson who were taking their donkey to the market to sell. On the way, someone remarked, "Look at the fools. They don't know how to use a donkey." Hearing this, the old man put the child on the donkey. But shortly thereafter somebody else commented, "Look how spoiled that child is! He is riding the donkey while the poor old man is dragging his feet." The child felt badly and switched positions with his grandpa. Well, another person scoffed, "The old man is so selfish. If the donkey can carry his weight, can it not carry that of the little child as well?" So he put the child in his lap and was riding happily until someone said, "They will definitely kill the donkey before they reach the market." Finally he thought of the "right" solution. They tied the donkey's legs and, with the help of his walking stick, carried it to the market. Needless to say, many others laughed at their folly.

I find that, unless we learn to control it, we are deluged with free advice. We should note that the value of free advice is only equal to its price. There is a French saying, "Conseilleurs ne sont pas payeurs." Translated it means, "The advisers don't have to pay." In accepting free advice, remember that you are the one who will have to pay the price.

How much should we listen? Well, based upon my personal experience and wisdom, I believe that we should

- avoid listening to the vast majority; nearly eighty per cent of the people, who barely make it through their own lives;

- listen fairly well to the select group of less than five per cent who have been very successful in their own career or profession; and

- listen religiously to the advice of our own inner voice (our conscience).

21

Putting Pareto's Principle
Into Practice

Although Pareto's 80/20 formula has been universally acclaimed as "extremely beneficial", very few people can apply it successfully. The challenge lies in putting all your activities in the order of their value. The problem is compounded if some new important activities suddenly fall into your lap during the middle of the day. After being frustrated by these, most people give up trying and say, "Well, it's not for me."

This essay shows how you can facilitate the task by first making a short-list of activities and then trying to put them into the order.

Read also essay numbers 19 and 35.

V ilfredo Pareto, a nineteenth century Italian economist, once became interested in knowing who controlled most of the wealth of his country. After exhaustive research, he found that only twenty per cent of all Italians controlled nearly eighty per cent of the national wealth. He felt that there was definitely something wrong. He then studied the wealth of some other countries and found that the 80/20 ratio applied roughly to all of them too. This was a startling revelation. He became so interested in his finding that he extended his research to many other areas of life and found that the 80/20 ratio appeared to be some kind of a universal rule. For example, consider that:

you use 20 per cent of your wardrobe for 80 per cent of the time;

80 per cent of results come from 20 per cent of your activities;

20 per cent of the salespersons bring 80 per cent of the business;

20 per cent of the products of a company bring about 80 per cent of the revenue;

20 per cent of the students cause 80 per cent of the problems in the class;

and so on.

The percentages may vary slightly, but the ratio comes out very close to the 80 and 20.

Pareto's discovery has been found to be specially important in the area of time-management. If twenty per cent of all one's activities account for nearly eighty per cent of the results, why not focus on the important twenty per cent?

A number of years ago, a man by the name of Mr. Ivy Lee visited Charles Schwab, the then President of Bethlehem Steel Company. He claimed that he was an expert Management Consultant and suggested that he had something very valuable to offer. Noticing that Mr. Schwab was a very busy man, he went straight to the point. He asked Mr. Schwab to write down every activity that he thought he needed to do the next day. When Mr. Schwab had done so, he said, "Now put them in the order of their priority. Tomorrow morning, pick up item number one from that list and work on it until it is finished. Pick up item number two only when you are through with item number one, and proceed through your list only in that order. If you cannot accomplish more using this technique, I guarantee, you will not be able to accomplish more using any other technique. Try this for as long as you like and then send me a cheque for whatever value you think this technique is worth to you."

The next day Mr. Schwab started working on it. At the end of the day he realized that he had accomplished more than what he would have done otherwise. He continued using this technique for a few days. Then he asked his immediate subordinates to try it. Everyone was overwhelmed by the results. At the end of thirty days, Mr. Schwab mailed a cheque of twenty-five thousand dollars to Mr. Lee. Remember, that was a lot of money in those days.

Ivy Lee's technique is simply an application of Pareto's principle. If you put all your activities in the order of their importance, the top twenty per cent of them will bring you approximately eighty per cent of the results; the top four per cent will bring you approximately sixty-four per cent of the results and the top one per cent will bring you approximately fifty per cent of the results! Think of that. Even if you do only the top one per cent of your activities, you can achieve nearly fifty per cent of the results. What a saving of your time and your headaches!

No Time Management training is complete without a reference to the Pareto's 80/20 formula. Everyone admires it and resolves to put it into practice. But then something happens. In a short time, the vast majority quit trying it. Those who master it, benefit tremendously from it. Every high achiever, consciously or unconsciously, uses this technique. Why is it that the vast majority are unable to take advantage of this great technique?

I believe that the greatest challenge lies in "putting the activities in the order of their importance and then disciplining oneself to handling them only in that order".

Most of us have trouble listing what we need to do today. Some make the list in the morning and, by the afternoon, discover half a dozen extra items that should have been included. Then, we seem to get confused in deciding the order of their importance. What appeared to be of lesser importance in the morning, may look to be much more important in the afternoon. Even worse is the fact that some activities, which are not on the list, may demand a higher priority. Many emergencies creep in and throw everything out of whack. The result is that in a short time we admit, "It's a good tool, but I am not suited for it."

But there is a way out. The following pointers can help you alleviate your puzzle.

1. Keep your main goal in focus.

Every activity should have a purpose. Ask yourself, "Why do I want to do it?" or, "Why do I have to do it? Is this consistent with what I am trying to accomplish today, this week or sometimes in the future? What would happen if I did not do this activity at all?"

2. Recognize that every activity counts.

There is actually no activity that is truly neutral. Each activity moves you in some direction. If a certain activity does not move you in the direction of your goal, it definitely moves (or at least holds) you away from your goal. Every activity takes some of your time and attention. If it is not moving you towards your goal then you are wasting some of your resources, which you could have used in some other activity that could move you towards your goal.

3. Judge every activity in the light of your goal.

To decide the priorities, we generally start comparing the importance of one activity against that of another. This is wrong. We need to check each activity against our goal. For example, if neither of the two activities move you towards your goal, wisdom suggests that you do not include either of them on your list. Each activity should be accepted as a step towards the goal, not an activity for the sake of keeping ourselves busy.

4. Keep your list short.

We have a tendency to overcrowd our lists. Perhaps we feel that bigger is generally better. This may not be so. Think quality and not quantity. Remember that only twenty per cent of important activities can bring you eighty per cent of the total results. If you keep your main goal in mind then only the important activities will surface . If you keep your list short, you will be more likely to concentrate on it until finished. I recommend that you include only six important items on your list each day. If your list contains more than six, ask yourself, "Out of these, which six are really important for my goals?" Once you have a list of only six items, you will find it much easier to put them in order of priority.

5. Learn to be "single task minded".

Cultivate the habit of keeping all thoughts, except those related to the present task, out of your mind. Keep telling yourself, "This one thing I do." Thinking about more than one task at one time is like feeding the data of more than one problem in the computer - none of the problems can be solved properly. When some distracting thought comes to your mind, tell yourself, "This can wait for a moment." Have you noticed how a doctor works? While examining one patient, the doctor thinks only of the problems or the symptoms of that one patient. You can act in the same way. Remember the movie, "Heaven Can Wait". Yes, even heaven can wait, if you form the habit of concentrating on one task at a time. Refuse to react immediately. Don't pick up the phone on the first ring. If the call is important, the caller will hold for the second ring. Act as if you are important, you are in charge.

I find the above guidelines to be very helpful in deciding the priorities of my activities. Once you learn how to decide the priorities, you are well on your way to putting Pareto's principle into practice.

22

Make Yourself More Valuable

Do you sometimes feel discriminated against? Or, did you have an occasion when you felt that you should have been promoted, but you were passed over?

Life may occasionally appear to be unfair. But in the long run the truth must win.

The life of Abraham Lincoln is a classic example of repeated failures. But Lincoln never wasted any time ruminating over his past failures. He focussed all his energy in making himself a better person.

There is generally only a fine difference between the winner and the runner up. Therefore, it is extremely important that we save every bit of our energy, and use it in making ourselves more valuable.

Read also essay numbers 10, 32, 51 and 90.

D o you sometimes feel that you are not receiving the help, the recognition or the promotion that you deserve?

I have often felt discriminated against; I should have been selected to be the speaker for a certain occasion, but someone beat me to the punch. What do I do? I ask, "Is it possible that I have not prepared myself enough?"

The Bible says, "When the pupil is ready, the teacher appears." Perhaps this advice may be extended to many areas of our lives. For example, "When the man with the idea is ready, the financier appears"; "When the author is ready, the publisher appears"; or "When you are ready for the next promotion, the position appears."

You may say, "Well, life is not so straight and fair." Perhaps you are right. But the odds suggest that when you are truly ready, someone will spot you and help you move up.

There is a story of a grocery boy who worked extremely hard. Whenever he was short of an item in his own store, he would run to the next store, borrow the item and sell it to his customer. As he was making such a run one day, a customer curiously asked the owner of the other store, "Why is that boy always running?" The owner replied, "He is working for his promotion." The customer then asked, "How do you know that, when he does not even work for you?" "Well," replied the owner, "from the looks I can tell you that he is working for his promotion." The customer then added, "And what if he doesn't get the promotion?" To this the owner quickly replied, "If he doesn't receive the promotion there pretty soon, I will hire him."

If your boss resigned (or died) this moment, can you handle his functions right away? The vast majority can't. We tend to see little value in preparing for a situation that has not come yet. But when it does, someone else, who has taken the pain and the initiative to prepare, steps in. Opportunity after opportunity comes and goes and we keep sitting like a duck.

Have you noticed that most reorganizations are done to suit the capabilities of the people? Look at any government administration. A cabinet is formed from among the elected persons. The departments are organized to suit the strengths and weakness of the ministers and the entire structure is carefully worked out according to the capabilities of the people available.

Private organizations do this even more drastically. A new Chief Executive Officer can slash many positions and create others almost overnight. A person is generally assigned only that much responsibility (and the corresponding power) for which he has prepared himself.

What you have today is what you prepared yourself for, until today. And what you prepare for today, you will have tomorrow. To have more tomorrow, you must prepare yourself more today.

"Do your duty and do not worry for the result", is perhaps the most important teaching of Bhagwad Gita, the Hindu Scripture. What does it really mean? How can we motivate ourselves without thinking of the expected result?

Gita does not ask us not to think of the result. However, it advises us against worrying for the result. We must think of our objectives, our goals and choose the proper activities that would take us to that goal. Every result is the effect of a certain cause. You cannot control the effect, but you can control the cause. Therefore, wisdom lies in focussing all your attention and energy on the proper execution of the cause (the right activities).

The cause in our situation is "Preparing ourselves for the next level". The recognition or the promotion is the effect. You can influence the result only by controlling your part - making yourself more valuable. Not receiving the desired effect (the result) simply means that the corresponding cause is not strong enough. The remedy is to improve upon the cause. The attention or the energy that you invest in worrying about the result, should be better used in improving the cause - better preparing yourself.

But how much preparation is adequate preparation?

Perhaps the sky is the only limit. During the 1988 Winter Olympic, Karen Percy lost the Silver medal because she took one-hundredth of a second longer (in an eighty second race). In fact, the difference of one per cent made the difference between winning the Gold medal and not winning any medal at all. Brian Orser had an almost similar experience.

How tall does a tree grow?

It grows as tall as it can grow. We also must grow as tall as we are capable of growing. We can do this only by concentrating fully on the task of preparing ourselves.

Perhaps no one experienced more defeats, frustrations and humiliations than Abraham Lincoln. Let me give you a brief run down.

1832: Lost job and was defeated for the Legislature.
1833: Failed in business.
1834: Elected to the Legislature.
1835: His fiancée died.
1836: Suffered nervous breakdown.
1838: Defeated for Speaker.
1843: Defeated for nomination for Congress.
1846: Elected to Congress.
1848: Lost his renomination for Congress.
1849: Rejected for Land Officer's job.
1854: Defeated for the Senate.
1856: Defeated for the nomination for the Vice-President.
1860: Elected President of the United States.

Lincoln's formula was, "I will prepare myself and my time will come." All his life he concentrated on making himself more valuable. He focussed on the cause and the result had to follow.

You can control your results only by controlling that which is within your power - your power to improve yourself, to make yourself more valuable, to prepare yourself for the next move. How well you perform at the present level will determine how quickly you can move to the next higher level.

Every little drop counts. In fact, one little drop may make the significant difference as Karen Percy and Brian Orser found out. Religiously focus on preparing yourself, and your opportunity will come.

"If a man can write a better book, preach a better sermon, or make a better mouse-trap, than his neighbour, though he builds his house in the woods, the world will make a beaten path to his door."

- Ralph Waldo Emerson

23

Your Attitude Can Make
The Difference

Our attitude determines how we are going to react to a given situation. Once a direction has been chosen, it becomes very difficult to change it.

Attitude plays a very important role in selling. The prospect is more influenced by the attitude of the salesperson than by the product or the service being sold.

This essay describes five different elements of attitude and suggests that our attitude to ourselves is the most important element.

Read also essay number 24.

Y ou must have heard of Pareto's 80/20 principle which says, "If all things are put in the order of their value, eighty per cent of the total value would come from the top twenty per cent of the things." With slight variations in the ratio, this formula has been found to apply to almost every walk of life.

In the Life Insurance industry, seventy-five per cent of sales are brought by the top twenty-five per cent of the sales persons and those in the bottom twenty-five per cent get only five per cent of the total business. Only the top five per cent of the sales persons qualify for membership in the Million Dollar Round Table (by selling policies worth one million dollars during the year).

What differentiates the top performers from the bottom ones? Is it their education, age, territory, organizational support or something else?

Each of these factors counts but little. For example, a good education is considered to be an asset but then there are many who, with little education, have proven to be high producers! The same applies to most of the other factors. But there is one factor which is responsible for this great disparity. It is attitude.

What is attitude?

Five different persons will most likely give you five entirely different answers. I heard one person comment, "When people do not know where to pin-point the problem, they say it's the attitude."

I think that attitude means the way you feel about the situation. The key word here is **feel**.

Since feeling is an emotion, it is purely subjective. It is your interpretation of a situation, based upon your past experiences. Often we do not know why we feel in a certain way, but we try to rationalize it by some logical reasoning.

Every piece of information is stored in our memory together with its associated feeling. Some may be weak and some strong but the element of feeling is always present. When you recall a past experience, the associated feeling pops out. Think of some song that you heard five or ten years ago. You will notice that you immediately recall some of the feelings you experienced when you heard that song for the first time.

Our mind tries to relate all new information with some information already existing in our memory. Thus, based upon whether a related experience had been negative or positive, the present situation appears to be negative or positive.

But how does attitude affect performance?

Our attitude determines how we react to our situations.

A shoe company sent two of their sales persons to a certain part of Africa to explore the market. Within a week one person sent a telegram, "There is no market. No one wears shoes here." At the same time the company received a telegram from the other person, "Tremendous opportunity. Almost every one needs shoes here."

It is not only possible but quite usual for two different persons to perceive the same situation in entirely different ways.

You may not get what you want to get, but you generally get what you expect to get, and you generally see what you expect to see. With a negative attitude, you are likely to see a problem in every situation. But, with a positive attitude, you can find an opportunity in every problem.

There are five elements of attitude: Your attitude toward (1) yourself, (2) others, (3) your product, (4) your company or employer and (5) your profession.

Your attitude toward yourself decides how much you like yourself, how proud you feel about the kind of person that you think you are.

Your attitude toward others determines how you are going to treat them. According to the law of expectation, people generally behave the way that you expect them to behave. Pressure creates pressure.

Your attitude toward your product tells how you feel about what you produce, create or sell.

Your attitude toward your company or employer reveals how you feel about being a part of that family. Do you feel proud of belonging there, or do you feel being trapped?

And, finally, your attitude toward your profession tells how worthwhile you consider the contribution of your profession to the service of the community (or the mankind). This generally controls your career accomplishments.

Since attitude is related to feelings, it is almost always conveyed by non-verbal signals, which are very difficult to be hidden. It is extremely rare to feel one way and to act in an entirely different way.

Your attitude toward yourself is the most important element. It is difficult for you to like others if you dislike yourself. No one can like you more than you like yourself.

Your liking of your product, your company or your profession, is possible only when you build some pride in yourself. The more you like yourself, the more you enjoy the world around you, the more you put your heart in what you do and the better you perform. You experience the rewards and gain additional pride in being the type of person you think you are.

People do business with people they like. When you cry, you are left alone to cry. But when you laugh, and have fun, every one wants to share it with you. No one likes to join the losers. Every one loves to do business with winners.

You can be a winner. Take a moment to review the five elements of your attitude. Change your attitude and you can change your world. Yes, attitude makes all the difference.

"Doing easily what others find difficult is talent; doing what is impossible for talent is genius.
- Henri F. Amiel

24

The Root Of Happiness Is Self-Esteem

Real happiness comes from the feeling of having been useful to other human beings, while making the best use of our own skills. This builds our self-esteem and success, because the latter is directly proportional to our self-esteem.

This essay suggests that whenever we try competing with the Joneses, we are likely to hurt ourselves. Our real competition should be against ourselves, against our current capabilities

Read also essay numbers 47, 57, 75 and 99.

A re you happy with your accomplishments? If not, perhaps you should look at your self-esteem.

It is difficult to be proud of yourself when you feel that you are not accomplishing what you would like. On the other hand, the more you accomplish, the prouder you feel about yourself. Thus, "the sense of pride in yourself" and "your level of accomplishment" are definitely related. The question is, "Which governs which?"

An accomplishment is a result. The right effort and the right attitude are some of its aids. We can control most of our attitudes, but sometimes it takes effort to control our negative impulses. Wisdom lies in concentrating on doing that which is within our control and in leaving the rest to the Supreme power. Sooner or later, every effort will bring the desired result.

Survey after survey reveals that nearly ninety per cent of all people consider themselves to be inferior. Isn't that ridiculous? Mathematically, only fifty per cent would fall below the average line. It is true that there may be some error in the survey, but not of that magnitude!

A below par accomplishment fits very well with a below average self image. To improve the level of our accomplishments, we must explore the means of improving it.

Why do we put ourselves down?

One reason is that "pride in oneself" is often confused with vanity, which is considered to be a sinful trait. But there is a difference between the two. The demarcation may be a thin line, but it is there. At times, this difference becomes a matter of perspective. It is possible to remain humble without losing an inner sense of pride in ourselves.

There is another reason which, perhaps, is more important.

We are brought up in a society which keeps pointing to our weakness. If a child gets honours in one subject, the parents ask for his position in the class. If the child wins a position, the parent asks, "Why not the trophy?" The push continues. No matter how well the child does, he finds himself inferior to someone. This pushing game is common in every walk of life. We fail to realize that everyone will remain poor compared to someone.

Do you know the origin of the word, "make-up"?

One lady felt that she was not beautiful enough. She envisioned an ideal, beautiful lady and started thinking how she could make up for the difference between her beauty and that of her ideal lady. Hence the term, "make-up". But the trouble is that no matter how much one uses make-up, there will always remain a gap between oneself and the ideal. Thus, the feeling of inferiority can't be completely eliminated.

Whenever we compare one of our abilities with that of others, we risk lowering our self-esteem. The moment we start thinking of surpassing someone, in some area, that person sets up some negative vibrations to counter our effort. Up to a limit, these vibrations are beneficial, but beyond that they become overwhelming and defeat us.

But, instead of competing with somebody else, why not compete with yourself? Why not concentrate on making better use of the potential that the Creator blessed you with?

Experts claim that an average person uses less than ten per cent of his God-given potential. Imagine how much room is left for us to grow!

Someone asked George Bernard Shaw, "If you had to relive your life, what would you like to become?" He quickly replied, "I would like to become the George Bernard Shaw that was capable of becoming."

Until we forget external competitions, we cannot truly focus on the internal one. The scope of growth in the inner competition is enormous and in that we enjoy everyone's support because no one perceives himself (or herself) as our competitor. As we succeed in our inner competition, we excel in the real world as well.

To cultivate our self-esteem, psychologists suggest that we use some affirmations such as, "I am the best", "I am the strongest", or "I am the richest". Although I strongly believe in the power of affirmations (that we truly become what we think of most of the time), I feel that many affirmations lead us to frustrations.

Let's suppose that you affirm, "I am the best". This statement implies, "best among a given number of persons". Now, let's remember that no one will concede that you are better without giving you a good fight. When everyone starts fighting you, your chances of meeting your goal diminish. You keep affirming, but after a while doubt sets in. You start feeling frustrated. The less you believe, the less you act. Finally, you reach the point when you give up completely and say, "Well, affirmations do not work for me."

Now, let's think of an internal competition. Since riches come to us in direct proportion to the value that we provide to others, we should focus on becoming more and more valuable. Consider the affirmation, "I am already a valuable person and every single day I am becoming even more valuable." You will immediately believe it because you realize that it contains the truth and nothing but the truth. Right now, you are more valuable than you think you are and by concentrating on the ways that you could become even more valuable, you will start seeing those opportunities and moving towards them.

Real happiness comes only by becoming useful to others. The more you visualize yourself as being useful, the happier you become and the longer you live. The moment you sincerely feel that you are of absolutely no use to any one, you die spiritually, and physical death follows soon after.

Don't expect to win a trophy in every line of activity. Find out your niche and develop it. Serve others by becoming the best in your particular niche. Allow others to excel in their areas while you excel in yours. In this way, your accomplishments will soar and you will experience real happiness.

Let's not strive for the kind of community in which everyone became an expert baker but no one cared to cultivate the wheat.

25

Responsibility   Brings   Freedom

The word "responsibility" appears to convey a negative connotation. It seems to mean "being tied up" or "liable to be punished". But in reality "responsibility" is always an asset. It always brings some associated power.

Responsibility also brings freedom. The more responsibility you are willing to assume, the more freedom you are allowed in the choice of the means that you would like to employ, in order to execute that responsibility.

This essay advises us to re-examine our image of "responsibility" and suggests that responsibility and freedom are two sides of the same coin.

Read also essay numbers 17, 34, 50 and 66.

"**R**esponsibility" is generally associated with the feeling of bad luck, burden or being tied down. Some times it is seen as a handicap to creativity. I have often heard people say, 'I wish I could do that but I have the responsibility of the family, I have to pay the bills etc.' Often a responsibility is perceived as something that one has to do and therefore appears as an external, undesirable force working on the individual. As a result, one envisions an external pressure, some stress and a feeling of misery in its presence.

Like a coin, every issue has two sides. You can find a beautiful flower in the middle of some thorns. There is some benefit associated with every loss. Unfortunately, we rarely see both sides of an issue. We generally notice only that which we pay attention to. In this essay I want to share with you my perceptions of the other side of the coin of responsibility.

What is responsibility?

Responsibility means taking independent action and then being prepared to accept all outcomes (good or bad) resulting from that action. The goal is to take those actions that will bring some desired, beneficial result.

It implies choosing one of a number of possible actions and making the best (within the capability of the individual) use of the resources available. It teaches us what to expect when we take (or neglect to take) a certain action. As we use it, we become better at it and get ready for assuming bigger, more difficult or more complicated responsibilities.

Every responsibility provides us with an opportunity to grow. What physical push-ups do to the building of our physical strength, responsibilities do to the building of our spiritual strength. Yes, it is true that responsibilities tie us down, but we grow only when we have to work against some restraints. A kite rises only against a wind. We train our muscles only by stretching them.

What is the opposite of responsibility?

If you ask a number of people what they consider to be the opposite of responsibility, the most common answer would be "freedom". The argument is that freedom means being able to do what one likes (or wants) to do. Here one feels in control.

Since real happiness comes only when we feel that we are able to do what we want to do, responsibility is perceived as a curse to happiness. But this picture is highly distorted.

Responsibility and freedom go hand in hand. Anyone deprived of all responsibilities is totally dependent on others and is therefore not a free person. Babies have no responsibility and little freedom. Prisoners have little responsibility and little freedom. Look at any nation. The less responsibility the citizens have, the less freedom they enjoy.

As a child grows and assumes some responsibility for his affairs, he is given some freedom on how he wishes to spend his time and other resources. The more responsibility that he can assume, the more freedom he is allowed. The moment he starts neglecting some of his responsibilities, he loses some of his previous freedom. This relationship applies in every walk of our life. The more responsibility we assume, the greater freedom we are given.

Can we convert our "have to" into our "want to"?

Yes, to a large extent we can do that. You will find some such ideas in essay number 17, "Get Control Over Your Have-To Activities". But you may still find some activities that you must accept. Rather than feel miserable about this, why not accept these activities boldly, as a challenge? Remember the advice from the Bible, "Do and you will gain the strength."

We cannot ignore the laws of nature. For example, whether we like it or not, the law of gravity is going to stay with us. We have no choice but to obey it. However, by learning how it works, we can use it to our advantage.

Similarly, we must accept some essential responsibilities. If we do not accept them willingly, someone will impose them on us. The choice is ours.

The skill of accepting and handling responsibility is developed like any other skill. We must start small and keep stretching bit by bit. We cannot expect to lift four hundred pounds of weight on the first day. But, with constant training, some day, we can do that.

Stretching too much too quickly can work against us by frustrating and depressing instead of encouraging us. Also, remember that what was a stretch for you yesterday, may not be a stretch for you today. Always strive for a bit beyond your perceived limit.

No matter where you are, right now you have assumed, or you are given, certain responsibility. How you handle this one determines how quickly you will be given the next higher responsibility. You, and only you, determine the limit to which you can rise.

If freedom and responsibility go hand in hand, then what is the opposite of responsibility?

I believe that the opposite of "responsibility" is "blame". We blame external circumstances only when we do not want to share our piece of the responsibility. Blaming others, or external circumstances, weakens us. Accepting the responsibility, and tackling it as a challenge, strengthens us.

George Bernard Shaw once commented, "People are always blaming their circumstances for what they are. I don't believe in circumstances. The people who get on in this world are the people who get up and look for the circumstances they want and if they can't find them, make them."

If you want to have and maintain real freedom, welcome the responsibilities that come your way and focus on doing your best. Very soon you will experience more freedom than you ever dreamed possible. Responsibility and freedom are two sides of the same coin.

"All business depends upon men fulfilling their responsibilities."
-Mahatma Gandhi

26

Only Worthy Goals Excite Us

Why is it that some goals excite us, while others don't? This essay suggests that only worthy goals can excite us and that worthy goals are characterised by the fact that they benefit everyone. They harm no one. There is no loser.

Before you start working toward achieving a certain goal, examine it in the light of the benefits that it would provide to others. If it benefits, then it is worthy. It it doesn't, just drop it and look for some other worthy goal.

Read also essay number 13, and 22.

E arle Nightingale defined success as "The progressive realization of a worthy ideal". The question is, "What is a worthy ideal?"

The inventive genius Charles Kettering said, "A problem well defined is a problem half solved." As an extension of this statement many experts claim that a goal properly set is a goal half achieved. Again the question arises, "What is a proper goal?"

David Henry Thoreau said, "At the age of twenty-five most people are full of dreams and enthusiasm. However, within a few years, the great majority abandon their dreams and accept a life of quiet desperation. They become frustrated in their efforts or feel overwhelmed by their obstacles." What is the main cause of this rapid drop?

Perhaps the main reason is the absence of worthy ideals. The path of success is full of pot-holes, and only a powerful force of worthy ideals can pull you out of those holes and keep you on track.

A good ideal draws positive forces - forces that steer us in the right direction. But wrong or vague ideals generate conflicting forces, some of which immobilize us, or even cause us to move away from the desired destination. Progress is possible only when we have a clear picture of the desired destination and a strong inner feeling that the chosen destination is worthy. To build the necessary force (or the pressure) that could propel us in the right direction, we must maintain that strong feeling. Any doubt in that feeling works like a leakage in the main pressure chamber - the storehouse of our drive and enthusiasm.

Let's look at some characteristics of a worthy ideal.

A child is told that he can have anything that he can dream of or desire. Is that always true? No, and in my opinion, this is the root of most of our frustrations.

The universe is governed by certain laws of checks and balances, and we must abide by them. Therefore, we should discover the checks that apply to us and make the full use of the latitude that is provided within them. As long as we operate within those checks, we can achieve anything that we desire or dream of. Our worthy ideal should be the highest possible ideal within our limits.

One of nature's limits requires that we must not do anything that would hurt someone. Yes, it is true that nature allows destruction, but only for overall benefit. To verify whether your ideal is worthy or not, you should check if it is going to benefit others. If it helps, then find out how, and to how many. The more beneficial it is to others, the worthier it is, and the more excited you will feel about it. That means, the more support you will receive from others for its achievement.

We commonly notice the games where one person wins while another loses and we accept this as the norm of all games. However, in the important games of life, there are no losers.

Suppose your ideal is to earn a certain amount of money. You can achieve it in one of two ways. You can either go for a bigger piece of the pie, or you can somehow try to enlarge the existing pie and then share part of it. By both methods you would have the possibility of getting more of the pie than what you had before. But there is a tremendous difference in the repercussions of the two methods. The moment you intend to grab a slightly bigger piece than your share of the pie, you create some opposing forces. No one likes to give up any of his or her share easily. The more you intend to grab, the more opposing forces you set up. Consequently, you either do not get what you want to get, or experience the Pyrrhic victory (a victory gained at too great a cost). But if you enlarge the pie, you create an opportunity for everybody else to get a little extra piece as well. Everyone will like you for doing this and will help you to achieve your chosen ideal.

By nature, we experience happiness only when we are able to increase the happiness of others. When we get something at the expense of someone, we generally do not feel good about ourselves.

A worthy ideal is an ideal that does not harm anyone and benefits a great number of people. You not only achieve that ideal, but through its achievement, you also experience some new self-esteem, enthusiasm and overall happiness in your life.

Another way of looking at ideals is to think of the characteristics that you would like others to acquire. What would you like your children and students to become? What would those ideal characteristics be? Why do you think those will help them? If you really feel strongly about these characteristics, why don't you go ahead and try to acquire them yourself? Do you feel that you are too old to undertake that challenge? No, you are never too old. If you do the best that you can do, you will convince others that you really believe in what you are preaching.

Remember, everyone is a teacher in some respect. We teach others every single moment by the way we behave and live our own life. Everyone who ever came in contact with you, took a little piece of your character. Those who respect you more, or love you more, copy you more. There are only two ways that we learn something, by imitation or by defiance. We imitate the characteristics that we admire, or believe to be good and we defy those that we believe to be wrong. We are exposed to different ideas either directly by a person or through the media of books, magazines, tapes etc.. Thus, whether you realize it or not, you are playing a definite role in influencing the lives of others.

When we talk of setting an ideal most people think of having something, money or possessions or facilities that money can buy. It is interesting to note that money is a by-product. It comes to us in direct proportion to the service that we provide to others. The more valuable service that you can offer, the more money will come to you. One way of doing this is to make yourself more valuable, more useful. The focus of a worthy goal therefore should be to make yourself more valuable. You would then be competing against yourself, rather than competing against someone else. The moment you stop competing against others, they start helping you, and you find yourself in a win-win situation.

Jim Rohn suggests that we should go for the reasons. Think of all the reasons why you want to achieve that ideal. When you have enough reasons - and feel good about being able to help others - you have a worthy ideal.

The best time to start something is now. Take a few days off and reflect on where you are and where you would like to be. Think of some worthy ideals by keeping "service to others" in the fore front of your mind.

"I have learned this, by my experiment, that if one advances confidently in the direction of his dreams, and endeavours to live the life which he has imagined, he will meet with a success unexpected in common hours."
- Henry David Thoreau

27

Fund-Raising
Can Be A Win-Win Game

Almost every week we meet someone who is trying to raise funds for some good cause. In most campaigns this effort simply results in the transfer of funds from one pocket to another, which also means that some person gains while many others lose.

This essay presents some ideas by which both parties can win.

Read also essay number 46 and 56.

F und-raising is perhaps one of the most important challenges of many volunteer organizations. It demands time and energy and often frustrates the persons involved.

Although most people like to support a good cause, beyond a certain limit they get fed up. There is hardly a week when someone or other is not running a fund-raising campaign!

I have often noticed people buying an item, or making a pledge, for the sake of, 'You scratch my back and I will scratch yours.' Does it create a net winner?

I believe that every fund-raising project should meet two basic needs, namely, (1) it should be moral and ethical, and (2) it should result in a win-win situation.

Contrary to common belief, not all existing methods are moral and ethical. I feel that raising funds through lotteries, Bingos or Casinos is not moral because we are really taking money mostly from those who are poor and who themselves need help. They have no realistic dream for their life, no definite goal, no ambition. They are desperately looking for any 'get-rich-quick' scheme. After having lost all their hopes they seek help from charities and add to the problem that your organization is trying to alleviate.

I realize that this topic is controversial, and I do not wish to waste valuable space debating it. Therefore, let's look at the second basic requirement.

If you donate ten dollars to me, I become richer, while you become poorer by ten dollars. In other words, I win while you lose. In that case, there is a good chance that, deep down in your heart, you do not feel happy about it.

And what about me? Do I really feel happy about having milked you of the ten dollars? No, I don't, because basic human nature is to help others. We feel happy only when we are able to increase others' happiness. Any action that makes others a bit uncomfortable, also makes us feel a little guilty.

But how are we to raise the funds then?

A better way is to strive for the win-win situation.

Suppose I provide you with a useful service, at some bargain rate, in exchange for the ten dollars. You would be happy and I would enjoy the task and learn an honourable and useful skill "selling" at the same time! This is a win-win situation because it enriches both parties.

You may ask, "But what can the fund-raiser sell?"

You can find many people who are willing to donate their services for a good cause. For example, I would rather donate a full day of my time giving a seminar than four hours of time working in a Bingo hall! Almost every professional would be willing to donate a piece of his or her service. Make a list of those services and auction them. The net profit would be the funds raised.

Examples of such services would be: preparing a will, providing a certain amount of accounting service; landscaping; dry-walling; painting; furnace cleaning; car tune-up; tire service; gift certificate from various stores; old furniture; used clothes; etc. etc.

This will definitely require some planning and preparation, but can generate funds while maintaining the spirits of the persons involved.

You can add "class" to the auction event, by inviting some celebrities and/or respected members of your community. Consider also inviting some individuals who, in the past, have benefited greatly from your services. They are proof of the cause for which you are raising the fund.

Consider soliciting the services or materials that you would buy from those funds. Review your last year's expenses and think of people who could have donated some of the items or services that you paid for. I am sure, you will find several.

Mahatma Gandhi was perhaps one of the best fund raisers. He raised huge funds (using only ethical and moral means) from people who were literally starving. His technique was simple. He said, "Give me a piece of whatever you have." Later on, he auctioned everything and collected the money.

People think twice before parting with their money, but they are relatively liberal in parting with their material possessions or donating their time or services. Any donation, worth even a penny, is proof of that person's moral support for your cause.

Gandhi spent a lot of his time building public awareness for his cause. You may be providing a really valuable service, but what makes you think that the general public knows about it? Prepare promotional brochures about your services and encourage some of your members to speak to the various service clubs. The members of those clubs could be in positions to offer you help that would otherwise cost a lot of money.

Perhaps the most important factor is your personal belief in the cause that you are representing. Over ninety per cent of our messages are conveyed non-verbally. It is extremely hard for us to hide our feelings. The person whom you approach reads your inner feelings and enthusiasm and decides whether or not to help you. To succeed in raising funds, you need to sell your ideas to others, but first you yourself have to be totally sold on it.

Let me share with you an interesting incident.

Many years ago, Dr. Frank Gunsaulus was giving a talk on "What I Would Do If I Had a Million Dollars". He described his dream of starting a college where the students could receive some practical training.

At the end of the talk, a man by the name of Phillip D. Armour approached him and said, 'I believed every word that you said and just to prove it, I am going to give you the million dollars, if you will come to my office tomorrow morning.' This is a true story. This is how The Armour Institute of Technology, now known as The Illinois Institute of Technology, was started.

If you sincerely believe in your cause, money will never be the main obstacle. There are many ways of raising funds. I recommend that you go for the win-win alternatives.

If you are content with your present methods, by all means keep using them. But if you are experiencing frustration, why not try one of the ideas suggested in this essay?

"Common people do not pray; they only beg."
-George Bernard Shaw

28

Unselfish Service Brings Lasting Happiness

The more we try to find happiness, the more it appears to evade us. First we believe that more money will bring us more happiness. But that proves to be purely an illusion. Few people discover, in a systematic, scientific, way, the secret of real happiness. Some lucky people just stumble upon it.

Real happiness comes only from rendering some unselfish service. The service need not be on a grandiose scale. In fact, any service, within your capabilities, can bring you real happiness, provided that you render it without expecting, or accepting any compensation in return.

Read also essay numbers 11, 17, 24 and 37.

L ife is full of challenges - some we enjoy, some we fear, and some we treat with a degree of apprehension.

Those that frighten us, depress us and often immobilize us; those that apprehend us keep us on our toes; and those that excite us provide us with reason for our living. We keep looking for challenges. We thrive on them. In fact, in their total absence, we die spiritually.

Of all the different varieties of challenges, perhaps the one that intrigues us the most is our search for real happiness.

Most people have the illusion that once they earn a certain amount of money, they will be happy. This is not true.

Yes, money is essential, and one must apply his knowledge and skills to earn enough money to meet all his financial needs. But money alone does not bring real happiness.

If your needs keep growing faster than your ability to earn the money to satisfy them, you may spend all your life like a dog chasing his own tail.

One day a lady told me that the main cause of most marriage problems was "the lack of sufficient funds between the couples". Had this been a universal truth, Elizabeth Taylor would not have married Richard Burton twice!

I believe that there are two important ingredients of real happiness, (1) the feeling of having control over one's life and (2) the feeling of being useful to others.

I have deliberately used the term "feeling". You may have full control over your life but, unless you **feel** that you have that control, you cannot experience real happiness.

Similarly, you may be a very valuable citizen but, if you feel that you are not making any worthwhile contribution, then you will remain unhappy.

What do we mean by having control over our life?

Look at your daily activities and notice that there are some that you have to do and there are others that you want to do.

When you do an activity that you feel you have to do, then you are not really in your control, you are being controlled by some external force. You may do something to please someone, or to conform to some norms, or simply to compete with the Joneses. But when you do something that you want to do, then only are you in control.

Every external force is a drag on your life and every internal force works like the upward thrust of a rocket engine which can lift you to tremendous heights. Common sense suggests that we strive for more internal and less external control.

But the reality is that over ninety per cent of people live most of their lives driven by external forces. And the tragedy is that they go through their entire life without even realizing it.

But what is the solution?

Well, to find the solution, you must first have a good grasp of the problem. A prisoner will make no effort to get out of prison until he realizes that he is imprisoned, isn't that right?

Become aware of the activities that you feel you have to do. Analyse them. Ask yourself, "Why do I have to do this? Is there some way that I could avoid it? Can I trade it for some other activity that I choose to do?"

Every time that you replace one of your have-to activities by one of your want-to activities, you gain a little more control over your own life.

By consciously looking for them, and by using discipline, you will be able to make a marked difference in the quality of your life. You will not only attain more happiness but will also accomplish more.

The common denominator of all great achievers of the world has been that they engaged themselves mostly in the activities that they wanted to do.

To discuss the second ingredient, let me ask you another question. If you had a choice, what kind of activities would you really like to do?

Fun and pleasure are good for a while but, in the long run, everybody sincerely wants to make a meaningful contribution to society because the basic human nature is to serve.

Have you not experienced a sense of inner happiness when you helped a needy person? Of course you did, because at that moment, you felt that you were a worthwhile person.

To help others, you must first make yourself more capable of helping. You are a unique creation of God. Experts tell us that most of us go to our graves with nearly ninety per cent of our potential left unrealized. Don't let that happen to you. Devote some time discovering your unique strengths and resolve to develop them.

Martin Luther King, Jr. once said, "He who has not found a cause to die for, has not learned how to live."

It is only through providing some unselfish service that you can discover your cause for life.

Make it a point to do one thing every day for the sole purpose of helping some needy person. Refuse to accept any compensation for this act. Even the little courtesy of helping some elderly or handicapped person will make a noticeable increase in your self-esteem. Once you have the ball rolling, it will not take long for it to assume a giant proportion.

Reflect for a moment on these two ingredients - having control over your life and making yourself more useful to others, and you will see that as you practice them, you attain real happiness. And that is the important challenge of life.

"The best training any parent can give a child is to train the child to train himself."

- A. P. Gouthey

29

"But" and "However" Impede Communication

A normal person speaks at the rate of approximately one hundred and fifty words per minute and processes information at about two thousand words per minute. This allows him a substantial amount of free time to "entertain" some other thoughts in-between.

A speaker must make some effort to ensure that his listener's attention is maintained, and continually brought back, when necessary. This is generally accomplished through the use of some attention-capturing words or non-verbal signals.

Two words, which are quite commonly used, and which prove to be deadly for effective communication, are "but" and "however". "But" negates, or nullifies, everything that has been said until that moment. "However" is only slightly less destructive than "But".

This essay points out how "But" and "However" hurt us and how we can get around them.

Read also essay numbers 20 and 36.

The ability to communicate is one of the rare gifts that the Creator has given us. Because of this gift we are able to take advantage of the vast storehouse of knowledge and experience collected by every other human being, living or dead.

Speaking is one facet of communication. With its aid we not only express our ideas, but often determine the extent to which we allow others to express theirs. Communication is greatly influenced by the prevailing mood of the environment.

It is interesting to note that we can absorb information at a rate somewhere between four hundred and two thousand words a minute, whereas we generally speak at a rate of between one hundred and two hundred words a minute. Thus, while we are speaking, our listener(s) have a lot of "free time" to entertain other thoughts if they wish. When we speak, it is our responsibility to maintain the attention of our listener(s). Therefore, we should use words and non-verbal signals with thought and care.

Some words are effective in maintaining, or bringing back, the attention of the listener. For example, every time that you use your listener's name, you capture his attention. When you talk about a matter that interests him, you have his attention.

There are some words that may cause your listener to lose all (or at least partial) interest in what you are saying. It is not possible for me to provide you with a list of such words or phrases - these will vary from person to person and from situation to situation - but I will try to capture your awareness of this important element of communication. Select some words, notice their uses and make your own judgment of their influence on the effectiveness of the communication.

Let me draw your attention to the influence of two seemingly harmless conjunctions - "but" and "however" - which are very commonly used in everyday discussions.

Let's imagine that you have just expressed an idea or an argument and your listener responds by saying, "You are right, but...." What does he really mean? Does he sincerely mean that he agrees with your argument? I doubt it. In my opinion, he either means that you are wrong or that your argument is irrelevant to the topic. In both cases, he has nullified what you were trying to accomplish.

The use of the conjunction "but" virtually negates everything that has been said up to that moment.

The conjunction "however" is not so forceful, but it also has a cancelling effect. If a person says to you, "You are right, however....", he is actually drawing your attention to an important point or consideration that he thinks you have overlooked.

The psychological influence of these conjunctions is profound.

The moment someone counters your statement by using "but" or "however", he stops paying full attention to your arguments. You may try to counter his, but he is not really listening to you! Consequently, a good part of your argument is lost. This is similar to creating a thin film or screen as barrier to the communication process. If the transaction continues like this, the barrier will become stronger and stronger and very soon you will find that no one is listening. That's why I say that "but" and "however" may impede communication.

You may notice that people who respond with either "but" or "however" are generally very eager to give their opinion on what you have just said. In many cases, they may even start speaking before you have completed your sentence. This proves that they are not really listening to you. If you doubt it, try stopping in the middle of your sentence. The person may not even notice that you have stopped talking.

But what is the solution?

The first step to solving any problem is developing awareness of the existence of the problem. Recognize the negative influence of these words, and see if you can maintain the discussion without using them.

Try pausing for a few seconds after the other person has finished his sentence. This will give you not only time to think of an appropriate response, but it will also generate an atmosphere of courtesy, respect and mutual trust. Whatever you say after that pause will command more power and will result in better understanding.

While someone was speaking to him, Mahatma Gandhi listened with all his attention. When everyone had his or her turn, then, and only then, he spoke. Since he had respectfully listened to others, they felt obliged to listen to his arguments or views. In this way he commanded a good deal of attention.

Try replacing "but" and "however" with the conjunction "and". For example, you may say, 'You are right, and here is something else that's also true', or 'You are right, and here is another way to think about it.' In this way, you are supporting the area of agreement and exploring some additional area where agreement may be reached. This will ensure ending the discussion on a win-win feeling.

On some occasions, the use of "but" and "however" may be appropriate. If you want to tear the other person's argument apart, you may like to try it. But I believe that it is much better to gain the cooperation of the other fellow than to try to crush him.

Challenge yourself to eliminate the use of "Yes, but.." and "yes, however..." from your discussions and notice the marked improvement in your communication ability.

"Discretion of speech is more than eloquence."
- Francis Bacon

30

Imitation is the Mother of Learning

We acquire habits either through imitation or by defiance. In most cases we use imitation.

If you are not happy with one of your behaviours, look around and try to identify the person who is "feeding" you, or supporting you in maintaining, that behaviour.

This essay suggests that the simplest way of acquiring a new skill is to literally surround yourself with some people who already possess that skill. If you cannot get surrounded by such people, surround yourself by their portraits, products or anything that could symbolize them. If you do so, then soon you will acquire that skill almost magically.

Read also essay numbers 49 and 54.

D o you realize what role "imitation" plays in the shaping of your life? Well, it is much greater than what you or I would be willing to accept.

Our life is governed by habits. It is estimated that we perform more than ninety per cent of our everyday tasks unconsciously, guided solely by our habits. And these habits we have acquired by imitating someone to whom we were exposed.

The second child in most families often learns faster than the first one. The reason is simple. He does not have to go far to find someone whom he can imitate. The same is true for subsequent children in the family, provided the difference in age is not too great.

The learning of a language is a classic example of the role of imitation. Every child learns to speak long before he or she learns to read or write. I am told that in the language of the Canadian Indians, there is no word equivalent to the word "stuttering". The explanation is that a Canadian Indian child did not have the occasion to see any one stutter, therefore, he did not learn to stutter.

Every single habit or skill of yours, you have acquired by some form of imitation. You imitated your parents, your siblings, your friends, your teachers or someone with whom you came in touch. From some of them, you may have acquired many habits, whereas from others maybe just a few. Generally, we imitate those whom we admire or respect - the more the respect, the greater the degree of imitation.

Sometimes we acquire a habit as a form of defiance. For example, my father was a chain smoker. My elder brother imitated this habit, while I defied it completely. As a result I have never smoked a cigarette in my life.

Imitation is basic to human nature. You may have noticed that when one person in a room yawns, there is an immediate and automatic yawning by many others in the same room. The weeping or the smiling of one person causes others to do the same. It's difficult to hide the powerful impulse to imitate what we see around.

Our whole character or personality is built, piece by piece, on imitation. Since, to imitate, you must first see someone else's behaviour, your total personality is simply the sum of the little pieces of various characteristics that you picked up from people to whom you have been exposed. Even your value system is influenced by those people who surround you.

It has been observed that, with the passage of time, husband and wife pick up each other's characteristics - mostly by imitating them unconsciously.

If a man of "good" character happens to find himself among men of "bad" character, he will most likely hate or abhor the habits of his new company but, after a while, will start tolerating them. If he remains in their company long, then in due course, he will start accepting them, understanding them, and then, even supporting them. This phenomenon has been found to hold true in countless cases. It takes an extremely strong will and character to fight the influence of immediate environments.

If you think that you have a bad habit, ask yourself, 'From whom did I pick up this habit?' If you are honest, you will have no difficulty tracing the person. It is virtually impossible to pick up a habit out of the blue.

For a habit to stay with you, you must feed it regularly and adequately - similar to feeding a fire. This is provided by someone who is an important part of your life.

If you sincerely want to rid yourself of a certain habit, find out who is feeding that habit (by way of accompanying you in maintaining that habit) and resolve to stay away from that person until you get control of that habit and kick it completely. Identifying the person and disassociating with him constitutes more than eighty per cent of the battle. The person will resist your efforts, because he too needs those who can feed his habit.

Creating a physical distance is very effective but not always possible since you may not want to hurt that person. However, you can always create and maintain the distance in your mind.

Tell yourself that you are assuming full control over your life and that you refuse to allow anyone to impress his behaviour on you. This you can cultivate fairly easily.

Since nature abhors vacuums, it is difficult to simply throw away an existing habit. It is far easier to replace one habit with another. Think of a habit that you would like to acquire, and keep diverting your attention from thinking about the bad habit to thinking about the good one. Let the good habit take root and then it will take care of itself. It is said that first a man makes a habit and then the habit makes the man.

Seek out a person with a good habit that you would like to acquire. Look for avenues of bringing yourself close to him and very soon you will find yourself acquiring that habit.

The key is to surround yourself with people who already have the habits (or the characteristics) that you wish to acquire. Slowly but surely, by some process of osmosis, you will find yourself picking up those habits.

Try this technique consciously for the next twenty-one days and notice the improvement in the quality of your life.

It is our inherent nature to imitate the habits of the people around us. We learn by imitation. In fact, imitation is the mother of man's personality.

"To see things in the seed is genius."
- Lao Tze

31

We Attract Circumstances

On the surface it appears that many innocent people get victimized. But this essay suggests that the victims themselves, through non-verbal signals or thought vibrations, attract the circumstances that lead them to being victimized.

This theory is substantiated in this essay through a review of a series of situations that led to Mahatma Gandhi's assassination. The review reveals that the main cause of his assassination was his loss of a will to live.

This essay suggests that by taking control of our own thoughts and actions, we can easily protect ourselves from being victimized.

Read also essay number 70.

O nce in a while, everyone feels that he or she has been victimized in some way or other. Does this happen just by chance, or do we do something voluntarily to ask for it?

Try to recall a situation where you felt you were victimized. Did you feel that it happened all of a sudden, or perhaps it was the culmination of a number of little incidents? Did you play any role in creating the condition, or were you simply victimized? Chances are that the situation built up piece by piece and that you did voluntarily contribute to it.

According to the Law of Thought Vibrations, our mind transmits signals describing our current dominant thought. These signals are received and reacted to by many other minds. Both the transmitting and the receiving takes place at the unconscious level of the mind.

You may have experienced situations when you were thinking of someone and all of a sudden that person called you, wrote to you or bumped into you in the most unexpected place. You may be thinking of something and your friend or somebody else happened to have exactly the same thought. Between husband and wife it is a common occurrence that as one thinks of a tune, the other starts to sing it. They often convey their choice or decision to each other without sharing any word. All these are caused by thought vibrations.

Not only do we mentally express our thoughts and desires, but we also literally describe how we like others to treat us. Every single action of ours is a message which is received consciously or unconsciously by every other mind. The minds that are interested in this message act upon it accordingly. Thus, through the use of thought vibrations, all minds communicate with each other and thereby specify how they wish to be treated. No one ever treats us contrary to the message that we are sending out, at the particular moment.

When a mugger is on the prowl, he looks around for possible victims and generally selects the person who appears to offer the minimum resistance. Although this reading (or observation) takes place at the subconscious level, the fact remains that the victim plays a definite role in being selected as the target for an attack.

By means of our thoughts, we attract other minds and thereby attract related situations or conditions. These situations keep building up, piece by piece, and culminate in the actual victimizing circumstances. It is easy to cry over apparent helplessness, but the truth is that we always have at least some control over the matter.

Let's briefly look at the assassination circumstances of Mahatma Gandhi.

On January 20, 1948, two persons attended his evening prayer meeting, with the sole purpose of assassinating him. According to their plan, one person would throw a bomb in one direction, creating a panic and diverting the attention of the mass. That would leave Gandhi unattended, and the other person would then come close to Gandhi and shoot him. The bomb was thrown and a wall was demolished. There was a slight panic, but within seconds Gandhi urged everyone to remain calm, which they did. As a result, the would be assassin had no chance to shoot.

The person who threw the bomb was arrested and charged. Gandhi pleaded for his release, but he was kept in detention. The other person easily escaped and went to Bombay to regroup and make new plans.

Immediately following the bombing, one member of that group had broken out, and tried to inform the Bombay police of the plot. However, nobody believed him! He even approached one of the provincial cabinet ministers. Everyone thought that the man was insane. After all, who would ever think of assassinating the Mahatma?

The government offered the services of a personal body-guard, but Gandhi declined the offer. Because of his recent fast he was too weak to walk, but he mixed with the crowd as usual. Communal tension was so strong that no one's life was considered safe and yet Gandhi refused any protection.

On January 30, 1948 Mahatma Gandhi was assassinated by the very same person who had escaped after the January 20 attempt. Could this not have been prevented?

It is true that there was a definite conspiracy, but I believe that Gandhi spawned the seed of that conspiracy and helped to foster it. I believe that we ourselves are responsible for every situation in which we ultimately find ourselves.

You surely have heard of the law of cause and effect. It has been described in many ways. "As you sow, so shall you reap." Every cause has a definite and corresponding effect. Good cause produces good effect. Poor cause produces poor effect.

The process of victimization is an effect. The corresponding cause is the dominant thought in the victim's mind. No one can force you to think in any given way. You have total control over your thoughts. If you assume this control fully and entertain only the right thoughts, you cannot be victimized (or at least, you minimize the chances of being victimized).

You may argue that this is not true in every case. You may be right. But may I suggest that this philosophy could prepare and protect you against most threatening circumstances.

The moment you take control of your thoughts, you start radiating vibrations of self-confidence. You let the other person know that you won't allow yourself to be victimized without putting up a good fight. This message itself will discourage most attackers from coming close to you.

This approach will bring you yet another valuable advantage.

In some respect, your life is meaningful only to the extent that you take control over it. When you feel total lack of control, there is literally no life left in your life.

By assuming that you have no control over being victimized, you are giving up part of your right to live.

I believe that there are no victims - only volunteers, because we ourselves attract every circumstance.

32

The Law of 250
Can Work Miracles For You

This essay describes how Joe Girard, using the Law of 250, sold over 1,300 individual cars each year, for five consecutive years and earned a mention in the Guiness Bookof Records.

Ray Kroc built his MacDonald's Empire and Walt Disney built his Disneyland and Disney World, using basically the same principle.

By learning, and by applying this technique, you also can expand your business to any limit that you want.

Read also essay numbers 22 and 48.

J oe Girard holds the world record for selling the maximum number of cars in a year. Between 1972 and 1976, he sold an average of over 1,300 cars each year, none of which were fleet sales.

To my knowledge, this outstanding achievement has not been paralleled by any one since then. What was the main reason for this extraordinary feat?

Although it is not easy to single out, Joe says that the most important reason for his phenomenal success was his discovery of the law of 250.

Once when he was attending a funeral, a question suddenly came into his mind, "How do they know how many invitation cards to print?" He posed the question to the funeral director who said that having learned from experience, he printed 250 cards, and that those were adequate in most cases - being neither too many nor too few.

Next, when attending a wedding reception, the same question popped into his mind. He talked to the catering manager, who said, "Well, that's easy, 250 from each side."

Joe continued to research the number 250. He found that most auditoriums had a seating capacity of 250; most reception areas had a standing capacity of 250, and so on. He then concluded that 250 was a magic number.

People like to talk a lot to other people about what they bought and what they plan to buy. They offer advice about where to buy what, and how much to pay. Those who are in the market to buy, want advice but, suspecting the honesty of a salesperson, prefer to ask persons they know. Generally, they make their buying decision based on that advice - even though that may not be the best, or the right advice, for the particular circumstance.

Joe asked himself, "What would be the consequence if every single customer of mine talked to the 250 persons he or she knows?" The answer to this question boggled his mind. One satisfied (or dissatisfied) customer will share his experience with 250 other prospects. If you have served 250 customers (which is not a large number in any business) then 250 times 250, or up to 62,500 persons will sooner or later receive words about the kind of service that you provide! Every time you turn off just one prospect, you turn off 250 more!! Can you afford to ignore even a single prospect?

Instead of seeing the one prospect sitting across his table, Joe started visualizing him (or her) as the representative of a group of 250 prospects. He gave him the best possible service, and in time, each person in this large network of people became a salesperson for Joe Girard! Joe confesses that without this strategy, he could not have sold an average of more than five cars every single working day for six years.

This strategy can be very powerful. Suppose you are trying to sell a product to someone, and that your net profit from the sale would be just one dollar. Well, one little dollar may not motivate you much and you may even ignore that prospect. But imagine that he is overwhelmed by the quality of your service, talks to the 250 persons he knows, brings them to you and that you are able to sell to every one of them. This would mean a net profit of two hundred and fifty dollars to you! Your motivation will suddenly soar, will it not?

Let's move one step further. Imagine that you provided your best service to every one of those 250 persons. They felt overwhelmed and in turn each one of them talked about it to the 250 persons they knew. There would be some duplication, but chances are that they would bring in thousands of prospects which would mean thousands of dollars of net profit - all as a result of one totally satisfied customer!

This strategy has been religiously followed by at least two persons I know. When Walt Disney built Disneyland, his policy was, "Make it so nice that anyone who visits it once comes again and brings his friends with him." Cleanliness, enjoyment, hospitality, relaxed atmosphere and many other similar amenities were provided, but the main focus was on impressing the visitor so much that he would want to visit again. And of course he talked to everyone that he knew. Invariably, the visit to Disneyland became the highlight of that person's vacation that year. No wonder the business has been very successful.

The other person is Ray Kroc. His main policy in building the MacDonald's chain was, "Do your best to make absolutely sure that not one person walks away dissatisfied." I believe that it is this policy and the power of 250 that enabled the MacDonald's franchise to become so popular all over the world.

There is abundance in the universe. There is always room for you and me. If you focus on improving your product or service and giving your best to every prospect you meet, you also can build an empire like the Disneyland or MacDonald's.

Look at every presentation as the tip of an iceberg. If you deal successfully with the tip, you can capture the entire iceberg. But if you neglect it, or goof up, you lose not only the visible tip but also the invisible part of the iceberg, which in this case could represent as much as ninety-nine per cent of the total.

I might suggest that you also bear in mind that "Birds of the same feather flock together." A teacher will talk to 250 teachers, a farmer to 250 farmers, a lawyer to 250 lawyers, and so on. If you want to serve a select market, choose a representative of that portion of the market, provide your best service to each particular prospect and let the law of 250 work miracles for you.

Assume that every person you meet has
a sign around his neck which reads,
"Please make me feel important."

33

Treat Every day
As A New Day

Are you unnecessarily carrying some negative experiences of the yesterdays? If you are an average person, then you are doing so, without even being aware of the fact.

Yesterday's negative experiences work like a partial brake on your present performance. Use them only for learning some valuable lessons and then bury them permanently.

You can unleash a great deal of your latent potential if you learn to treat each day as a new day.

Read also essay numbers 14, 18, 23 and 97.

If you were to participate in a one hundred meter race, would you carry a twenty-five pound sack on your back? No, that would be unnecessary. But don't we do the same thing in the actual game of life?

Every day we do a few things right and a few things wrong. But somehow we seem to remember less of the good and more of the wrong experiences. Consequently, we generally end up having a net "wrong" on the balance sheet of our day. These "wrongs" keep accumulating.

Imagine driving your car with a brake that sticks just a little bit - so little that you don't even suspect that it sticks. You get used to it and perhaps believe that that is the normal performance of your car.

What would happen if the amount of "sticking" increased slowly, week after week? You would not get a good performance from your car and would ruin it much sooner than its normal expected life.

In some respect, that's exactly what's happening to us. The negative experiences of our past act as inhibitors, the sticking brake or the unnecessary burden on our back. They curb our normal, natural growth and performance.

The sticking brake is a mechanical problem and you may have to take your car to a mechanic for correction. The problem of carrying the negative experiences of your past is totally mental. Just like tossing away that unnecessary sack, you can discard them as soon as you become conscious of their presence and influence.

Life provides us with negative experiences so that we could learn from them. Unless we experience a very hot and humid day, we may not appreciate a cool breeze. Negative experiences force us to think, to devise ways of handling new problems and thereby to develop our talents. In their complete absence, all our talents will atrophy in a short time and then life will become not only dull but also meaningless.

Let's say you had a negative experience. All your cussing cannot undo anything. So why waste your energy? Why not look for the good? Every adversity is supposed to carry a seed of equal or superior gain. If you look for that seed, you will discover it.

The trouble is that most seeds are too tiny and of a form very different from the fruit that they will eventually bear. Therefore, we either overlook or fail to identify them. The average person pays attention only to fruits and ignores the seeds. But a wise man goes for the seed because the latter, when properly nourished, could be much more valuable than the fruit.

A seed requires care and nourishment during the early stage of its growth. As it matures, it is able to sustain itself and ultimately bear hundreds of fruits.

Look for the seed of advantage in your negative experience. Focus your thoughts only on that seed and dismiss forever the rest of the experience from your mind.

Think of each day as a new life to you. Yesterday is gone, and tomorrow is in the future. Today is the only day over which you have any control.

The French philosopher Montaigne once said, "My life has been full of terrible misfortunes, most of which never happened."

When we worry about our future, we tend to imagine mostly the negative things that might happen. The very thought of those terrible things often paralyses us to such an extent that we lose sight of things that are presently within our control.

Do not worry if you have lost control of your life. You can regain control almost instantly. All it takes is an awakening.

Mahatma Gandhi, as a child, was very shy. He could not speak in front of two or more persons. Early in his life, he must have had some negative experience of speaking to a group. Every time that he attempted to speak, he remembered his past failure and promptly failed again. These experiences kept building up. He literally blacked out on several occasions.

But within one week of his arrival in South Africa, he discovered that he could speak with full confidence, for about an hour, to a group of over one thousand strangers! What caused this tremendous transformation? My guess is that in the new land he found nothing that could remind him of his past failure as a speaker. The moment that self-imposed inhibition was lifted, his natural talent surfaced.

You and I have many useful talents eager to unfold, if only we could remove some of our inhibitions.

Ralph Waldo Emerson once said, "Most of us are born as a butterfly and grow up into a cocoon." Isn't that sad?

Every child has great ambitions and lofty dreams. But as he grows, the fire within him cools. By the time he reaches his adulthood he finds himself totally compressed into the standard mold - one of the crowd. You can tell a child is grown up when he stops asking questions for which you have no answers.

Let's get out of that sad mold. Let's provide an opportunity for our life to bloom. Let's not unnecessarily carry the burdens of yesterdays. Let's toss away that unnecessary sack. Let's treat each day as a new life for us.

On my office wall, I have a poster of a rising sun. It reminds me to look at this day as a new life for me. This has definitely enhanced my outlook on life. Any such image will do the same for you. If you can't get a poster, you surely can imagine, can't you? As you leave your bed in the morning, think of the day as a new life to you, and it will be so.

"Hating people is like burning down your own house to get rid of a rat."
                                        -Harry Emerson Fosdick

34

You can Lessen
Your Dependence On Others

Is your productivity hampered because you keep waiting for some decisions or guidance from your superiors? If so, there is a way of alleviating this problem.

This essay describes several practical ways of lessening your dependence on others. You will not only become freerin your activities, but also gain some extra self-confidence and self-esteem.

Read also essay numbers 24 and 25.

$\mathbf{R}$ ecently one person commented, "All week I wait for the Monday morning meeting and then my boss does not show up! This not only slows down the actions that I need to take but also affects my morale."

"How can you maintain your morale and productivity if your boss is never available for consultation or guidance?"

Many members of my audience have asked me this question. I have tried to give them some specific solutions to their particular situations. Here I am going to discuss this problem in a more general way.

We rarely work in total isolation. We predominantly operate as members of a team. One person's productivity (or lack of productivity) affects that of the team. If you miss your own target date, you may affect that of several others and vice versa. Your boss (or supervisor) plays a particularly important role. You may need his (or her) approval or consultation before taking a certain action. What do you do if he is hardly ever available to you?

Whenever you feel that your life is being controlled by the pull of others' strings, your morale, and thereby your productivity suffers.

Here are my suggestions for overcoming this problem.

1. Make a list of all items for which you think you require consultation.

As long as you keep the items in your head, you may remain confused about the exact nature of the help that you need. Writing them down will protect you from fighting the fog.

2. Analyze the items and shorten the list.

Listing the items allows you to be objective, to separate your emotions from the actual problem. It is much easier to dissect something which is not a part of you. It is relatively easier for you to analyze somebody else's problem than your own. Even a surgeon finds it difficult to operate on his own body, no matter how simple the operation might be.

When you write your problem down, you give it a separate identity - separate from you. Then you can scrutinize it, without feeling hurt yourself. You may discover that you could go ahead with some of the activities without seeking the consultation that you previously thought was essential. By striking off, you can shorten your list.

3. Find out exactly what consultation you require.

If you got an opportunity to talk to that person for a very brief moment, what would you ask? What do you consider to be the core of the matter? Why do you really need his or her help?

By asking yourself such questions, you may find most of the problems to simply disappear and those that are left will generally be reduced in size and complexity.

4. Put your request in writing.

Write a concise memo describing the nature and the cause of the problem. Include your recommendation. How would you handle it if you were in his position? A written request draws much more attention, and quicker response, than a verbal one.

If possible, type your request. This will show that you seriously need the help that you are seeking. A type written request carries more weight and therefore commands more attention than a hand written note. Yes, this will take some of your time, but the result will more than justify the investment.

5. Assume that you have the authority to go ahead on your own.

If you assume more independence, and demonstrate that you are capable of handling your functions, you will generally be allowed some more freedom. Keep your boss posted on the actions you take and the results you experience. Most likely he will interfere only if he detects some grave flaws in what you are doing. In that case you will promptly receive the advice that you had been seeking.

The heavier the load you can carry for your boss, the happier he will become. He will then find time and energy for enhancing his own areas of responsibility. But please do not overdo this. You may easily threaten him by becoming overly aggressive. Everyone likes to protect his own position and importance. Let him know that you do need him and that you go ahead only when you notice that he is too busy to spare enough time for you.

6. Rather than ruminating over what is not within your control, focus on carrying out that part of the activity which you feel is within your control.

As you proceed, you will discover that you have, in fact, control over many more things than what you believed earlier. Remember the age-old advice, "Go as far as you can see, and when you get there, you will see some more." Similarly, when you finish doing all that is within your control, you will notice a few more things falling within your control.

7. Consult him in your imagination.

If you cannot at all proceed without consulting him, try using your imagination. Mentally put yourself in his position and ask yourself, 'What would I do if I were in his shoes?' You will be surprised by the pieces of advice that you will receive. Abandon all fear and simply put that advice into action.

Life is complex and dynamic. It is virtually impossible to find a recipe that will solve every problem in every situation. The above guidelines have helped many who have sincerely tried them. If you are facing a similar problem, why not try them and verify their strengths?

> "He, who every morning plans the transactions of the day, and follows out that plan, carries a thread that will guide him through the labyrinth of the most busy life."
>
> - Victor Hugo

35

How To Get Out Of A Swamp

Do you sometimes feel that your next step is too big for you to try a move? If so, there is a solution.

Imagine that you have been provided with a high, energetic and obedient assistant. Your task has been reduced to supplying a rough plan for this man to work on. As you think of the plan, you will start realizing that the task is not as overwhelming as you had thought it to be.

This simple method can get you out of most swamps. Read also essay numbers 21 and 41.

Do you sometimes find that you have an important task to do, but for some unknown reason you just can't get started? If you do, don't feel bad. You belong to a very large group.

By nature, we postpone starting any new task. After all, we have seen others do the same and quite often we discover that we can work wonders under pressure, don't we?

Sometimes we have the strange feeling that if we keep ignoring the task, it may disappear, or shrink in magnitude, or maybe someone will chip in to help us out. But in most cases that is only a dream. We behave like the ostrich that buries its head in the sand and hopes that the danger will go away.

Why do we keep postponing doing something that we know we must do?

There are many reasons. We may perceive the task to be too difficult, too boring, thankless, humiliating, or something like that. We may fear that the result could be unpleasant or that we could discover one of our weaknesses.

Perhaps the most important reason is that we perceive the task to be too difficult. If we were confident that we could do it easily, and that we would enjoy doing it, we would tackle it right away, wouldn't we?

Charles Kettering used to say, "A problem well analyzed is a problem half solved." Similarly, a project well planned is a project half completed. But the trouble is that planning requires some skills, patience and peace of mind.

Any problem, even an overwhelming one, can be broken into bite size pieces, organized in proper sequence and then tackled piece by piece. Everyone knows it and yet very few capitalize on this principle. Most people fear the fact that they may end up doing the dirty work and that some pieces may turn out to be unpalatable. I am going to share with you one technique that may get you out of this plight.

Imagine that you have been provided with a very obedient assistant. He will do anything, at any time that you ask. But you must utilize his assistance. The moment you leave him idle, you risk losing him. Are you willing to accept this challenge?

Although he is a hard worker, he is not creative. He does not use his own initiative. You must tell him exactly what to do, where to start, in which order to proceed, where to find the needed resources, where to receive guidance when necessary, how to know when to quit perfecting a certain piece of the task, some do's and don'ts, and so on.

He will work for you for one week on a trial basis. If he proves to be valuable to you, you may keep him longer. Of course, you don't have to pay him a penny. Would you like to try him out?

If you want, he can start working for you in about ten minutes. In the meantime you should scribble some instructions for him. You need not work out a comprehensive plan. You can fill in the details later. For the moment, just jot down the important ideas that come to your mind.

Don't fidget if you perceive some part of the task to be too difficult. It may not be too difficult for your assistant. And remember, you don't have to carry it out yourself, anyway.

Since the fellow has not arrived yet, spend just a few minutes reviewing your notes. Add, delete or rearrange a few ideas if you so wish. Neatness is not important. Simply brainstorm for ideas.

While you wait for your assistant, imagine him sitting across from you at your table and trying to understand your scribbling. He feels the task to be overwhelming. You try to console him. He has difficulty deciphering some symbols. You explain what they mean and try to simplify them.

You begin to feel impatient as you wait for him, but he is late. You go and get a drink and as you sip it, you try to relax. A few minutes later, some more ideas come to your mind and you simply add them to your list.

While you are waiting, you look at your notes and start thinking which activities appear easy for you.

You discover that one or two of them are not only very easy but are ones that you would find enjoyable to do yourself. You are tempted, but you resist because these are for your assistant to do. You wiggle your thumbs and feel restless.

Because you are anxious to use your time to advantage, you start on the activity that you think you would enjoy most. As you work on it, you notice something else that could also be fun for you to do. Some other activities that previously appeared to be very hard, now appear to be less difficult. You say, "To heck with that assistant, I will finish this task myself and receive all the glory."

This is a magic technique for getting started on a tough task. Once you detach yourself from the fear of the drudgery of doing the task, you can analyze it, work out a plan, see all the pieces of the puzzle and slowly put them in the right order. As you get the ball rolling, the momentum will overcome most of the hurdles on the way.

A word of caution. This technique suggests that you start with the most pleasant activity. This does not mean that you continue doing only the pleasant activities. The most pleasant activity is seldom the most productive. Once you conquer your inertia, start looking for the items that will bring you the maximum result.

Remember the Pareto principle, "If all activities are arranged in the order of their value, the top twenty per cent generally represent nearly eighty per cent of the total value." Before picking up the next activity, ask yourself, "Is this one of my top twenty per cent most valuable activities?" If the answer is no, drop it and tackle the high value activities first.

> "Those who know how to think
> need no teachers."
>   - Mahatma Gandhi

36

Too Much Knowledge
Can Be Harmful

We have often heard that 'A little learning is a dangerous thing'. But what about the other end of the spectrum? This essay suggests that too much knowledge can also be harmful.

Communication between two persons is smoothest when they are both talking "on the same frequency". As the gap in the knowledge between the two persons increases, there is a risk that they may not be able to speak on the same frequency.

There is no harm in learning and making yourself wiser, but don't let it become a barrier for you.

Read also essay number 29.

This may sound paradoxical but too much knowledge can be harmful.

When a person has a lot of knowledge (compared to the person with whom he is communicating), he tends to be a poor listener. He feels that he has far more knowledge to share than to receive. Consequently, he keeps talking and talking. He hardly allows the other person to say anything. He interrupts the other person in the middle of his sentence or idea. The moment he hears the first few words, he thinks he can see the whole picture. Often, the picture that he sees is totally wrong or highly distorted.

Whenever you prevent someone from expressing himself, you impede effective communication. In addition, you can hurt his feelings. Such interruptions are considered to be impolite and offensive. The trouble is that when you are extremely knowledgeable, it is very hard to be humble.

The moment your listener senses the height of your knowledge, he finds it uncomfortable to maintain a free and frank discussion with you. He feels scared, overwhelmed and sometimes almost paralysed.

Too much knowledge may create over confidence. You start screening out the "ignorant" people. You think you know it all, that you have seen it before, and therefore, you do not want to waste your time. The other person soon notices it and may tune you out too!

The main cause of a communication gap between parents and their teen-age children is the vast difference in the worldly knowledge of the two parties.

When a patient does not respond to a certain treatment, a psychologist often says, "Well, he was not ready for the treatment." But whom can you blame?

Acquiring knowledge sometimes becomes an addiction. Some people acquire knowledge simply for the sake of acquiring knowledge. They live in their own world. Some of them spend their entire life studying the root. They never find a chance to study or harvest the fruit.

After earning my Master's degree, I approached a professor at McGill University to enquire about the possibility of pursuing my research towards a Doctorate degree. He talked me into "Nip Mechanics". After an hour long interview with him I learned that the world was dying for the solution to a certain problem in "Nip Mechanics". It took me nearly four years to solve that problem. Then I eagerly waited for the world to beat a path to my house, but no one ever showed up. When you acquire knowledge for the sake of knowledge, you end up living in an ivory tower, all by yourself.

Every teacher faces the problem of the knowledge gap. He is far more knowledgeable than his students. The first challenge is to win the trust of his students by narrowing the gap and building rapport.

Abraham Lincoln advised, "If you want to win an argument, first convince the person that you are his sincere friend." Every piece of teaching requires some form of convincing on the part of the teacher.

You can win the trust of your students by making them believe that you are not a superman but an ordinary human being just like them. Refer occasionally to your shortcomings, your personal difficulties in trying to learn what you are now trying to teach. Try to mix in some humour wherever possible.

Although you can see the bigger picture, and can analyze the problem faster, resist the temptation of rushing to the goal line.

Socrates said, "If you teach a man something, he will never learn." Yes, learning is more effective when the knowledge is discovered by the student. The word "educate" comes from the root word "educare" which means "to draw out". To be really effective as a teacher, we must let our students draw out the learning.

This can be accomplished by encouraging them to participate in analyzing the problem. Socrates was extremely skillful at this. He led the other person to the discovery of the right knowledge by asking them the right questions. He was sentenced to death for the crime, "asking too many questions".

I want to share with you three simple ideas that will enhance your skill of asking questions.

1. Let them know, in advance, that a question is coming.

Often we ask a question without giving any notice. Half of our audience fail to hear it because they were preoccupied with some other important thought. They feel embarrassed. They try to fake the answer and end up resenting us. You can avoid this situation by pre-ambling, "Let me ask you a question..." This will draw their attention. They will love you for giving them a chance to save face.

2. Ask them questions whose answers they know.

If they do not know the answer to the question, they feel inferior. They assume that those who could answer the question are smart. Avoid creating a situation that could reveal their ignorance.

3. Ask them questions whose answers are pleasant for them.

An unpleasant answer lowers self-esteem and obstructs learning.

Keep asking the right questions until the right ideas are expressed through their answers. Your task is simply to lead them in the right direction, by means of the appropriate questions.

Allow them the time to cultivate the ideas. Be patient. Sometimes you may find their ideas to be superior to yours. Even if a certain idea happens to be exactly the same as yours, let it come from them.

A friend of mine had a poultry farm. One day I watched him feeding the chickens. He spread some corn on the floor and then covered them with some straw. I asked why he took the trouble of covering the corn. He said, "For two reasons: (1) it provides the chickens some exercise in trying to remove the straw and (2) they feel smart. They think that I was trying to hide the corns from them, but they had no problem discovering it."

Why not use the same technique with the people that you are trying to communicate? Why not purposely provide them with the opportunity of thinking that they are smart?

Every time that they come up with a new idea, no matter how insignificant, reward them. This technique is used in almost all animal training. The trainer rewards the animal every time that it does something in the direction of the desired training. Ken Blanchard says, "Catch them doing something approximately right." Keep rewarding and lead them gently towards what you are trying to teach.

No, there is no harm in being knowledgeable, as long as we do not allow it to shine too brightly. Let's be wise but appear like an ordinary person. Let's remember that the greatest teachers have been the most humble persons. While we are involved in teaching, let's forget ourselves and our knowledge. Let's focus all our attention on the process of the communication - encouraging our audience to discover for themselves the knowledge that we wish to impart.

"When I am getting ready to reason with a man, I spend one-third of my time thinking about myself and what I am going to say and two-thirds about him and what he is going to say."
                              - Abraham Lincoln

37

Care For The Gretzky Of
Your   Organization

This essay was written as a reaction to Wayne Gretzky's trade to Los Angeles Kings. It draws our attention to the Wayne Gretzky, the outstanding performer, of our own organization.

What would you do if your Gretzky left you today? Are you taking some measures to ensure that he stays with you?

Why do super-performers leave?

This essay provides some practical tips for developing and maintaining a healthy organization.

Read also essay number 28.

The Wayne Gretzky trade is perhaps the most important current (August 1988) issue for most Canadians. We do not know the main driving forces, but the unexpected has happened. Wayne Gretzky is gone.

This trade has raised many questions. Are we living in a truly free society? If Paul Coffey is right, then even a person of Wayne's calibre is treated like any other commodity (like "meat" in Coffey's parlance). Do we have any consideration left for "humanity" or "spirituality"? I lack the wisdom to judge the case. I can only pose questions.

Everyone seems to be talking about "loyalty", "patriotism", "trust" and so on. These are subjective topics. Their interpretations depend almost entirely on the prevailing feelings of the persons involved.

How does Wayne feel about the whole development? Nobody knows for certain. Even his close friends, along with sports experts, are only speculating. I doubt if we will ever find out the whole truth.

Every adversity has some valuable lesson imbedded within itself. To look for the lesson in this trade, let's ask ourselves the question: "What would we do if we lost our most valuable person?"

God forbid, but this may happen to us. There is no guarantee against traffic accidents. In our society, every person is free to make his own choice. Should such a calamity strike you, how would you react? You may already have faced, and successfully coped with, such a situation. If so, I would sincerely like to know about your approach.

I am going to share with you my way of dealing with this type of problem.

1. Accept the fact that such a calamity can happen.

If we are prepared to accept it, we can react to it with cool minds. Otherwise, we get panicky and find ourselves incapable of picking up the remaining pieces.

2. Keep preparing for such eventualities.

There is wisdom in fire-drill. It may be too late to rehearse when an actual fire starts. During the drill we may notice many things that we might otherwise overlook.

The instructor of one of my defensive driving courses once said, "Look frequently in your rear view mirror. Observe the traffic behind you and try to guess their manoeuvres. Imagine that you have been asked to provide a running commentary about the activity of the traffic behind you. Doing so will reduce your chances of getting involved in an accident."

In a similar course, the instructor advised, "Imagine that you are forced to leave the pavement. Where would you steer your car to minimize injuries and damage? Always keep looking for an escape route."

These suggestions have helped me cultivate my awareness of the possible influence of external forces. They have made me think, in advance, how I would react should a problem arise.

3. Develop your number two person.

Most of us have a tendency to brag about our number one producer (or the most valuable person in our organization) and neglect the rest.

A vast gap between the number one and the number two person is actually harmful to the organization. The number one person finds little challenge and the number two person generally lacks the courage to aim for the number one spot. Narrowing this gap keeps the number one person on his toes and motivates the number two person to "try for the Gold".

Perhaps the most important trait of a good leader is his ability and desire to train his replacement. Poor leaders avoid this. They are afraid that they would be threatening their own position. This is a wrong assumption.

The more we share our knowledge and skills, the more we grow ourselves. If we are really good, then we should be able to maintain an edge, even when we try to give away all that we have got.

The more we are eager to share our knowledge and skills with others, the more cooperation we receive from them. This is a key to building any team. I believe Gretzky became what he is today because of his passion for sharing all his skills with his team-mates. Yes, money changed hands during this trade, but this trait stayed with him, and with this he will build a strong team wherever he goes.

The cultivation of the number two person can be fostered by allowing him some opportunity to perform in the absence of the number one person. A strong number one can overshadow, and thereby smother the creativity of the rest of the team. Since he clearly understood this human dynamics, President Kennedy often purposely removed himself from some discussions involving a sensitive national matter.

A narrow gap between the number one and the number two producers is a healthy sign for any organization.

I am deeply hurt to see Gretzky leave Edmonton. I know he will be number one wherever he goes. He does not need my wishes. He has the necessary wisdom and skills.

Let's look at the Wayne Gretzky of our own organization and hope that he stays with us. But, should he leave us some day, let's be prepared. Let's keep looking for our escape routes. Let's keep cultivating our number two person. It is highly unlikely that we would lose both of them at the same time.

Common sense is not so common.

38

"Natural Talent" Is The Key To Super Performance

Mahatma Gandhi often said, "There is no lazy person. There are only some people who have not found the right work."

Our performance largely depends upon the degree of utilization of our natural talents. If our work could harmonize totally with our natural talents, there would be no limit to our accomplishments.

Natural talents can sometimes be discovered during the course of normal work but a better way is to seek professional help, such as that one offered by Johnson O'Connor Research Foundation Laboratories.

For more information read "Your Natural Gifts" by Margaret E. Broadley.

Read also essay numbers 60 and 72.

O nly a few people seem to enjoy success naturally and easily, while the vast majority struggles to barely make a living. Just look at the success that Wayne Gretzky has had by the age of twenty-seven whereas, in the same city, province or country, thousands (and maybe even millions) have found themselves "crawling" even at the age of thirty-seven, forty-seven or even fifty-seven!

Has God been partial to Wayne Gretzky? Or, are we failing to make use of something?

I have been studying "the causes of success" for many years. I find that "having a clear purpose", "perseverance", "the right education", "the right environment" and many similar traits are helpful, but there is another factor which, acting like a catalyst, brings and binds all the necessary traits together.

Everyone is born with some natural talents. The average person spends nearly half of his life exploring a number of areas where he feels he can fit. He has some inkling of his natural talents but often compromises them for "other worldly considerations". By the age of forty, he starts experiencing a vague sense of having wasted part of his life.

There are many theories of success or failure. Each one is right in its own interpretation. The one I found to be very interesting says,"The root of all failures lies in the inability of the individual to discover and utilize his natural talents."

Imagine how you would feel if you possessed some valuable asset but somehow you did not know about it - or that you knew about it but somehow failed to make use of it. It is the same with our natural talents. They are our assets - perhaps our most valuable assets. The realization that we are not using those assets causes restlessness and frustrations. We can mask these frustrations for only so long.

But how do we discover our natural talents?

There are several ways. We can discover them simply by paying attention to our true personal likes and dislikes.

Recall some activities in which you were totally absorbed. You had literally lost your awareness of the environment or of even your bodily needs. You experienced a great sense of delight and excitement in what you were doing. You actually felt energized instead of feeling drained. Those activities utilized some of your natural talents. What are those talents?

The right work (the one that can use our natural talents) unlocks our creative imagination.

Thomas Carlyle once said, "Blessed is the man who has found his work. Let him ask for no other blessedness."

We can also discover our natural talents by taking some kind of an aptitude test, such as the one offered by the Johnson O'Connor Research Foundation Laboratories. Their Boston centre is known as the Human Engineering Laboratory.

They have identified about twenty unique, basic, personality traits. According to them, an average person is born with six such traits. Most jobs use only one or two traits. This results in several natural traits (or talents) remaining unused. This is the main cause of frustration in adults.

It is lucky to find a job which could use all talents. But you can supplement your job by getting involved in a hobby that could make use of your unused talents.

The greater tragedy is the fact that nearly eighty per cent of us get trapped in jobs where we do not use any of our main natural talents.

Some people, who experience failure in their endeavours believe that they lack talents. But lack of talent is seldom the main cause of frustration or failures. In most cases, it is the presence of some unused talent that causes frustration. The person who can identify his only natural talent is truly lucky, because he can easily decide what he should be doing.

People with many aptitudes generally find themselves torn in all directions. No recognized occupation uses more than four or five of the basic aptitudes. The probability of success actually decreases with more than five aptitudes.

Some aptitudes are mutually exclusive. For example, an extremely subjective personality and strong structural visualization do not fit together. They pull the person in opposing directions. Similarly, Ideaphoria and Graphoria are restless companions.

Learning any skill in the area of our natural talents is child's play. We find them not only easy but also gratifying. Yes, we can learn some skills in other areas, but would find them to be burdensome and, in times of stress or pressure, we tend to forget them.

If you want to get into a business but feel that you lack one of the necessary aptitudes, the best solution is to form a partnership with someone who has strong aptitude in that area. The most successful partners complement each other.

The great French philosopher Montaigne advised: "Follow the order of nature. For God's sake follow it. It will lead them who follow, and those who will not, it will drag them anyway, along with their tempers and medicines."

To enjoy life, and to accomplish some extraordinary feats, let's be ourselves. Let's develop some awareness of our natural talents and use them, preferably with some goal in mind. Soon we will find that all competitions are fading away.

> Your talent is God's gift to you;
> what you do with it is your gift to God."
> - Karl Malden

39

Even Severe Handicaps
Can Be Overcome

Do you feel stymied by some of your own handicaps? Here is the story of a man who was not only born with some serious handicaps but was also struck by polio twice (a rare occurrence). But he did not let his handicaps stop him. He fought every obstacle and became one of the leading psychiatrists of North America.

This essay will erase your myth about your personal handicaps. If Milton H. Erickson could overcome his, you surely can overcome yours.

For more information read "Healing in Hypnosis" by Milton H. Erickson.

Read also essay numbers 63 and 92.

D o you sometimes feel that life has not been fair to you? Well, don't worry. We all feel that way sometimes. The following story may cheer you up.

Milton H. Erickson was born in 1902, with several handicaps. He suffered from a kind of colour-blindness. He was tone-deaf, which means that he could neither recognize nor execute the typical rhythm of music and song. He was dyslexic. At the age of six he could not differentiate between the number "3" and the letter "m". He went through most of his schooling without realizing the alphabetical arrangement of words in a dictionary. His father was a poor, uneducated farmer.

At the age of seventeen Milton had a bout of polio, and as he lay in his bed, he heard the doctor say to his mother, 'This boy will die tomorrow morning'. Wishing to see one more sunset, he begged his mother to move the dresser which was obstructing the view through the window. As the sun set that evening, he slipped into unconsciousness and remained unconscious for the next three days.

Milton did not die, but was left severely paralysed. He could hear; he could see; he could move his eyes; but he could not move his body and, with great difficulty, he could speak only a few words.

He had been paralysed for about a year when his mother tied him in a rocking chair and left him in the middle of the room, as she went about her farm chores. Somehow, she forgot completely about her son, and Milton found himself to be totally helpless.

Suddenly he noticed that his rocking chair was oscillating slightly. He concluded that his thoughts of rocking must have caused the chair to rock. He then stared at his hand and tried to recall how he used it to hold a pitchfork. After hours of concentration, he felt some twitching in his fingers.

From that day, he spent all his time recalling how he climbed trees, jumped like a monkey, and used his body for different functions. He kept staring at his hands and feet, until he could feel some movement in them.

Fortunately, at that time, his youngest sister was learning to walk. He watched her all day and mentally tried to copy her. Within a year of his self-rehabilitation program, he was able to walk with crutches!

He then enroled at the University of Wisconsin. He was a slow student, but he received everyone's sympathy and cooperation. A campus physician suggested that he spend the summer outdoors with nature to heal his body and mind. So Milton decided to undertake a canoe trip.He got permission from his parents. A friend, who had agreed to accompany him, dropped out at the last minute, but Milton decided not to postpone the trip. With two weeks' supply of rations, other necessary supplies and four dollars in his pocket, he started on his adventure all alone, and on crutches.

He planned to go downstream for a few days, rest and gain some strength, and then return upstream. Often, he got stuck but other campers rescued him. He shared his funny stories with them and they became his friends. He even did some light work for others to earn money to buy his necessary supplies.

When he started his return trip, he had gained enough strength to fight the current. He had stopped using the crutches. The total trip took ten weeks during which he covered twelve hundred   river-miles, returning home with eight dollars in his pocket. But most important, he returned as a robust boy with a good deal of self-confidence. He never used those crutches again, although he limped a little.

At the age of twenty-six, Milton H. Erickson graduated from the University of Wisconsin with M.A. and M.D. degrees. He practised medicine but became more interested in hypnosis. Slowly he became a national authority on hypnotherapy.

At the age of fifty-one, he had a second attack of polio (an extremely rare occurrence). This time his recovery was much faster, partly because he had a previous experience and partly because he used self-hypnosis. But his leg muscles were giving up on him and he became mostly confined to wheelchairs.

In 1957, he founded the American Society of Clinical Hypnosis and served as its President for the first two years. In 1958, he initiated the American Journal of Clinical Hypnosis and served as its editor until 1968.

He was recognized as America's top hypnotherapist, and the most difficult cases were referred to him. Hundreds of his papers have been published in many scholarly magazines. His papers and case studies, compiled in book form, are considered to be standard text books on hypnotherapy. He invented the spectacular pantomime techniques of hypnotic induction.

In 1977, he was awarded the Ben Franklin Gold Medal for his outstanding work in Hypnotherapy.

He died in 1980, at the age of seventy-eight!

Milton Erickson managed to work through his handicaps. His will, and not his physical abilities, caused him to succeed.

Many of us hide behind our handicaps. We blame them for our inaction. What we don't realize is that if we learn to recognize them, accept them, work with them, and have a strong desire to succeed, then we can succeed. Seen in that light, our handicaps and misfortunes become opportunities for struggling and building strength.

Let's not pay too much attention to our personal misfortunes. Let's look at them in the light of the misfortunes of others like Milton Erickson. Our personal misfortune may well pale compared to Milton's and, by his example, we may well go on to success.

"Nothing happens to any man which he is not formed by nature to bear."
                                                    - Marcus Aurelius

40

When It Rains,
Just Let It Rain

We are often reluctant to try a new or a different approach, for fear of being criticized or even ridiculed. But no matter what you do, you will be criticized by some people, because it is impossible to satisfy every single person.

This essay discusses an effective way of dealing with the rain of criticism. It further points out that criticism can be helpful and, therefore, desirable.

Read also essay number 20.

What do we do when it rains, and rains and rains?

There is no way that we can stop the rain even if we wish so. Getting irritated about it doesn't help a bit. All our griping doesn't make any difference either. It continues to rain and it will stop on its own.

Every action in nature has a definite purpose. Yes, even the rain on a parade has a purpose. Therefore, we should accept it as part of nature. We can enjoy it, if we can see it as a blessing.

Fortunately, life always provides us with more than one option. Even during rain, we have several options. We can fume and gripe, or use the rain to some advantage.

We can get out of the rain and stay indoors until it stops. We can convert the rain-time into thinking-time. We can even use the opportunity to draw our loved ones together. Yes, if we want, we can prevent the rain from affecting us, both physically and emotionally.

There is another kind of rain that affects our lives, the rain of criticism. Just like nature's rain, it comes without our asking. Sometimes it rains lightly. Other times, it pours. Sometimes it is endurable, but other times it creates frustration. It may even appear to threaten our mere existence.

Let's look at the cause of the rain of criticism.

It is human nature to explore and to comment on everything which is different. As long as we live, we will continuously want to do something differently and that will invite criticism from some source. Criticism is a sure sign of being alive. The more important the person, the more severe is the criticism of his deeds.

Criticism can either help or hinder us. If we become too sensitive to it, it may restrict our movement in the new direction. But if we use it to discover our weakness, the criticism can become a good ally.

The signals gathered by our sensors are mixed - and thereby tainted - by our emotions and feelings. We therefore see the same criticism differently, depending upon the state of our emotions at the time.

To be helpful, the criticism must be analyzed as objectively as possible. This is often a big challenge. This skill differentiates the great achievers from those who barely live.

There are five possible kinds of response to criticism. These are: (1) over-response, (2) opposite-response, (3) non-response, (4) under-response and (5) delayed-response.

Over-response is generally caused by anger and violence, as the result of taking a criticism personally. We perceive our ego as being hurt. We become very defensive. We are in a deep emotional state. We tend to see everything as being against us.

The purpose of opposite-response is to shut up the person who is criticising. This is actually the sign of a weak personality. To prove his individuality, the person makes the opposite response.

A non-response may be seen as a response which is being contemplated. Most criticism dies out with time. We may not have to make a response. This saves time and energy. If properly done, the skill of doing nothing becomes a great asset.

Under-response gives us some control. We maintain the option of responding fully later and it placates the criticiser.

Perhaps the best response is the delayed-response. You listen to the criticism and decide to evaluate it later, when you will be in a quieter mood. Almost every comment, criticism or suggestion looks different when we view it a few moments later. We are much more objective in analyzing it.

But this response has a few drawbacks as well. It can lead to procrastination. Delay often allows a problem to grow in magnitude. Remember the age old aphorism, "A stitch in time, saves nine."

If you keep entertaining criticisms, and postponing actions on them, you may soon find a big pile of criticisms hanging over your head.

President Lincoln once remarked, "If I care to listen to every criticism, let alone act on them, then this shop may as well be closed for all other business. I have learned to do my best, and if the end result is good then I do not care for any criticism, but if the end result is not good, then even the praise of ten angels would not make the difference."

Criticism is actually quite desirable. It keeps us alive and on our toes. Its mere presence is proof that what we are doing is important and worthwhile.

Many historians believe that the main cause of Hitler's downfall was the fact that he had censored all criticisms. He started punishing the bearers of bad news. Consequently, a time came when no one dared to bring him any bad news. He literally lived in an ivory tower.

When subjected to the rain of criticism, let's not curse the rain. Let's accept it as a part of life. Let's remember that the more criticism we can successfully handle, the more zest we will experience in our lives.

Let's not shy away from the rain of criticism. Let's not allow it to run our lives either. When it rains, just let it rain, but let's get indoors where we can analyze the rain with a peaceful mind.

"Reviewers are usually people who would have been poets, historians, biographers, if they could. They have tried their talents at one or the other, and have failed. Therefore, they turn critics."
                                        - S. T. Coleridge

41

See Your Work As "Play"

What is the difference between "work" and "play"?

Work is any activity that you feel you are obliged to do, while play is an activity that you do without any obligation.

While engaged in a "work" type activity we rarely do our best. But we put our whole heart in a "play" type activity

"Work" or "play" is often a matter of perception. This essay suggests that one way to enhance our productivity, and thereby the quality of our life, is to see some element of "play" in our routine work.

Read also essay numbers 15, 17 and 74.

To recover from the tension of a long and strenuous week, an executive goes fishing. He puts in many hours of hard physical labour and still finds it to be fun and relaxing. But a fisherman does not experience the same fun and relaxation in fishing. For him this is work. When he is exhausted or frustrated, he takes time to do something completely different, such as gardening. And how does a gardener feel? Well, for him gardening is not really relaxing. He does it to earn his living. To relax he goes to town and does some window-shopping.

It is evident that what is work for one person could be play for another and vice-versa. What then is the difference between work and play?

Work is any activity that we feel we have to do. It implies a feeling of compulsion. We do it to earn a living, to please someone or to meet some obligation.

"Play" on the other hand is some activity in which we feel a sense of freedom. We do it simply because we want to do it.

If the same activity can be "work" for one person and "play" for the other, then the actual difference must depend upon our perception of the particular activity. Therefore, with a change in our perception, a "work activity" can become a "play activity" and vice versa.

We rarely do our best when we are involved in a "work activity". On the contrary, the more "play" that we perceive in an activity, the more vigour, zest, enthusiasm we put into it.

Life is a mixture of work and play. The ratio varies from person to person. The average person experiences little play in his life. He works like a mule and yet, at the end of his life finds little to show as accomplishments.

Work builds tension and drains the battery of our life. Play releases that tension and recharges the battery.

A balanced life includes both work and play. They should be intermixed. When we are engaged in work-type activities for a long time, we must take some play-time to replenish our used energy. Thus even the play becomes a must for us. What a tragedy!

If you are lucky to be engaged in play-type activities then you require little of the so-called vacation. Thus you find more time to do what you really like to do.

The greater the ratio of play to work in your life, the greater will be your accomplishments. The common denominator of all high achievers is that they get themselves involved in doing mostly the play-type activities.

If somehow we could convert some of our "work" into "play", we could accomplish more. This would bring us more satisfaction and happiness.

It is within our power to change our perception and to even alter the nature of the activity life demands from us.

Next time you perceive an activity as "work" ask yourself some questions such as, "Why do I have to do this? Who is running my life? What would happen if I did not accept it in its entirety?"

Answers to such questions make us realize that we are not as restricted as we thought we were. By being able to make even the slightest modification in the extent of the activity, we start seeing that we do have some control. We have lost this control mostly because of default or lack of use. We can reclaim it, slowly but positively.

If you had a chance to choose, what would you choose?

The first step, in taking charge, is knowing what you want to accomplish in your life. What would you like to do if you were totally free from all obligations? If you do not know where you want to go then you will either follow someone who knows where he wants to go, or you will end up going round in circles.

Letting others know, what we truly like or dislike, can make a change in the type of "work" that we are asked to do at the moment. If we do not clarify it ourselves, others assume that they can read our mind.

The other day I read the story of a couple celebrating their twenty-fifth anniversary.

The morning after their wedding the husband had served bread and jam for breakfast. He gave the middle pieces of the bread to his wife and kept the end pieces for himself. They enjoyed the breakfast so much that they repeated the ritual every week for the next twenty-five years.

On the twenty-fifth anniversary the wife got up early and served their favourite breakfast - jam and bread, the end pieces for him and the middle pieces for her. At this moment, with tears in his eyes, the husband said, "No! Not on our twenty-fifth anniversary!"

With great surprise the wife asked, "What do you mean? I served you something that you like most." To this the husband replied, "I always served you the middle pieces because they taste better than the end pieces. At least on our twenty-fifth anniversary I did not expect to eat the end pieces."

The wife said, "It's funny. I don't like bread and jam, but have been eating it for last twenty-five years simply to please you."

We can please others more by being honest and revealing our real self.

Our most important duty is to make some meaningful contribution to life. This can be done better if we could perceive more play in our routine activities, or if we could choose our play-type activities to make up the bulk of our daily activities.

Every change takes time. Getting started is the most difficult part. Even a one per cent additional control over the choice of our activities will make a significant improvement.

Whenever Mahatma Gandhi recruited someone for a task, he said, "You either do it willingly and happily, or don't do it at all."

Let's heed Gandhi's advice. Let's choose the activities which we would do willingly and happily. Then we will have fun and will leave society with the legacy of some great contribution.

"The rule of my life is
to make business a pleasure, and
pleasure my business."
- Aaron Burr

42

To Slow Down Aging,
Get Involved

This essay suggests that as long as we keep learning something, we maintain an active mind which, in turn, prolongs our life. Therefore, we should never stop learning.

Enroling in a formal course is not the only way of maintaining learning. This essay discusses several avenues, suitable for a broad spectrum of people, for facilitating learning.

Read also essay numbers 72 and 90.

As soon as school starts, I notice significant changes in the behaviour of the children that I know. Most of them look forward to their new challenge. They become too occupied to pay attention to soap operas. They find little time for unnecessarily bothering others and stay out of "mischief".

Those who are enroled at a university or college seem to have definite goals for their lives and they plan to work steadily toward achieving them.

Some adults have either already enroled, or are thinking of enroling themselves, in continuing education courses. Even those who have university degrees, or who have spent a good deal of their life educating themselves, seem to be eager to learn something new.

I earned my Ph.D. degree in May, 1972. Since then, with the exception of a few days of holidays each year, I do not recall one week when I was not actively engaged in learning something new. The older I get, the stronger my desire for learning seems to become.

Why do we take the trouble of continually educating ourselves? Where do we really want to go?

Our mind is a monstrous slave. It has almost unlimited power. But it cannot remain idle and it serves us only when we control it. If we neglect to do so, it wanders and may even become self-destructive. Thus the saying, "An idle mind is a devil's workshop."

We can control our mind by demanding it to perform some definite tasks such as learning a new skill.

Everybody likes to enjoy the benefits of learning, but few like to work for it. Fortunately, you need not work to learn. Learning should be a natural, easy process. If you are not enjoying what you are learning, most likely you are going after the wrong fish. Yes, there are millions of fish in the ocean of life.

Since our brain is ever curious, it enjoys learning. It keeps looking for new things, new areas, new avenues to explore. In fact, it becomes bored if it is asked to do things that it already knows how to.

Contrary to common belief, with age, our brain does not lose its learning ability, nor does it reach its learning capacity. Continual learning is good for the health of not only our mind but also our body.

As long as we keep learning, our mind stays young, fresh and interested in life itself. To a great extent, the health of our body is controlled by the health of our mind. A healthy mind slows down the aging of the body.

Even after realizing the importance of continual learning, if you are too shy to enrol in a formal course, here are some ideas that you might like to try.

1. Consider joining a Toastmasters' club.

Every time that one learns a new subject, or a new skill, one gains some additional self-confidence, and thereby self-esteem. The skill that builds one's self-confidence the most, is the ability to speak in public. Without any hesitation I say that my public speaking ability has been the greatest gift of my life.

Anyone, irrespective of age, sex, education or ethnic background, can acquire this skill. I recommend Toastmasters because it offers a highly structured, non-threatening program. It cannot be described accurately. One must attend a meeting to get first hand experience.

2. Consider joining a service club.

If you are not already a member of a service club, such as Lions, Kiwanis, Kinsmen or Rotary, you are missing a great thrill. Join one and soon you will discover that voluntary service is very healthy for the soul. Volunteer to be a member of their executive, or of one of their committees. There is nothing life-threatening in any of these assignments. It is fun, exciting and a good challenge for our ever inquisitive mind.

3. Visit your local library regularly.

Set a definite day and a definite hour every week to visit your library. Don't force yourself to learn anything. Just go there simply to relax, to be away from daily chores.

Just browse through some newspapers and magazines, or wander through some of the aisles and read the titles of some of the books that draw your interest. Soon you will find something of interest. By reading only that which interests you, you will soon find yourself engaged in an organized learning program.

4. Listen to some audio tapes or records.

If you cannot invest some time in the library on a regular basis, make it a ritual to borrow one record or one cassette every week. During the week play it a few times, not to learn, but simply to stimulate your mind. You will find it to be very relaxing and, in due course, you will learn at the same time.

5. Form a habit of writing.

If you can write, you should allocate one hour every week, preferably on the same day and at the same hour, to write some of your thoughts or experiences, not for publication, but for your own personal benefit. This may turn out to be an invaluable legacy for your children. At the same time, this will enhance the quality of your life. Your outlook will improve and you will better understand why others behave the way they behave.

Life is dynamic. We are either progressing or regressing. The moment we stop learning, we start dying first mentally and then physically. It is true that some day we must die, but we can slow down our aging, and enjoy a better quality of life, if we keep learning.

Knowledge does not obey the law of diminishing returns.

43

What Does It Take
To Win Gold Medals?

To most viewers a goal medal performance looks like many other activities. But if we dig deeply into the training that goes behind each gold medal, we would be appalled.

Here is a brief account of the training of two outstanding athletes, Greg Louganis and Pat McCormick. Each of them put in about twenty-five thousand hours of rigourous training. They were totally focussed on their goal and never let any comment, criticism or political climate deter them.

This essay suggests that with an equal amount of determination, perseverance and self-discipline, anyone can win the equivalent of an Olympic Gold Medal, in the field of his or her endeavour

Read also essay number 2.

D uring Olympic Games, we witness some athletes performing effortlessly, and winning gold medals. Occasionally, we also come across some unbelievable stories such as that of Greg Louganis.

While attempting a dive from the springboard, Greg hit his head, which required five stitches. Within twenty-four hours, he was back in the competition, attempted the same dive, and won the gold medal for that particular event.

What does it take to win the gold medal? Is it the mental preparation, the physical preparation, dedication, luck or simply being crazy about it? I do not really know, because so far I have not received any valuable medal like that. But, I can't stop myself from marvelling at the performance of these athletes, and am ever interested in knowing the causes that push them to those limits.

Greg Louganis had participated in the 1976 Olympics, and was very disappointed to win just a Silver medal. Determined to win the Gold medal, he trained himself for another four years. But, unfortunately, United States decided to boycott the 1980 Olympics in Moscow. Greg continued to train himself for four more years, for the next Olympic competition.

During the 1984 Olympics, at Los Angeles, he won Gold medals for diving from the springboard and from the tower. But, he was not fully satisfied, partly because he did not consider it to be a full competition, since the Soviet Union had boycotted it, and partly because he wanted to tie a long standing record of winning those two gold medals at two successive Olympic competitions. So, he continued training himself for four more years! That would mean a total of sixteen years of training, from 1972 to 1988!!

During the 1988 Olympics, Greg Louganis won those two gold medals, even after hurting himself during the competitions, and thereby tied the record.

The record, of winning gold medals for diving from both the springboard and the tower, in two consecutive Olympic Games, was set by Pat McCormick in 1956. This extraordinary feat had not been duplicated in thirty-two years! What was so outstanding about Pat? Let's briefly look at her training.

In one of her writings, Pat confesses that she did not have any unusual talent for diving. In fact, during her early years, one of her coaches had once told her, "You are a nice little diver, Pat, and a really hard worker, but you will never be good enough for national or Olympic competition."

At that moment, Pat had considered quitting diving completely. But then she thought, "Why should I let one person's opinion determine my future?" Therefore, she continued training herself for diving and decided to prove that she was good.

By the time she had received her first Gold medal, Pat says that she had put in approximately twenty-five thousand hours of training for diving. She further adds that anyone who is willing to put in twenty-five thousand hours of dedicated effort in one single interest, can win the equivalent of an Olympic Gold medal.

If you put in ten hours a day for every single day, it would take you seven years to accumulate those twenty-five thousand hours. With this amount of dedication, self-discipline and single-minded pursuit, I believe that very few goals can remain to be a mere dream.

After receiving the two Gold medals in 1952, she continued to train herself for the next Olympics. In the meantime she got married to her coach, and had a family. Three months before the trials for the 1956 Olympics began, she gave birth to a baby boy. Can you imagine how she pursued her training, for diving, under those conditions? But, she walked away with two more Gold medals and a new Olympic record!

Her son, Tim, was active in baseball but did not pursue sports seriously. Her daughter, Kelly, started with diving, but, being the daughter of a four-time Gold medalist and her coach, created enormous expectations from her. Unable to cope with that pressure, she quit diving, and tried gymnastics. But she did not make much headway.

Reluctantly, she then returned to diving. To relieve some pressure, her parents absented themselves from the competitions in which she participated. Kelly ended up winning the Silver medal, for diving from the springboard, at the 1984 Olympics in Los Angeles. Never has there been a similar mother-daughter combination in the history of the Olympic games!

Why was Pat able to win four Olympic Gold medals when her coach had predicted that she would never make a national team? And what about Kelly? Pat says, "If I had Kelly's natural abilities for diving, I would still be a competitive diver." Why did Kelly, with her natural ability, proper coaching and all the necessary support and encouragement, settle for a mere Silver medal?

I feel, that the only ingredient lacking in Kelly was "single-mindedness". Had she not wasted some of her attention in the pursuit of gymnastics, she could have beaten, or at least equalled, her mother's record.

There is a parallel to this in our common lives. Most of us are not sure of what we want. We go through most, and sometimes all, of our life without deciding the area in which we would like to focus. Before entering her teens, Pat had decided that she would dedicate her life to the pursuit of diving.

After the independence of India, one reporter asked Mahatma Gandhi, "How do you feel having liberated India from the mighty stronghold of the British Empire?" Gandhi replied, "I have not accomplished anything extraordinary. I believe that anyone can accomplish what I have accomplished, provided that he or she maintains the same degree of determination and faith."

We may be too old to participate in the Olympics, but we still have many avenues open to us. Let's not cry over what is gone. Let's start working for what's still available and let's go for the gold.

44

What Made Gandhi
A Multi-cultural Man?

*This essay was written during Multi-Cultural Week.
It briefly discusses the environment in which Gandhi
grew up and which helped him cultivate his "open
personality".*

Read also essay number 6.

M ohandas Gandhi's father was the prime adviser to the local princely state. In that capacity he had to see and listen to all kinds of people. This task required him to remain unbiased and open-minded toward everyone who came to see him.

Just before Mohandas's marriage, his father was injured in an accident and remained confined to bed until his death three years later. Being the youngest child, it became Mohandas's duty to nurse his ailing father. During those three years (between the age of thirteen and sixteen) Mohandas had the opportunity of listening to countless discussions, on a variety of religious beliefs (Hinduism, Jainism, Islam, Buddhism, Christianity etc.). It was in that environment that Mohandas (later known as Mahatma) Gandhi grew up.

At the age of eighteen, Mohandas went to England to study law, where he spent the next three years. During that period he not only remained tolerant of other cultures, but also tried his best to pick up their good points. He adopted the European dress, learned table manners, and even took lessons in ballroom dancing.

After returning to India, he spent about one year in Bombay, trying to practice law. This provided him another opportunity of meeting a wide variety of people of various religions and cultures.

He then received a temporary assignment to work in South Africa, but ended up living there for the next twenty-one years. It was there that his love of people of all cultural backgrounds was firmly implanted. Even the Indians living in South Africa came from vastly different heritages.

The lawyer he assisted was a devout Christian. Under his influence, within one year, Gandhi studied over eighty books on Christianity. He was tempted to change to Christianity, but thought that he should first study his own religion. The more he studied Hinduism, the more he felt that he would not gain anything from the change, and believed that all religions were good and that there was no need for anyone to switch to another.

When asked by some of his friends, "When are you going to become a Christian?" he occasionally quipped, "As soon as I meet a true Christian."

He was so accommodating that he could easily become a part of anyone's family and all his friends behaved as if they had always been a member of the Gandhi family.

Some of his strongest supporters and followers were Jews and Christians. Herman Kallenbach (a Jew) donated eleven hundred acres of land for Gandhi's ashram, and went to jail several times for Gandhi's cause.

Reverend Joseph Doke, a priest, nursed Gandhi for three weeks when Gandhi had been brutally attacked by Mir Alam. Reverend Doke also wrote the first biography of Gandhi, in 1910, much before the world had any indication of the birth of the "Mahatma".

Romain Rolland, the Nobelaureat, once remarked, "Gandhi is another Christ."

Gandhi never let culture or religion stand as a barrier. Relentlessly, he fought for "the equality of all human beings". As a result, he always ended up supporting the "weak". In South Africa it was the "coolies", in India it was the "untouchables" and so on. He resented women being called the "weaker sex". He renamed the untouchables "Harijans", which literally means "the children of God".

According to Gandhi, the good of all lies in the good of the individual and therefore, until every single person is properly looked after, there can be no lasting peace.

Uniting the three hundred million people of India, who spoke six hundred different dialects, and winning the independence of India, were simply some by-products of Gandhi's main mission of "universal brotherhood".

The more I study his life, the more I believe that Mahatma Gandhi was an Idol of multi-culturalism.

45

Sometimes Doing Nothing
Is Very Beneficial

We live in a very fast world. Everyone seems to be always rushing for something. We literally feel guilty if we waste even a minute here or there. Sometimes we try to cram several activities together. Does that enhance our overall productivity?

This essay suggests that by rushing too much we are likely to be less effective. There is no sense in doing a task perfectly if there was no need of doing that task in the first place. Before we jump into working on the task, we need to slow down, relax and think of "the most important task at the moment".

The essay provides several tips for finding the necessary time for relaxing and thinking

Read also essay numbers 76 and 81.

H ave you sometimes felt that you had just too many things to do? Well, on many such occasions, your best course could be to do nothing. That's right, do absolutely nothing!

This may appear to be deceiving, or even sarcastic, but "doing nothing" often proves to be very beneficial.

I am not suggesting that we do nothing all the time. I am only suggesting that we do nothing once in a while.

Whenever we find ourselves in a situation where we feel we have too many things to do, we tend to freeze. Our mind slows down, and may even black out. We find ourselves incapable of making rational decisions. In some respect, we become partially blinded, and therefore, fail to see what is still available, and within our control.

The greater the pressure, the greater the panic and, therefore, the greater the degree of the blindness.

According to Pareto's principle, approximately eighty per cent of all values lie in the top twenty per cent of our activities, provided that we arrange our activities in the order of their value, and we handle the high value activities first.

Thus, before we start working on any activity, we should take some time to find out its respective value. We should also ascertain the extent of the resources available to us. This requires a quiet, relaxed mind. Therefore, for a while, we should do nothing but think quietly.

But how long should we do nothing?

Only as long as it takes to unfreeze our mind, to remove its excessive pressure, to review the list of our activities, and to assess their relative values. This can normally be accomplished in just a few minutes.

Doing nothing means cutting down the activities of the mind. It means refraining from all activities, including listening to the radio or watching the television. It means no eating, drinking, or talking. Total silence should be observed. With your eyes closed you should sit, or lie down, totally still.

Since approximately eighty per cent of all external signals reach our mind through our eyes, keeping them closed cuts down on the largest part of the stimuli that prevents our mind from being quiet. The quieter the mind, the better it can think, and therefore, the more efficient it becomes.

If you can't remain still, you may try walking around calmly. You may look at the sky and watch the clouds, the rain drops or the snow flakes. You may watch a water fountain or a stream, if one is available nearby. The idea is to free your mind temporarily from some of its regular duties and pressure.

Whenever Leonardo da Vinci needed new ideas, he used to stare at the burning woods, and their ashes, in his fire place. He kept staring at them until he forgot himself and his surroundings. Ideas then started flowing into his mind.

A relaxed body induces relaxation in the mind. Deep and slow breathing brings additional relaxation to both the body and the mind.

Normally we carry a lot of mental chatter. We can reduce this by continually telling ourselves that for a few minutes we are off-duty, to relax. We should take the attitude that even heaven can wait for a moment.

If you are unable to cut down this chatter, try recalling some situation when you were able to cope with a similar pressure. Try affirming that you are strong, and that you will be able to handle this challenge. This will build your self-confidence.

As your mind quietens, you will start receiving useful ideas. You will start seeing your activities in the light of their values. You will become aware of some additional resources that you could use. You will notice some tasks that you could delegate. In brief, you will start seeing the bigger picture.

Within minutes you may feel that you have received enough useful ideas. You may be tempted to rush back to your regular chores. But you should resist. You should take your full time to relax your mind. A few extra minutes of relaxation will eventually bring many more valuable ideas.

When you feel that you have relaxed enough,you have some sense of control over your situation, and that you have received some valuable ideas, you should jot those ideas down, preferably on a blank sheet of paper. A clean slate protects the new ideas from being coloured by our past biases. The task then is reduced to implementing those ideas one by one.

Within certain limits, every hour of time spent in planning something saves at least two hours of the time spent in doing it. Good planning improves co-ordination, reduces delays, clarifies different roles, and therefore expedites execution. It saves resources in the long run.

Quietening the mind allows us to listen to our inner voice, which is our best guide, especially in an emergency situation.

'How often should you do nothing?'

You should do this at least once, and preferably twice, every day. Early in the morning is the best time, because it enables you to plan and, therefore, make the best use of your day. Doing nothing for at least five minutes just before you start your day's work, is also very beneficial. In addition, whenever you find yourself struck by a panic situation, just remember to take a minute, to do nothing.

The proof of the pudding is in the eating. You can realize the usefulness of doing nothing only if you try it. Why not try it right now?

Take a short break. You deserve it. Sit comfortably. Close your eyes. Remain still. Relax your body, and quieten your mind, as much as you can. You will discover a new life. Go ahead and check it out.

> "The best thinking has been done in solitude."
> - Thomas Edison

46

Abracadabra:

Speak The Blessing

"Abracadabra", the mystic word for every magician, means "speak the blessing". No matter what happens, a magician is advised to speak only of the good things, and therefore, to ignore the things (the motions) that went wrong.

By focusing their attention only on the good things, they keep on noticing only the good motions or good alternatives. Thus they are able to salvage most of their errors and the audience gets the feeling that even the error was one of the planned acts.

This essay suggests that we can use the mystic power of "abracadabra" in our daily life. If we keep looking for something good, we will find something good, in almost every situation

Read also essay number 94.

No matter how many times we have seen the trick, we still wonder how a magician pulls a rabbit out of a hat. What appears to be real magic is actually no magic at all. The rabbit had been hiding in the hat all the time. The magician simply goes through a certain routine, in some proper order, and in some proper way.

Sometimes he fails in his trick, but he doesn't waste any moment thinking of the failure. He goes through some other motions and makes us believe that the failure had been intentional, as part of the routine.

When he fails, he goes right back to the basics. He practices the correct manoeuvres and perfects the trick.

As he performs, he keeps affirming "Abracadabra". This mantra seems to do the needed magic for him. What is the secret?

The dictionary meaning of "Abracadabra" is, "gibberish" or "An incantation or magical word". Thus according to several current dictionaries, "Abracadabra" does not have any specific meaning. This is not entirely true.

After some research, I found that the original meaning of "Abracadabra" was "Speak the blessing". But since this word was very heavily used by magicians, the general public thought it to be some kind of gibberish. After decades of "lack of use" its original meaning has been totally lost, and now even dictionaries define it as "gibberish".

A magician is trained to think always of the blessing. By doing so, he focuses his attention on the good things, and therefore expects good outcomes. Can we not apply the same philosophy in our every day situations?

If we bless our current condition, we will be seeing more good things. Every situation carries some favourable and some adverse elements. It is true that generally the adverse elements outweigh the favourable ones, but it is still to our advantage to look for the favourable elements.

If you were mining for gold, you would handle approximately four tons of dirt before you would collect one ounce of the precious metal. Wisdom lies in not giving up the mining process, but in focussing our eyes on the ultimate goal, the ounce of gold.

The more burdensome it is to separate the precious metal from the dirt, the more valuable that metal proves to be.

This analogy has a direct bearing in the affairs of our lives. There is some gold in every situation, in every problem. If we look for it, and strive for it, we are likely to find it.

Many events in life appear to be magical, because they happen as surprises. But in reality, nothing is magical. The rabbit had been put in the hat beforehand and anyone, who has learned the routine, can easily surprise the audience by pulling it magically out of that hat.

The whole universe is governed by the law of cause and effect. If we learn to take charge of the cause, we would not be surprised by its corresponding effect. Understanding this law, and making effective use of it, is one of the greatest challenges of life.

Yes, we make errors and so do magicians. But unlike them, we seem to dwell upon our errors. We forget that the natural, proper course, is the successful working of the trick.

Let's learn from the magicians. Let's affirm "Abracadabra" in all situations. Let's bless the situation that we are in. Let's look for the hidden gold, the opportunity for us to grow.

I keep a card bearing the words "Thank You" on my desk. It acts as my constant reminder to be thankful. Occasionally I question myself, "Thankful for what?" As I look for the answer, I notice several genuine blessings for which I should be thankful. I am amazed that even the most serious problems carry some benefit for which I should be thankful.

A friend of mine told his little girl one day, "Today something wonderful is going to happen to you at school. I want you to look for it and to tell us in the evening." Something wonderful did happen to her that day. Thinking that that was just a coincidence, he repeated the game for the next few days and found that every day something wonderful did happen to her.

We generally notice what we pay attention to, and overlook the rest. Perhaps that's why the Bible says, "There are people who have eyes but who can't see." The act of seeing must first take place at the mental level before it can take place on the physical level.

God has provided each one of us with enough talents to be able to live a happy life.

"Happy the man whose wish and care
A few paternal acres bound,
Content to breathe his native air
In his own ground."
                              - Alexander Pope

47

Everyone   Counts

Do you feel your role in your company, or society to be insignificant?

No role is actually insignificant. What appears to be almost insignificant today, may turn out to be very significant tomorrow.

This essay points out that just as a nail can become very important for a war, your role can, and in fact is, very important

It is up to God to distribute the tasks. Our duty is to perform our share of the task. It is only by making the best use of the current task that we can expect a more challenging task tomorrow.

Read also essay numbers 24 and 80.

R ecently I noticed that this year's annual theme of one service club in town, was, "Every member counts." After some deliberation, I felt that not only every member of a service club, but every single person in the world counts.

No matter what you do, or what your role or position is, you are making some contribution by doing your part. You should be counted simply for rendering your share of the service to society. I believe that you are important, and that you count much more than what you think you do.

If you think that I am simply trying to please you, try disappearing for a few days and notice the resulting chaos. In the very least, your presence is preventing the occurrence of that chaos.

The best way to contribute is to do our part best. By doing our part we help our team. The more we help our team, the faster, and higher, we can rise in the hierarchy of our own team.

Some roles are perceived to be more important than the others. But in its proper place, every role is important, and any role can become vital.

Some years ago I read a poem entitled, "For the want of a nail". It goes like this:

"For the want of a nail a horse-shoe was lost;
For the want of a shoe a horse was lost;
For the want of a horse a soldier was lost;
For the want of a soldier a battle was lost;
For the want of a battle the war was lost."

Imagine that! Even a simple nail can count toward the ultimate success of a war. In the same way, every single person counts toward the ultimate success of the team.

Behind every worthwhile accomplishment, there has been a cohesive and harmonious team working toward the overall goal. The individual contributions of many members may not attract the spot light, but that does not mean that those little contributions are not needed.

Often I receive some accolade for some of my work, but I know that I could not have accomplished that if my wife and my children would not have helped, by taking care of their part, and by maintaining a harmonious atmosphere within the family.

Each role may be seen as the contribution of one of the pillars of a structure, that finally support a huge mansion. Individually the importance of a certain pillar may appear to be trite, but remove it and it may upset the stability, and thereby the viability, of the entire mansion. Remove one nail from a wall, and you introduce a local weakness, which may soon loosen the neighbouring nails. The little weakness will soon propagate and weaken the entire wall. That's why the phrase, "A stitch in time, saves nine".

Don't underestimate the importance of your current role. How you handle a one dollar assignment today, determines how quickly you can get the opportunity to handle a thousand dollar assignment. The more heart you put into doing your best on your current assignment, the faster you can move to the next rung in the ladder of success.

The essence of each role is to serve others. There are infinite ways of serving. We can serve by becoming a brick of the superstructure, or the rock of the foundation. In one case we would be highly visible. In the other we would lie silently, unnoticed and may even remain unrewarded. But perhaps the foundation plays more important role than does the superstructure.

It is nice to be rewarded, to be recognized for the service that we render. But the real reward comes from our inner feeling of having made significant use of our lives, of having used our God-given talents.

Some people feel that they are too old to be counted. This may be a totally false assumption. Except for sports, it has been found that most men make their significant contributions only after they pass the age of forty. It seems that until that time they remain preoccupied with other interests such as education, earning a living, raising a family, etc. Once they are over the age of forty, they suddenly realize that they do not have many years left and that they must do something to leave a meaningful legacy behind.

No matter how old you are, you can still contribute. Many men have made more contributions to society in a matter of just a few years than they did in their previous decade(s). The turning point came when they experienced a change in their attitude to life.

This change invariably comes through introspection, by asking some soul-searching questions, such as, "What have I done so far? Where am I headed? Am I happy with my accomplishments? What could I do to experience more happiness from my life?"

We are activity-centered creatures. We want to use every single minute of our time doing "something". Often we do something without giving much thought to our long term objective.

Wisdom suggests that for every so many hours of actual running time we take at least some time to look back and review the grounds that we have covered so far. We should ask ourselves, "In which direction, and toward what purpose, am I running?"

Fifteen minutes of thinking time, or self-assessment time, every day, can make a tremendous difference in our productivity, in our meaningful contributions to society.

You and I may never catch up with a superstar, and there is no need for that, but we can certainly outperform many of them in the area of our unique talents.

The Creator has blessed every one of us with at least one unique talent. Our task is simply to discover that talent and to work consistently toward cultivating it. We can do this through a regular period of introspection.

We cannot change our past. We must start from where we are and with what we have. Making the decision that we want to make a more significant contribution to our society is the first step.

Let's stop downplaying the importance of our individual roles.   Let's put our whole heart in it, because every role does count, and therefore every person counts.

> "The road to success is filled with
> women pushing their husbands along."
> - Lord Thomas Dewar

48

People Do Business
With People They Like

This essay suggests that people make decisions based more on "personality-matching" than on the likeability of the product or the service. Therefore, if you want to increase the sale of your product or service, first try improving your human relations skills. The more people like you, the more they will do business with you.

The essay points out that perception, mental filter and non-verbal signals play important roles in building human relations skill.

Read also essay numbers 6, 15 and 32.

Do you know of a situation where two sales persons were trying to sell the same thing, and where, for some reason, the prospect bought from the one and not from the other?

This happens all the time. But, does it happen simply by luck, or is there some definite motivation behind it?

Let's analyze the situation and see if we can find a pattern.

All wise persons have advised us, 'know thyself'. It is only when we begin to understand ourselves that we begin to understand the motivations of others. Therefore, let's take a moment to understand how we express ourselves and how we read others.

Recall some cases when you either bought, or decided not to buy, something. How did you make your choice? Why did you choose one salesperson and not the other? Try also to recall some people who chose to do business with you. Why did they choose you, and not your competitor?

Do you see any trend?

Of course there is a definite trend. People do business with people that they like.

You would not walk into a new town, enter an unknown store and ask an unknown salesperson to sell you an item that is totally unknown to you, would you? No, that would be silly.

Among the many variables, the like or dislike of the person involved in the transaction plays the most important role. The greater the degrees of liking each other, the quicker, and the more pleasant is the transaction.

The best way to be liked, is to become one of them. But how can we become one of them for each of our prospects? There is a danger we could go crazy.

We can perhaps take a lesson from our family lives. Anyone who has more than one child recognizes that each child has his own individual personality. Somehow the parent carefully molds his approach to deal effectively with each. We can do the same in dealing with our prospects.

You may say that the parent has the advantage of knowing the child since his birth. He had ample time to study the child. In addition, the child is dependent on his parent for most of his needs.

You are totally right. You have the advantage of "having more background information" on your children, than you have on your prospects. However, you can develop the skill to quickly discover the uniqueness of a prospect and then adapt yourself accordingly, while dealing with that prospect. This is tantamount to learning how to act different roles and then actually acting one of those roles in a moment's notice.

Liking begins with the discovery of some common ground. The more common ground we share, the more we like each other.

But all common grounds do not create the same degree of bondage. Those that carry some emotional attachments go straight to our hearts and create strong bonds.

It is claimed that all decisions are made by the heart. We first make a decision based on our dominant emotions, and then we try to rationalize it by some suitable logic.

The fastest way of reaching someone's heart is by talking to that person in his own language. This works like magic.

We are normally conscious only of the verbal component of a language. But there is another component, the non-verbal, which plays a more important role. It includes, but is not limited to, body language.

It is estimated that nearly ninety-three per cent of the signals that we receive, reach us through sight, tone, touch or some imagination related to sight, sound or feeling. These are commonly known as the visual, auditory and kinesthetic components of a signal. We use some combination of these three components to express most of our thoughts.

Each of us has our own preferred set of combination of these three components of message. This constitutes our unique filter, which determines the importance, or the relative value, of the different component of the incoming signals, reaching our mind.

For example, to express himself, person A could use eighty per cent visual, five per cent auditory and fifteen per cent kinesthetic signal components. Person B, on the other hand, could use twenty per cent visual, fifteen per cent auditory and sixty-five per cent kinesthetic signals.

Irrespective of the make-up of the incoming signals, person A (who is strongly visual) will notice mostly the visual components. If the same signal was aimed at person B, he would notice mostly the kinesthetic part and would almost ignore the visual and auditory parts.

If A and B talk to each other without realizing the difference between their filters, they would miss the greater part of each other's message and would have a tendency to make up the gap with their own guess. With time, the new pieces of information would get highly distorted and the communication would eventually break down.

This problem can be alleviated by (1) cultivating the awareness that different persons have different filters, (2) understanding the unique filter of the prospect that we are dealing with and (3) trying to understand his real message in the light of our knowledge of his filter.

Fortunately, we are not stuck with one set of filters for the rest of our lives. With our experience our filters change. Moreover, we can consciously modify them, to a great extent, to suit the particular occasion.

This task is not as difficult as it sounds. Like any other skill, this one can be cultivated, if one works at it taking small regular steps.

For the moment let's remember that people do business with people they like and that people like those who speak their unique language.

We may have the world's best product or service to offer. We may be most sincere in trying to help our prospect. But we can't succeed in our endeavour unless we understand and use the prospect's unique language.

It's not what we hear or say that counts. It's what our prospect hears, understands and takes to heart that really counts. Let's invest in learning the most important language, the language of expressing oneself using compatible visual, auditory and kinesthetic signals.

"If my theory of relativity is proven successful, Germany will claim me as a German and France will declare that I am a citizen of the world. Should my theory prove untrue, France will say that I am a German and Germany will declare that I am a Jew."

- Albert Einstein

49

Emulation

Is The Best Homage

This essay was written as a homage to the soul of a young teacher who suddenly passed away.

The essay refers to the life outlook of Ben Franklin and Mahatma Gandhi, and suggests that the best homage is to emulate the virtues of the departed soul.

Read also essay numbers 30 and 78.

Gurmit Singh Rai, a Chemistry teacher at Salisbury Composite High School, passed away at the age of fifty-five. He enjoyed good health and was an active person. Minutes before his death, he had returned from participating in some sport.

Gurmit was loved by both his family and his students. At his funeral, his sons, colleagues and students described how loving a man he had been.

His two children are getting well settled in their own lives. His wife has always been very supportive of him. From what I heard, I found no apparent sign of any serious stress in Gurmit's life. Despite this, why did he pass away at such an early age?

At the funeral I noticed that everyone had nothing but praise for Gurmit. But did Gurmit experience the same love and respect during his life?

Why is it that we keep finding faults with a person during his life, but when he departs we recall mostly his good virtues?

There was one speech that I found to be very unusual. About a month earlier, Gurmit's second son, Paul had written him a letter. At the funeral, Paul read that letter. That was his eulogy.

I found that to be very touching, because that was the only speech that Gurmit had heard during his life. Wouldn't it be nice if we could hear our eulogies while we are still alive?

Although technology has advanced considerably, and the average life-span is now around seventy-four years, there is no guarantee that anyone will live that long. A person meeting Gurmit a few hours before his death, would have no inkling of his abrupt departure.

In what condition would you leave your affairs if you had to leave right away? Would you like to touch someone before you leave? Would you like to finish something? Then don't wait. Do it right away. You never know when your number will be called.

What legacy would you be leaving behind, if you had to leave tonight? What improvements would you like to make in your legacy, if you were allowed one more day, one more week or one more month to stay? Don't wait. Get busy and do the most that you can do, while you still have the time.

Mahatma Gandhi, the great leader of India, was a relentless worker. He spent one-fourth of the last twenty-six years of his life in jail. Yet he organized more projects, more movements, than anybody else could. His writings have been collected into ninety volumes of approximately three hundred pages each. What was his secret?

When he was not in jail, every hour, every day he lived under the shadow of the possibility of being arrested. Therefore, he never postponed doing something that he could do right away. As he finished one task, he could see his next most important task. He did not stop until he was jailed.

Since we have little chance of being jailed, we are in no hurry to start something that we can postpone until tomorrow. Is that a blessing?

Ben Franklin was another great man. His accomplishments are unbelievable. Here is a short glimpse.

Although he had little education, he taught himself the classics, writing for publication, science, finance, politics, diplomacy and in four languages!

He was the first to discover positive and negative electricity and electrical charge. He invented the electrical battery, condenser, conductor and lightning rod. He invented a kitchen stool that folded over to become a step ladder, and a mechanical hand for lifting objects from high shelves.

He discovered that storms rotate while travelling forward. He charted the Gulf Stream. He discovered that water boils at lower temperature in thinner air and at high altitudes.

At the age of seventy-eight, he invented the bifocal lens. He organized the first service club in America, the first regular police force, the first fire department, the first insurance company. He founded the American Philosophical Society, the national academy of science, the first national library and museum, the first patent office. He started the great Pennsylvania Hospital. He founded the college which later became the University of Pennsylvania.

This is just a partial list. How did he find the time for all that, I don't know. But here is sage advice from him.

"Do you love life? Then don't waste your time, because that's the stuff that the life is made of."

Gandhi also believed in "doing your best" at the moment, and in not wasting any time in idle gossip. During the Independence movement of India, many important leaders passed away. Immediately after attending the funeral he urged everyone to start working on the "ideals" for which that man had lived. According to him, the best homage was to emulate the virtues of the departed soul, or to further his or her unfinished work.

Many Indians revered Gandhi like a god and would hang his picture on their neck. Noticing this Gandhi would say, "You would respect me more by following me in my footsteps."

He did not wish any formal funeral after his own death. He had advised Madeline Slade (also known as Mirabehn) not to rush to his funeral, and to continue doing what she was doing. Miss Slade was not in Delhi at the time of Gandhi's death. She was invited to come to his funeral. But recalling Gandhi's advice, she declined, and continued doing what she had been doing.

Perhaps a good homage to Gurmit's soul would be to strive for acquiring some of the traits that he symbolized. He was a model husband, father and teacher. we need not imitate him but we can create our own image of the ideal person and work toward achieving that ideal.

Time is life and life is uncertain. Capture it while it is still available. Express your love to your loved ones today. You do not know how much time you have left. Therefore, don't wait for tomorrow. Start this very moment.

50

Self-Discipline Leads To Self-Actualization

Discipline is a vital element of life, because in its total absence, life cannot sustain itself.

There are two kinds of discipline, internal and external. For a balanced living both kinds must be present, although their ratio may fluctuate considerably. As the proportion of one increases, that of the other must decrease.

This essay suggests that a person performs better when he is subjected more to internal discipline and less to external. As the component of self-discipline increases, the person moves towards attaining the ideal state of self-actualization.

Since it is within our power to cultivate self-discipline, it is possible for us to self-actualize

Read also essay numbers 25 and 45.

E very single moment of our life is governed by some kind of discipline, internal or external. The proportion of the two varies from person to person. It is obvious that the greater the presence of the one, the lesser will be that of the other.

Some discipline is essential for any organized life. If we do not obey it voluntarily, it is imposed upon us.

A good example is the life of a child. As long as he obeys the required rules of the family, he enjoys many liberties. But the moment he fails, some of his freedoms are slowly withdrawn.

This has a parallel in our daily lives. We have some duties to perform within certain prescribed limits. If we do, we enjoy freedom over our affairs. But if we fail, we are punished in some form or the other, by some outside force.

For society to function effectively, it develops some guidelines. We, as members of our society, participate in the formation of those guide-lines. But once developed, they exercise power over our lives.

These guidelines guarantee only the survival of the society and its members. For growth one must design, and abide by, some more strict discipline.

The more self-discipline we can exercise, the more freedom we are allowed, and therefore, the more opportunity we have to do what we really like to do. This is what self-actualization is all about, isn't that right?

But where do we begin?

We begin by changing our perception of "discipline", which is much more than simply a form of punishment.

Discipline demands just enough punishment to bring us back on our right course, if and when we go astray. In that light, the related punishment becomes a blessing.

But discipline is much more than punishment. When self-imposed, it enables the person to control his mind, for the best use of his life. In other words, to self-actualize.

According to Mahatma Gandhi, the greatest challenge for a person is to be able to control his mind, and to direct it to do what one would want it to do. But control of the mind is possible only after one has learned to control the body. The latter is impossible until one has learned to control the palate.

The seed of self-control, therefore, lies in the control of our palate. We are literally the slaves of the needs of our palates.

Try giving up one item of food for a few days and notice the change in your feelings. It may be a bit difficult in the beginning, but you will survive and will experience some extra inner strength. Your thought will move along the lines of "If I can control that, I can control other desires as well." This will lead you to self-mastery.

Another area, in which to practice self-discipline, is to observe silence for some specified duration. This means not only refraining from speaking but also cutting down most of the incoming sensory signals.

Two or three times a day, for a few minutes, keep your eyes closed, and sit still without doing anything. This will not only relax your body and mind, but will also build some inner strength. There is no need to feel guilty about wasting your time doing nothing. In fact, these few minutes may turn out to be very beneficial, because the quieter the mind, the more efficient it becomes.

Anyone who fails to master himself cannot master someone else. On the contrary, the more that one can master oneself, the more influence one can exert over others.

This perhaps was the main secret of Gandhi's rise from mediocrity to international influence. He earned the title of "Mahatma", which literally means, "The great soul", simply because he could demonstrate extraordinary self-control.

If some external discipline bothers you, try to mull over it objectively. Psychologists say that when a person relaxes physically, his mind relaxes and his anger evaporates. With a cool mind see if you can appreciate the rationale behind the required external discipline. If you can find some logical reason, accept that discipline happily. If you don't, then you may be missing some aspects of the rationale.

If you still feel that the obligatory discipline is not justified, take some immediate action to get it amended. Raise your concerns through proper channels. Get the unjustified discipline changed, but as long as it is not changed, obey it willingly.

We can change the perspective of a situation by modifying the associated discipline. Voluntarily accept, and impose, a self-discipline which is a little bit more strict than the external obligatory one, and you will find the pill more palatable.

It is important that we achieve some success, and gain some self-confidence, before we try more difficult challenges of self-discipline. Start by trying some relatively easy tasks such as being punctual or refraining from the use of some words that have a negative influence on our attitudes.

Don't worry if you fail in your first attempts. It simply means that your chosen step was too big for you. Reduce the size of your current step and try again. Continue reducing the step-size until you do succeed.

One successful experience is all that you need to get started on the road to self-actualization Success breeds success. One success, no matter how small, will inspire you to try another step, slightly larger and more difficult than the previous one. The momentum will continue and soon you will be taking even those large steps which are frightening you today. Just remember, whenever you feel scared, cut down the size of the step and go on.

Even a ninety per cent failure means ten per cent success, and ten per cent of something is more valuable than one hundred per cent of nothing.

You may not wish to become a Mahatma, but you can make the best use of the potential that the Creator has blessed you with. I do not know what it feels like to truly self-actualize, but I do know that if one ever reaches it, one should always strive for the ideal condition. Destination is important, but is is also important to know the direction toward that destination, and to make the first move.

Let's choose self-actualization to be our main destination and let's start moving towards it by choosing to build self-discipline today, and every day.

"The most valuable of all education is the ability to make yourself do the thing you have to do, when it has to be done, whether you like it or not."

- Aldous Huxley

51

Don't Curse The Darkness, Light A Candle

If life was full of "light' all the time, it would become very dull. To create some variety, and to challenge us, nature occasionally puts us in darkness. The average person, in that situation, curses the darkness. But a wise man accepts whatever comes his way, and then works to improve it.

This essay points out that many men were able to make outstanding accomplishments only when they were totally surrounded by "darkness".

Read also essay numbers 1, 22 and 53.

H ave you sometimes been struck by a sudden darkness? What did you do at that moment?

If you are a normal person, you would have cussed, complained, and hoped that the light reappeared soon.

But no amount of cussing or complaining is going to make the slightest difference unless, of course, the person responsible for the light can hear you, and decide to do something about it.

Cussing, complaining or hoping simply reveals our weakness. By affecting the peace of our mind, they prevent us from reacting to the situation properly.

If you are an above average person, you will not get frightened, or react violently. You may patiently wait for a moment for the light to return. If it does not, you will start thinking of the alternatives that you have. Can you let some light in by opening a window, a door or both? Will it help if you removed some drapes, blinds or some other objects that are presently obstructing the light? Do you have a match, a candle or some other source of temporary lighting? Can you call someone for help?

The main difference between an average and an above average person is that one panics while the other stays cool, thinks and decides to take some action to gain control over the situation.

I am not suggesting that we ignore a problem. But fretting about a problem rarely helps solve it. We should give the problem just enough attention so as to think of the cause, the consequences and the proper course of action at the moment.

We have often heard that success breeds success. By the same rule, failure breeds failure. How we handle the present problem, however small, determines how we would react to some future problems. Our reaction to the sudden darkness is a test of our maturity.

The more we talk about the seriousness of a problem, the more importance we attach to it. In that way, even a flimsy problem can gain in magnitude. We often lose our perspective and stop noticing the resources which are readily available to us. It is not the circumstances, but our reaction to them, that really matters.

I remember my engineering Machine Design exam. It was tough, and in addition, it contained some printing errors. No one at the place of the exam, had the authority to correct the errors. Perhaps we could identify the errors, correct them, and then solve the new problem. But that meant taking a big risk. We were in a state of panic. We stared at each other and even considered walking out of the room.

Suddenly an idea came to my mind. Rather than fuming over the situation, I decided to ignore the difficult parts, and to answer the ones that I thought were within my capability. As I solved one part, I noticed another that I could handle. One by one, I solved more than half of the problems. By this time I had gained enough confidence to correct what I thought was "printing errors." By refusing to panic, I was able to notice more things than I had noticed earlier.

Later I learned that I had earned the highest mark in the university in that particular paper!

If we stay cool, and accept the problem as a challenge, we become stronger, because future problems of similar complexity do not disturb us to the same degree.

The average person asks, "God, why me?" The above average person says, "God try me."

Dr. Norman Vincent Peale often prays, "Lord don't you trust me any more? How come you have not given me some new problems lately?"

But what about a blind man?

Actually, every one is blind in some respect. We are surrounded by many more things than our eyes or ears notice. We are often inundated with opportunities but we fail to notice them.

Thomas Edison often said, "Ideas are in the air. If I do not catch them, somebody else will."

Some people think that ignorance is bliss. By that count blindness can be a blessing too. But life means looking for, combating and solving problems. If you do not get disturbed by darkness, then there is something inherently wrong with you. Some disturbance is good. Just remember not to panic.

When faced with darkness, we generally feel handicapped. But there is a blessing in almost every handicap, and we can capitalize on it, if we stop cursing it and start looking for the blessing.

Darkness often provides us with an opportunity of solitude. This can be a tremendous blessing. Occasional solitude is very beneficial for our souls. All great achievers make it a point to create some regular periods of solitudes. I find that nothing great has ever been achieved by a person who did not make some use of the power of solitude.

Some people are blessed with solitude through illness, imprisonment or some other means of confinement.

Albert Einstein thought of the Theory of Relativity while he was confined to bed due to an illness. John Bunyan wrote Pilgrim's Progress when he was in prison. Mahatma Gandhi did most of his thinking while he was imprisoned. He found the solitude in prisons to be so helpful that he devised some means of creating solitude as often as he could. Every Monday, he practiced silence, mainly to gain some solitude.

Nature plays no favourites. The darkness strikes everyone alike. But the average person takes it as a curse, and panics, while the wise person takes it as an opportunity to test his mettle and to exercise his creativity.

Next time you are faced with darkness, don't panic. Look for your available alternatives. Try to make the best of what is still within your control, and accept that which you cannot change.

Let's remember the age-old saying, 'Go as far as you can go and when you reach there, you will see some more.' In most cases we do not see our second step until we have taken the first one. As we take the immediate step, no matter how small it may be, we start noticing a few more things that we had overlooked earlier.

Let's not curse our darkness. Let's learn to light a candle.

> "There is no king who has not had a slave among his ancestors, and no slave who has not had a king among his."
>
> - Helen Keller

52

Disagreements Signify Creativity

How do you feel when someone disagrees with you? Disagreement is not necessarily a sign of disrespect for the person. It may signify a different angle of viewing the same situation.

Since no two persons occupy exactly the same position, it is impossible for the two to perceive a situation identically. This creates an immediate disagreement. In that way, a disagreement indicates creativity. Therefore, we should not only tolerate disagreements but even encourage them.

This essay discusses several ways of converting disagreements into a win-win experience.

Read also essay number 83.

H ave you ever tried to do something that was in the best interest of the other person, but found that he disagreed with you? How did you feel when this happened? What did you do then?

Why do we see the same thing so differently? Why do we have disagreements?

Everyone sees a situation from his or her own perspective. Since no two persons have identical experience, no two persons see identically.

We disagree when we feel that what we are being asked to do is illogical or not conducive to our own welfare. We feel that there is a better way of handling the situation.

No one intentionally wants to hurt anyone else, and no one wants to be exploited either. When a person feels that he has a better perspective on a certain situation, or feels that he can adequately foresee and judge the outcome of his alternatives, he will want to follow his own conscience, even if it means disagreeing with some 'authority'.

Sometimes we disagree just because we want to explore the area that is forbidden to us. We want to test the limits, or the powers of the authority. We want to find out just how far we can bend the rules.

Being curious by nature, we want to try everything. We want to know "why?" We are seldom satisfied by someone else's explanation. We want to verify it ourselves.

Sometimes we disagree to express our defiance, or to demonstrate our right to be independent.

Is it bad to disagree?

Within certain limits, disagreement is a healthy trait. It is an indication of the fire, the life within the individual.

All inventions, all developments, have been the result of some form of disagreement or resistance. Someone could not accept certain conditions. Someone decided to prove that things could be better in some different way. Someone resolved to prove that he could do the impossible and fought it to the finish.

The birth of every new religion, every new piece of music, every new piece of literature, every new design, is due to someone who disagreed with the existing norms.

Every leader has been a dissenter of some kind. Mahatma Gandhi, one of the greatest spiritual leaders of this century, not only tolerated but also welcomed disagreements. He often said, "If you agree with me totally, then you have nothing to offer me." Gandhi himself was an example of a dissenter of the highest degree. He would disagree even if he happened to be the only person in the world on his side. He said, 'Truth is truth, whether it is supported by one person or by a million. I do what I consider to be the truth. I follow my own conscience, irrespective of what everybody else thinks of it.'

When analysed carefully, we find that the root of all creativity lies in the urge to be different, to crave what's not available.

But what can we do?

Here are some ways of handling disagreement without hurting the spirit of the other person.

1. Welcome disagreement.

Rather than being upset about it, welcome it. Individuals must have some individuality, some uniqueness. If everyone agreed one hundred per cent, we would end up with a bunch of robots. Disagreements prove that people have some originality.

2. Guide it.

Instead of trying to quell the disagreement, help channel it constructively. Direct confrontation always results in resistance. A better approach is to ask the person why he feels that way. Ask what he would do if he was in charge. Ask him to explain why he thinks that his approach is better.

By asking questions you encourage the other person to think. If you just tell someone something, he will tend to doubt you. However, if he himself discovers the strength or the weakness of an argument, he needs no further explanation or proof. Socrates used this method very effectively, to sell his ideas.

You may also advise him to save his resources for more valuable issues. Encourage him to ask himself, 'Is this issue really important to me?' If it is not, then it should be dropped. If it is, then it is his duty to stand for it.

3. Keep occupied with meaningful, challenging tasks.

Once Mr. Nehru, the first Prime Minister of India, asked Mr. Gandhi, "Why do Hindus and Muslims fight?" Gandhi replied, "Because they have nothing important to do."

Keeping our minds occupied with challenging tasks prevents us from mulling about some petty things. The easiest things are generally not very constructive. Remember the age-old saying, 'An idle mind is a devil's workshop'.

4. Brainstorm for ideas.

It is true that every disagreement signifies the presence of some problem. However, we should also remember that there can be more than one solution to any given problem. Your solution is just one of the possible solutions. Give him a chance to think of other solutions.

If you are dealing with a big group, try forming small sub-groups of four to six persons each, and ask the members within each subgroup to brainstorm for solutions to the problem that is causing the disagreement. Set a time limit, and ask them to choose a leader of their sub-group. At the end of the session ask the leader to present his sub-group's solutions to the entire group. Let the entire assembly analyze each solution and vote for the best solution.

5. Get a formal consensus from the group.

It is not enough to come up with a good solution. It is also important that every member of the group accept the solution and then try to implement it for a while. Ask them to appoint observers who would monitor the effectiveness of the solution, for an agreed period, and present their findings as a formal report to the whole group. This would give them another opportunity of exercising their responsibility.

6. Refrain from correcting immediately.

If you are more experienced, it may be easy for you to see some flaws in the other person's ideas. But refrain from pointing out the flaws right away. Give him a chance to discover them himself. It is possible that he may make mistakes, and may even get hurt, but there is no need to feel guilty about that. Most errors serve us by teaching us valuable lessons. We often learn more from our mistakes than we do from our right actions. A child learns to walk only my making a series of wrong moves and then correcting them.

7. Encourage creativity.

By focussing on his creative contributions, you can cut down on his destructive behaviours. Reward him immediately for each creative idea, and make the reward proportional to the value of the idea. Psychologists say that the behaviour that is rewarded, gets repeated.

How much disagreement should you welcome depends upon the nature of the group and your ability to deal with them tactfully. You need patience, courage and the belief that this technique will ultimately benefit you, as well as the members of your team.

When faced with a real tough challenge, ask your own conscience to help you out. It will provide you with the needed advice and direction. Trust and follow that advice. If you do so, you will produce a better team. You may yourself feel like disagreeing with some authorities. If so, congratulations.

> "Associate yourself with men of good quality if you esteem your own reputation; for it's better to be alone than in bad company."
> - George Washington

53

Blindness

Is A Matter Of Degree

Scientists estimate that about two million signals reach our central nervous system every second. However, only a tiny fraction of that is allowed to reach our consciousness. This is achieved by the use of a filtering system. Nature has provided this filter to protect us from unnecessary, or harmful, influences from environment.

However, this very filter prevents us from noticing many things around us. That is why the Bible says, "There are people who have eyes but who don't see." The very filter that protects us, makes us partially blind. Thus every person is blind. The difference is only a matter of degree.

This essay describes several ways of reducing the degree of our blindness.

Read also essay number 15.

O nce I was asked to speak to a group of blind people. The lady who was chairing the meeting met me about an hour before my talk. We chatted for a few minutes about the subject of my talk, and my background. She then continued with the meeting.

I was a bit concerned. How would she introduce me? Normally I carry a typed introduction. But I did not know where to get my introduction done in braille.

When my turn came, she stood up and made a crisp and very appropriate introduction. I was amazed. How could she remember all those facts and state them correctly? Even those who read the typed introduction, often make some mistakes!

Had someone read my written introduction to her and had I not known that she was blind, after hearing her introduction, I would not have suspected that she was blind.

Are we justified in attaching the label "blind" to those persons whose organic eyes are not functioning normally? What about those who have perfectly normal organic eyes but who miss noticing some of the things around them?

In one of my seminars, I marked a small black dot in the middle of the flip chart, and asked my audience to describe what they saw. Not one of those thirty persons talked about the flip chart. Everyone talked about the little black dot. Can you imagine? The flip chart was at least ten thousand times larger than that black dot, and yet every one, including those sitting in the back rows, mentioned the black dot, and not the flip chart!

The other day I watched a group of children playing a game. They would invite an outsider, someone who did not know the game before, ask him to lie down on the floor, and cover him with a blanket. Then they would tell him, "There is something on your body that you do not need. We want you to find out what it is, then remove it from your body and throw it on the floor."

The person would remove his shirt, or some item from his pocket, or the girl would remove an item of jewellery and throw it on the floor. But no one would think of the blanket as the unnecessary item!

My experience is not unique. I am sure that you have come across many situations where you, or somebody else, failed to notice the obvious.

We have been trained to notice only the uncommon things. Biologists tell us that a fish does not realize that it lives in water, and notices its absence only when it is pulled out.

In the same way, we live in a world full of countless items, ideas and opportunities, but like that flip chart, or that water, we don't notice them. We do, however, notice some little black dot that may come our way.

It is a marvel that only a tiny fraction, of the approximately two million signals per second, reach our consciousness, and that the rest are handled, and acted upon, appropriately and automatically. If we had to act upon every signal, we could not handle them and, therefore, we would die in a matter of minutes.

But this results in our being blinded to many things including the signals that are gathered by our own sensors. Nature had a choice to either grant us total awareness with no chance of survival, or partial blindness with secure life and sanity. Obviously, she elected for the latter. From this point of view, I feel that everyone is blind to some degree or the other.

But what kind of information is allowed to reach our consciousness, and why?

We are conscious of only that which we look for. We may be surrounded by a million things, but if we are not looking for them, we would literally miss noticing them.

Perception is also a matter of training. To a great degree, we are selfish and short-sighted. With some practice, we can train ourselves to notice even those things that we do not need right away, but which we might need sometime in the future. The following are some ideas for improving one's perception.

Cultivate the habit of looking at the common, everyday things from different angles. Rearrange your room, or your office, and try to notice something different, something new. Change the lighting; change a few things or simply remove an item and see how you cope without it.

Make little changes in your normal routine. Move your lunch time by thirty minutes, and notice the difference in the crowd, or in the type of people at the new time. Make a little change in the time at which you leave for work. Try taking a slightly different route, and observe the difference.

Try seeing the common things from somebody else's point of view. Buy some caps and label them, "Doctor," "Lawyer", "Teacher," "Accountant," "Farmer," "Child," etc.. The next time you are confronted with an insurmountable situation, put on one of those caps and start thinking how that particular person would see the same situation.

You will definitely observe more things, and more ideas will come to your mind, by simply wearing a different cap. Wear one cap for a moment, and when you can't see anything more, replace it with another. The more caps you put on, the more observant you will become.

There is a story of a lady who went Christmas shopping one day in downtown New York. She was in a rush, because she had to buy many gifts that day. She dressed her three-year-old child and dragged him from one department store to another. The child resisted and cried but the mother paid little attention to those.

Finally, the child complained about his loose shoe laces. When the mother knelt down to tie his laces, she noticed that from the child's level one could see nothing but peoples' legs, boots, tables' legs and the floor. Thinking of the misery she had put that child through for the past six hours, she started crying.

If you don't have access to enough caps, you can use your imagination. Just ask yourself, "How would a three-year-old child see this situation?"

There is a Chinese saying, "Do not complain of snow on your neighbour's roof when your own door steps are not clean."

Let's not talk about the blindness of some unfortunate blind people. Let's endeavour to reduce our own blindness, because everyone is blind. The difference is only in degree.

"To know that we know what we know, and that we do not know what we do not know, that is true knowledge."

- Henry David Thoreau

54

In Learning, Quantity Leads To Quality

Our mind learns by remembering both successful and unsuccessful past steps (or movements). It tries to repeat the successful steps, and avoid the unsuccessful ones. For this, it must have an adequate supply of both successful and unsuccessful steps. In other words, it requires a good quantity of mixed experiences. In fact, the bigger the supply, the better.

Using the analogy of a torpedo, this essay suggests that quantity can keep us nearest to the straight line path, and therefore, lead us to quality more quickly

Read also essay number 30.

There is often a debate over the issue of quality versus quantity. In some cases, quality is superior to quantity. For example, it is better to have a few treasures than a house full of junk. Wardrobe experts advise us to buy half as many clothes which are twice as expensive, and therefore twice as good, as we normally buy.

However, in the field of learning a new skill, it is better to aim for quantity, which is generally the fore-runner of quality. In fact, it is virtually impossible to acquire a quality skill without resorting to quantity.

Let's first qualify what we mean by learning.

Learning a new skill means being able to recognize, and to perform the necessary actions which lead to some favourable outcome.

The first step is to identify the relationship between our efforts and their corresponding effects.

The result of every action can be favourable, unfavourable, or partly both. Based on our previous knowledge and understanding, our mind identifies that part of our action which produces the favourable component. It stores that information and uses it later for achieving better success in similar situations. It is in this way that learning takes place.

The sifting process requires the availability of an ample supply of pertinent data. For this we must keep taking actions and observe the corresponding success or failure.

In the beginning there may be a much larger proportion of the component of the undesired result. But, through "learning" from each trial, the proportion of the desired result keeps improving. Thus it is evident that quantity leads to quality.

It's rare for someone to produce a masterpiece, a high quality work, on his very first attempt. What may appear to be the first attempt,is generally preceded by many attempts in piece-meal fashion.

Let's consider the example of learning to speak in public. The only way to learn and to improve this skill is to keep trying to speak in public, continually finding out what works for you, what doesn't, and doing more and more of what you find to be helpful for you. The more often you try to speak in public, the better you learn this skill. In this field, quantity is definitely preferable to quality. I believe that ten average-performance speeches are more valuable than one high-quality speech.

Let's remember, each high-quality speech demands a great deal of preparation before the speech. Each step of preparation is equivalent to some practice, and adds to the total quantity. In that respect, quantity is responsible for that quality.

Let's also remember that real life situations seldom allow us preparation time. Therefore, we can better prepare ourselves for real life situations if we strive for quantity.

As another example, let's consider learning the skill of sales presentation. Again, I believe that ten average sales presentations are more valuable than one quality sales presentation. The "close" is seldom based totally on the quality of the presentation. If the sales person remains aware of his efforts, and their corresponding successes and failures, then the more presentations that he makes, the better will become the quality of his future presentations. Moreover, according to the law of averages, quantity rather than quality will close more sales presentations.

Another important factor to consider is that it is better to strive for immediate action with a sixty per cent quality than to wait for a long time for a ninety per cent quality.

It should be noted that the sixty per cent or the ninety per cent quality is not an objective measure. What appears to you to be a ninety per cent quality today, may appear to be only seventy-five per cent quality tomorrow.

There is another drawback in aiming for quality without quantity. When we become too concerned about the quality of our performance, we hesitate to start. Consequently, we may keep postponing forever, and never take the first step.

Learning is an active process. We learn mostly by doing, through some form of trial and error. Unless we are willing to accept low quality performance in the beginning, we will never start, and therefore, end up not learning the skill at all. We cannot hope to harvest the fruit if we spend all our life studying the root.

Our inherent nature is to strive for quality. Our mind learns by sorting out the "good" of each trial. When we make a similar trial again, it uses the previous learning to enhance the result of the new trial. After each new trial, our mind assesses its success or failure. In this way, it either reinforces or refines its previous learning. The learning, therefore, keeps building.

To "learn" one must be able to distinguish between favourable and unfavourable variables of each operation. For this it is important that the number of unknown variables be small. The larger the step, the more variables may be involved, and the greater will be the probability of its leading us to confusion, instead of learning. The trick, therefore, is to learn by smaller, but more frequent steps.

A torpedo corrects its course as it moves, and reaches its target by making a series of errors. The more we can increase its total number of steps, and thereby reduce the size of each step, the closer it would stay on the straight line path between its point of launching and its target.

In the same way, if we forget about the fear of making errors, and decide to take a large number of very small steps, and consciously try to learn from each step, then we would reach our goal in the shortest time, because we would stay closest to the ideal, straight line, path.

If you are serious about learning a new skill, stop worrying about the quality of your performance in the initial trials. Go for quantity. Take small steps. Trust that your mind will sort out the favourable and the unfavourable components of that step and thereby, with every new trial, you will be lead to a higher quality performance.

When learning a new skill, remember that quantity leads to quality. Therefore, go for quantity and you will attain quality much more easily.

"When you are through improving yourself, you are out of the game.
You learn until your last breath."
- Richard A. Nelson

55

"Completed Tasks" Build Inner Strength

It has been said that success breeds success. In the same way, failure must breed failure.

What is success?

In simple terms, success is the feeling of having accomplished what one had planned to accomplish. Failure, on the other hand, is the feeling of being unable to accomplish, or to complete, what one had planned to accomplish.

Every time that we pursue a task to its completion, we gain a feeling of success, and therefore of strength. Every time that we fail to pursue a task to its completion, we experience a feeling of failure, and therefore of weakness.

This essay advises us not to abort any task before its completion, because that saps our inner strength.

Read also essay number 43.

S ome people seem to possess extraordinary inner strength. Give them any task and they will delve into it right away. Obstacles rarely mean obstacles to them. In fact, they seem to thrive on challenges and obstacles.

Then there are those, the vast majority, who appear to lack most of that strength. Often they seem to prefer to sit by the side of the pool.

What makes this tremendous difference? Is God partial to us?

Our inner strength is built by our experiences of completing, or failing to complete, the tasks that we undertake.

It is estimated that we spend approximately seventy per cent of our waking hours talking to ourselves. We seem to possess two distinct voices. One keeps prodding us by reminding us of our past successes in similar endeavours. The other keeps discouraging us by pin-pointing the instances where we failed to pursue a task to its completion. We are thus torn by the battle of our inner voices. The one that wins determines the action that we take. This is the foundation of our inner strength.

If your task is to swim across a lake, you would be considered to be successful only when you reach the other side. If you fail to start, or if you quit somewhere before reaching the other side, you would be counted as a failure. Every task, no matter how large or small, when completed successfully adds to our confidence and builds our inner strength.

The common reasons why we fail to complete a task are: we never start it; we abort it in the middle; we abort it almost at the end; or, we are reluctant to produce a less-than-perfect job.

We hesitate to start generally because of our fear of failure or ridicule. But strength is acquired by doing and is lost by staying idle. Inertia is perhaps the deadliest poison against building strength.

If you put a one inch piece of wood in front of each wheel of a stationary locomotive, and then release its throttle, the locomotive won't be able to budge, in spite of all its power. But remove those pieces of wood and let the same locomotive move for ten minutes under full throttle, then it can easily demolish a five-foot concrete wall.

Every one of us possesses the potential power of that locomotive, but we can't realize it unless we remove the little stoppers from in front of the wheels that drive us.

We abort a task in the middle mostly when we are overcome by our negative voice. This creates a vicious circle. The more we fail to pursue a task to its completion, the more likely we are to abort future tasks.

Aborting near the completion is most damaging. But the trouble is that one does not know how close one is to the completion. Nature seems to test us for our degree of commitment. She keeps building our obstacles. The closer we get to the finish line, the more formidable our obstacles appear to be. We generally give up because of the lack of confidence in our ability to handle obstacles of that magnitude.

Most great achievers say that their greatest achievements were realized just after the point where they thought that they had been totally overcome by their obstacles. Never give up. You may be just one step away from completing it.

"Perfection" is often a trap. We are loathe to put our name on something which is less than perfect, in our own estimation. But no matter how much you improve it, you will always find some ways of improving it further.

It is better to aim for eighty per cent perfection, and one task completed, than to hang on for ninety per cent perfection and no task completed. In most cases the time and energy invested for that additional amount of perfection is not worth it.

According to Pareto's principle, you can achieve eighty per cent perfection by putting in your twenty per cent well-directed effort. Save your remaining efforts for handling other tasks. Let's recall that in the long range, quantity-completions will improve their quality as well.

Building inner strength may be compared to building a snowball. It's difficult to build it unless you let it roll. In the beginning, do not worry about perfection. You may not catch as much snow as it should catch in each roll. Just keep rolling and soon you will be amazed at its size. You can work at perfecting its shape when you have built adequate size.

Sometimes we hang on to a task because we develop some kind of emotional attachment to it. We are afraid that the moment the task is completed, we would have to part with it.

Incomplete tasks often appear to provide a feeling of security. As long as you keep doing something related to the task, others seem to leave you alone.

A repertoire of completed tasks is the only way of building our inner strength. Every time that we pursue a task to its completion, we build a little more strength. Let's not worry about what others will say. Let's set small, achievable goals. Let's pursue them to completion and add them to our list of completed tasks.

The more tasks that we complete, the stronger we will become. Therefore, to build our inner strength, first let's strive for the number of completed tasks.

> "Time is not measured by the passing of years, but by what one does, what one feels and what one achieves."
>
> - Jawahar Lal Nehru

5 6

Is "Selecting The Right Gift" A Problem?

This essay was written during Christmas. It discusses the problem of choosing the right gift within the limits of one's budget, and suggests some possible solutions.

Since Christmas is a time for sharing, a common gift for the whole family, that would provide an opportunity of sharing some time together, would make sense.

Instead of giving any gift that suits one's budget, this essay suggests one way of discovering the true needs of the other person and then of making an attempt to fulfill that need.

Read also essay numbers 22, 28 and 72.

As Christmas day approaches, more and more frequently we hear the question, "Are your ready for the Christmas?"

For many, the most important task, in getting ready for Christmas, is buying gifts for all the loved ones.

Buying gifts is not a new task. We do it throughout the year. There are birthdays, anniversaries, baby showers, graduations and so on. But Christmas gift buying is something different. For other occasions, we buy only one gift at a time. For Christmas, we seem to need to buy for the whole world - for family members, close friends, teachers, boss, secretaries, mailman, paper boy and on and on.

Christmas gifts are unique in another way. For most other occasions there are some guidelines to help us decide the gift. For example, for a wedding we would buy something that would help the new couple get settled in their life. But for Christmas you can buy almost anything. The only guide, or limit, is the size of your budget.

In most cases "the budget" turns the pleasure of sharing gifts into a chore. We need to prove that we love each other.

I remember a classic episode on Sesame Street. Both Bert and Ernie were concerned about buying gifts for each other. Ernie knew that Bert loved Rubber Duckie and Bert knew that Ernie loved his paper clip collection. But neither of them had the money to buy the gift. Seeing no way out, Ernie sold his paper clip collection to buy a Rubber Duckie and Bert sold his Rubber Duckie to buy some paper clips.

Some of us go far beyond our means to prove that we love the other person.

In our society almost everything is measured by the yardstick of money. The more money we spend on someone, the more we are perceived to love that person. This creates the game of "topping over". We want to win by giving a gift which is slightly more expensive than the one that we receive. This sometimes results in disaster.

Christmas gift buying is unique in yet another way. We pretend that we are not buying any gift for the other person. We hide not only what we buy but also our activities of buying. There appears to be some special pleasure in being able to outfool the other person.

The duplication of items, or the receiving of items that one does not really need, is another problem. A man's closet may be full of shirts, and yet it is not uncommon to receive a few more shirts at Christmas. Half of the items that I have received, I would not have bought, if I was spending that amount on me. But to show appreciation for the love and consideration of the other person, we put on a mask, and say that that was the most needed item!

Newspapers and televisions seem to help us solve our unique problem. Most stores "advise" us about the perfect gift for our loved ones, within our budget - whatever it may be. This "help" often turns out to be a confusion. Having so much to choose from, we waste a great deal of our time, energy and peace of mind. Even after having done our best, we are rarely satisfied that we have bought the right gift.

A better way is to first think of a few items within the budget that would be useful for the other person and then to consider other's advice for making the final decision. In other words, first listening to your inner voice before listening to the outer voices.

Deciding what would be most useful is always a great challenge. I know of one family that has handled this problem very effectively. They use a chart entitled, "What I wish for this Christmas". About two months before Christmas, each person lists what he or she wishes to receive. Some items may be outrageous, but most are not. The Chart is left hanging on a wall where everyone, including their friends, can see it.

Everyone examines the list, privately and leisurely, and picks up item(s) within his or her limit. As the items are picked, they are crossed out. Those who have a limited budget, are the ones to check the list first. In this way, everyone receive mostly what he or she wishes.

In some cases it is better to pool the money for buying something valuable and useful.

In a family of four members, there would be a total of twelve gifts. Assuming the average cost of each gift to be ten dollars, there is one hundred hundred and twenty dollars involved. Most of those ten dollar items would turn out to be of little value. But one item of hundred and twenty dollars can be very valuable.

Unfortunately, we are taught that gifts must be individualized. This is only brain-washing or ego-satisfaction.

The bondage of a family lies in the act of sharing. As the sharing between two persons decreases, this bondage reduces and finally breaks down. We share the house, the car, the kitchen, the television and so on. Why can't we plan to buy a family gift for Christmas?

We can start a Christmas Gift Piggybank, pool all the money that we plan to spend on gifts, look at the total sum, have a family discussion, decide on a common item and then buy it for common use.

For the hundred and twenty dollars you can buy the Canadian Encyclopaedia. The family can share many hours together, reading and talking about the information found in it. This will enhance your family bondage. One valuable item can become a life-time treasure. But most ten dollar items are discarded within hours.

The same idea can be extended for gifts for the teacher, the boss and even the paper boy. Imagine the entire neighbourhood pooling a few bucks each and buying a bike or some similar item, for the paper boy. I would love to receive the bike rather than the fifty chocolate bars, if I were the paper boy.

> "Love is to life what sunshine is to plants and flowers."

57

Children Need Love
When They Least Deserve It

When do you give most love to your children, and when do they need it most?

Children need love more when they do something wrong, because they need some support. But since at such occasions they don't deserve any praise, they don't receive any love.

This essay suggests that it is good to give love to children during special occasions such as Christmas, Birthdays, Graduation etc., but it is essential to give them love when they get caught in some bad bind, especially if it was precipitated by their own fault.

Read also essay numbers 24, 97 and 98.

C hristmas is a very special time for most families to get together and to exchange gifts. This is a special occasion for "sharing and caring". The core of the entire festivity is "sharing love for each other".

The other day I read that, for proper growth, our brain requires nutrition, oxygen, information and love. Although everyone needs some amount of love, children need it the most, mainly because it affects their growth. They are our future, and it is important that we provide them with everything that they require, for their proper and full development.

Perhaps our forefathers started the tradition of Christmas gift exchange, and birthday celebrations, to foster an atmosphere of love in the family. Every child looks forward to these days and most adults recall the happy memories of their childhood Christmas days and birthdays.

Unfortunately, this loving atmosphere soon fades away. I have even noticed some people saying, "You love him more than you love me', or 'You did not really care for me." Such verbal exchanges often start right on Christmas morning. Some go through the ritual of exchanging gifts and the cards, simply to fulfil their obligation.

Children need love every day, not just a few days during the festive season or on their birthdays.

Some parents use love as a motivator for imparting proper training in their children. They say, "Papa will love you if you ...." The child does what his father wants him to do, mainly out of the fear of losing that love. This is conditional love, which has many harmful, long-term effects. A child experiencing this love, fails to develop his personality. He remains ever dependent on the source of that conditional love.

We often feel that too much love may spoil the child. This is not true. Sincere love cannot spoil anyone. Sincere love builds self-esteem. The stronger the self-esteem, the better the development of that person's personality.

The person who loves you most can exert the most discipline on you. In most cases we do not even have to spell out the wrong that has been done. True love is expressed by a variety of non-verbal signals, the most important being the tone of our voice.

When do we give most love to our child? Except for some special occasions, such as Christmas and birthdays, we give most love when the child makes us feel proud of him, when he does something praiseworthy. The hug for doing something good is a great incentive for him to repeat that behaviour. But what about the time when he does something wrong? Most parents feel so ashamed of that child that they do not even want to talk to him, or see him. What impact does this have on the child?

Our ego forces us to defend all our past behaviours. The child has an ego too. When we show our disapproval of his behaviour, his immediate reaction is to defend himself. He comes up with any argument that would support his behaviour. Consequently, he fails to learn from the error.

After a while, when the parent cools down, he tries to forget the wrong behaviour, and hopes that it won't be repeated. But since the child did not learn, did not know at the moment what should have been the appropriate behaviour, sooner or later he repeats it. The whole scenario is repeated, this time in a slightly greater magnitude. This creates a vicious cycle. The withdrawal of love, when the child did something wrong, is the single most important cause of juvenile delinquency.

The solution is simple. A child needs love all the time. But he needs it specially when he does something wrong. He needs it when he does not deserve it. His instinct tells him that he has done something wrong, but he is not mature enough to know what was wrong and how it could be avoided. He needs some support. If he feels that his parents will withdraw their love for him because of his behaviour, he tries to hide the matter. But if he understands that his parents love him unconditionally, he will go to them, tell them everything and seek advice or direction.

It is normal to give children more love when they deserve it, but it is essential to give them more love when they don't deserve it. In fact, they need the love most when they deserve it the least.

If you want your child to build solid self-esteem, assure him, and demonstrate to him, that you would love him no matter what he does, that your door will always remain open for him.

Once I read the story of a teenage boy who had committed a serious crime. His father hired the best lawyer in town, but the crime was so obvious that the court could not set the boy free. As the judge was ready to announce his judgment, the defending lawyer requested permission to produce one more piece of evidence. Although it was too late, the judge allowed him the opportunity. The lawyer then submitted a letter that he had received just a few seconds earlier.

It was a letter from the boy's father to the judge, stating that he considered himself to be fully responsible for the crime of his son, and pleading that he be jailed, in the place of his son.

This was an unusual letter. Believing that both the boy and his father had learned a valuable lesson from the case, the judge released the boy on a one-year probation. That unconditional love reformed the boy instantly.

We do not need a situation as serious as that to become better parents. Let's love our children for what they are. Let's thank God if our children deserve that love. If they do not deserve it, then also let's love them, because that's the only way of correcting or improving them.

"The supreme happiness of life
is the conviction that we are loved."
- Victor Hugo

5 8

Why Most Resolutions
Don't Work

We seem to be very quick in making new resolutions. It appears that we always have a stockpile of resolutions waiting on the tip of our tongue. However, in most cases, we abandon the resolution, because it doesn't work.

Making resolutions requires some exercise in thinking. This essay provides some guidelines that should be followed, for choosing workable resolutions. It is not the feasibility, or the unfeasibility, of a particular resolution, but your feelings towards it that really matters.

By following some simple ideas suggested in this essay, you can easily cultivate the necessary skill.

Read also essay number 59.

For many of us, one of the most important activities of commemorating the New Year is to make resolutions. We emit a sigh of relief for having made it through a difficult year, and feel excited about opening a new account.

In the majority of cases, that enthusiasm wanes in a matter of days. Life gets back to the same old grind and we wait for another new year to make new resolutions.

But for some, the new year proves to be a turning point. It seems to work like a booster shot.

One reason for this disparity is that we do not receive any training in the area of making resolutions. We hope to learn it by trial and error.

Making resolutions can be either helpful or harmful. If we are able to follow them, obey them, achieve them, we build self-confidence and gain inner strength. In that case, they help us.

But if we are unable to follow them, or to withstand their demands, we lose some self-confidence, and thereby a part of our self-esteem. In that case they harm us. We would be better off not making any resolution that we cannot keep.

Let me share with you some basic guidelines for making resolutions that work.

1. The resolution must be self-inspired.

The only resolution that inspires us is the one that we think of ourselves. Anything suggested by someone else, no matter how learned or wise, feels like a burden. We may follow it for a while but as soon as we notice the first flaw, we abandon it.

Sometimes we choose a resolution to conform to a group. This never works. Very few individuals can be motivated by a team resolution. I can't help laughing when I notice someone offering resolution ideas to others.

2. The resolution should be based on new thoughts.

Don't try a resolution which you have failed at previously. It is difficult to succeed when you start on a negative note. Any recollection of a previous failure hangs like a dark cloud and will prevent you from succeeding in the future.

You can overcome this problem by modifying an old resolution in such a way that you see it as an entirely new idea.

3. You must see the resolution as achievable for you.

We do not take any step on a project that we don't believe we can achieve. When we make a resolution far beyond our perceived capability, we keep on deferring it. But no resolution can be met without taking some appropriate actions.

You may not believe that you can double your business in one year. But you can believe that you can increase it by say ten per cent. In that case, make a resolution to increase it by only ten per cent. As you see yourself reaching it, you can revise it to twenty per cent, forty per cent and so on.

There is nothing wrong with revising, or even changing, your resolution(s) in mid-stream. Life is dynamic. We must adapt ourselves to current needs. Before the end of the year you may achieve your goal of doubling your business. But if you set "doubling" as the original resolution, you may not move on it at all, and abandon it within weeks.

4. The resolution must be measurable.

Only that which can be measured, can be achieved. Know what to expect when you get there. How would you know that you have successfully met your resolution?

5. The resolution should be broken up into its components.

Look for the activities, or intermediate accomplishments, that would be required for fully meeting the resolution. Have several mini-resolutions for each component and mark them off as you meet them.

6. The resolution should not be publicized.

It is extremely important that you maintain total confidentiality. Your resolutions are your personal matters. Telling others works against you in many ways. It gives others the opportunity to laugh at you when you encounter a temporary defeat. Moreover, unconsciously we seem to expect help from those who know about our resolution. This weakens our inner strength. Don't tell anyone. Work on it quietly and let others discover it from the results.

7. Design, and use, a symbol for the resolution.

Symbols help us concentrate. This is vital for the successful completion of any project.

Almost anything- words, pictures, objects - can serve as a symbol, as long as it can remind you of your resolution.

Don't reveal your symbol to anybody, but keep it in a place where you can see it as often as possible. It will inspire you. It will work magic for you. It will enable you to overcome most of your obstacles.

8. Allow the resolution a fair chance to develop.

We are creatures of habit. By the stroke of the clock, the year changes, but it takes approximately twenty-one days to make any permanent change in our biological clock. It takes several days of conscious effort to implement any new resolution.

Don't give up at the first sign of defeat. Keep at it, and soon you will wonder how you were leading that old life.

9. Seek advice from your inner voice.

Making resolution(s) should be a serious matter. Allow some thinking and deliberation time. Plan to have at least half an hour time to be all by yourself, to relax and to think. During this period of solitude, you will feel as if someone is trying to talk to you. This is your inner voice. Just relax and pay attention to what it says. It will provide you with some ideas for a more meaningful life. Use this guidance to work out your resolution(s).

> "The great thing in this world is not so much
> where we are, but in what direction we are
> going."   - Oliver Wendell Holmes

59

Make Room

For New Things To Come

If you suddenly acquired a new piece of furniture, where would you keep it? Obviously, you must make some room for the new item.

If you were too lazy to make the necessary room, it may have to stay out in the garage, or in the drive way. But even there it will take some room, which until now has been used for some other purpose. If you are too obstinate to make any adjustment, you will not be able to keep (or have) the additional item.

The same rule applies to resolutions. We are quick in describing the new items or services that we want, but too lazy in making the necessary adjustment, the necessary room, for them to come into our life.

This essay suggests that if you want new things to come into your life, then first start making the necessary room for them.

Read also essay number 58.

It is estimated that most resolutions are broken within one week. Soon after encountering the first frustration, most of us abandon them. We need patience and persistence, but there is another important factor that we seem to overlook.

For new things to come, we must make the necessary room for them. Where would you keep a new set of furniture unless you make some room for it?

Nature abhors vacuum. The moment one space is vacated by something, something else immediately rushes to fill it.

A lady in New York wanted a piano. She had no money but she cleared one corner of her living room where she would put it.

A few days days later, a piano salesman dropped by. She laughed and said, "I would love to have one, but I have absolutely no money for it."

A week later another piano salesman knocked on her door. Feeling that something was working, she kept that area completely empty for her piano.

For a month there was no sign of her piano. Then one evening, while riding a bus, she was seated next to an elderly lady. They glanced at each other occasionally, but did not exchange any word. Finally, the elderly lady got off the bus.

While preparing to leave the bus at the next stop, this lady noticed that the elderly lady had forgotten her umbrella on the seat of the bus. She grabbed the umbrella and ran after that lady.

After thanking her, the elderly lady said, "By the way, would you happen to know someone who would be willing to keep a piano? You see, my husband and I are going to Europe for two years. We do not want to sell our beautiful piano. We are looking for someone who could use it, in lieu of storing it for two years."

The next day she had a piano in her living room, and it fit the exact area that she had cleared for it!

This is not an isolated incident. In fact, this is precisely the way that nature works.

Most resolutions relate to having, or acquiring, something. For this to happen, we must first make the necessary room.

Generally we are quick in thinking what we want, but very slow in deciding what we want to give up. To have something extra, first we must give up something that we already possess. The game of life demands "trade-offs" at every moment.

Jesus advised us not to try to wear a new garment over the old one, nor to try to put new wine in an old bottle. First, we must remove the old garment, and make it possible for the new one to come. First we must have a clean bottle ready to accept the new wine.

This philosophy works for every walk of life. If you want a new wardrobe, then first discard some of the old clothes.

According to Pareto's principle, you wear approximately twenty per cent of your clothes for roughly eighty per cent of the time. This means that if you discarded eighty per cent of your least used clothes, you would miss them for only twenty per cent of the time.

The same is true for books, magazines, papers and in fact all our possessions. Perhaps the cancer of the accumulation problem is "saving something just in case". Go through everything. With few exceptions, if you have not used something for the last six months, chances are that you won't need it in the future either.

I am not suggesting that you discard eighty per cent of all your possessions. But you must appreciate the tremendous scope of discarding, and thereby of making room for new things to come.

Discarding does not mean that you put things in the garbage. Give them away to others who could use them. Give the clothes to the Salvation Army. Give old books and magazines to daycares, or other groups that could cut out some pictures, cartoons or articles for their use. The social services groups can help you in disposing of your less valuable items properly.

Just like the case of the man who was walking while carrying too many unnecessary objects (read essay number 14 for detail), we store, or carry, too many unnecessary items and burdens, and are not even aware of their presence. They were useful some day, but may be a dead weight today. We need to assess their current usefulness, and to discard some of them to make room for new, more useful, things to come into our lives.

If you are having a problem maintaining your resolutions, don't become disheartened. Change your focus for a moment. Instead of thinking what you want, look around and see what you have that you do not need, and then discard it. As you make room, the desired things, or behaviours, will automatically find their way into your life.

"One of the most tragic things I know about human nature is that all of us tend to put off living. We are all dreaming of some magical rose garden over the horizon - instead of enjoying the roses that are blooming outside our windows today."

- Dale Carnegie

60

Don't Take An I.Q. Test As Gospel

Living in a high-tech society, we consider every report produced by a computer to be almost gospel. But we forget that behind every computer output there is a human mind that wrote the program.

An I.Q. test is supposed to measure the true intelligence of the subject, and then predict whether or not he or she will be an average, an above-average or a below-average performer. But we should remember that an I.Q test measures mainly the development of the left brain, and not that of the right brain. Therefore, a person scoring low on an I.Q. test, may perform below-average in analytical skills but above-average in areas which require the use of the right brain, or creative skills.

Read also essay numbers 16 and 38.

S ome people feel that an I.Q. test is a magic wand that divulges the true growth conditions of the person's mind. Although this is the main objective of the test, this conclusion is not totally correct. Some other factors must also be considered, for the proper interpretation of the test score.

A typical test covers abilities in four major areas: Numbers, Verbal, Shapes and Forms, and Deductive Logic. These are predominantly the functions of the left brain. Even shapes and forms provided in the form of sketches demand logic, which is a left brain function.

The right brain is sometimes called the "mute" brain, because it is unable to express itself in any verbal form. It uses feelings and hunches to express itself. Since the test has no way of measuring feelings, it virtually ignores the right brain contribution. The result, therefore, reflects mostly the development of the left brain.

Using an I.Q. score for predicting a person's total personality is like testing someone's left eye only and assuming that his right eye would be the same.

A baby's left and right brains are developed to almost equal degrees. But by the age of six his left brain is far more developed than his right one. This is because of the predominantly logical society that we live in.

We want everything to happen according to some rule, some order, some logic. We must be on time. We must have some reason for every action. This causes our left brain to develop, often at the cost of the development of our right brain.

Some of the so-called abnormal babies simply do not follow their logical world. Because of the "higher-than-normal" growth of their right brain, they often feel "out-of-place".

In their childhood Winston Churchill, Thomas Edison and Albert Einstein were slow, unruly or lacked the necessary discipline. Had they taken the I.Q. test, they would probably have failed abysmally!

It was only after his formal schooling that Einstein could do what he really wanted to do, and it was then that he started showing the genius within him.

One child was far below average in his group. He barely moved from one grade to another. In the final high school examination he failed in three or four subjects and received zero in physics. After several attempts he cleared the requirements and graduated from school. Although he was miserable in most subjects, he was good in "doodling". Unfortunately the school did not offer such a course. After graduating he could not find any job that he liked. He wrote to the Disney Studio. They interviewed him, but did not find him to be suitable. Finally, he decided to create his own cartoons and to sell them. He created Peanuts and Charlie Brown. I think that he was far more intelligent than what his I.Q. test scores had indicated.

We often seem to get confused between intelligence and aptitude. We assume that a super-intelligent person would be able to perform well in any field. This is a myth. Aptitude is much more important than intelligence.

Provided that one has high aptitude in a given subject, his intelligence in that subject can be increased by means of some progressive exercises. Without the right aptitude, this would simply be a burden on him.

Some factors that significantly influence the scores of the I.Q. test are: the eagerness of the person taking the test; his physical and mental ease at the time; and the environmental conditions such as noise, temperature, lighting, ventilation, time of the day, the people watching or simply present there etc.

Unless the candidate is willing and able to try his best, the test result cannot be a true indicator of his mental abilities.

Another factor to watch is the influence of suggestions. The I.Q. tests are generally given to young children and the younger the child, the more vulnerable he is to other's suggestions. This may help or hinder his mental development.

Just before his death, J.C.Penny's father commented to one of his friends, "I am not worried about him. He will do all right." The little boy overheard this conversation and remembered it for the rest of his life. He faced crisis after crisis, but he knew that he would do all right, because his father had predicted so.

After three months of schooling, Edison's teacher sent a note to Edison's parents saying, "This child has no intelligence, and therefore, cannot be taught." Edison's mother went to see the teacher and told him, "My son has more intelligence than the intelligence of all of you combined." After that, she took over Edison's teaching.

Whenever confronted with an insurmountable problem, Edison believed that he had the intelligence to solve it, because his mother had said so.

But such incidents fall in the minority category. We are generally far quicker in pointing out faults rather than indicating strengths. Countless men give up trying because someone once told them that they did not have the right intelligence for the task.

The I.Q. test is not a predictor of what a person can do in life. It is simply one way of measuring the growth of one half of his brain. The data is often subjective and circumstantial, because it depends upon the cooperation of the subject and the conditions under which the test is conducted.

High achievement requires a good utilization of both sides of the brain.

I am not against I.Q. tests, but I recommend that we do not take the results as gospel. The person may have better aptitude for right brain type activities. A man of average intelligence, working in a field of his liking, will excel far more than one of super intelligence working in the wrong field.

61

You Can Eliminate
Most Of Your "Fire-fighting"

*Do you find yourself fighting fires most of the time?
If so, this essay can help you get out of that bind.*

*The main reason that you end up with the "fire-
fighting" tasks is that you have communicated, mostly
without your awareness, that you enjoy dealing with
that kind of task.*

*Most people who complain about having to fight
fires, generally take pride in the fact that they are
asked to fight fires. They would feel depressed if all
their fire-fighting tasks were suddenly taken away
from them.*

*This essay provides some simple ways of cutting
down at least some of your fire-fighting tasks almost
immediately.*

Read also essay numbers 12 and 64.

A manager recently shared with me some of his concerns related to "Having to fight fires all the time". He said, that because of new fires starting almost every day, he could not find any time for his other tasks. He had reached the limit of his scope of delegation, because all his subordinates were "up to their noses" as well. He had tried brainstorming occasionally, and that had generated some ideas, but no substantial improvement had been made.

I had a distinct feeling that he was sincere and intelligent, and that he had developed the best system within his capabilities. But he needed help.

Although many of us are in a similar situation, we are reluctant to divulge our inner conflicts. We prefer to suffer quietly, and hope that some divine help will come our way.

There is always room for improvement. No system is perfect. The best song is still to be composed. The best painting is still to be painted. The absolute-best idea will never be found.

To look for improvements, we must first admit that there can be flaws in the present system. We must resolve to ferret out those flaws, and to take the necessary corrective measures.

This is not an easy task. We all have the weakness of seeing our own creations as immaculate. We get used to their aberrations, and work with them almost unconsciously.

Fighting fires is more expensive than preventing them. We lose not only money, but also unnecessary energy - physically, mentally and emotionally. If sustained for a long period, it shortens our life.

Let's look at some possible causes of the origin of these fires.

No system can survive until it is being fed regularly. Whether we are conscious of it or not, there are always some pay-offs that justify the cost.

Some people pride themselves in fighting fires all the time. Such persons make no attempt to get out of their situation. On the contrary, and generally unconsciously, they ensure that new fires keep starting so they can maintain their "pride".

If all the fires were put out suddenly, such persons would suffer from "withdrawal" problems, similar to the withdrawal of nicotine for a nicotine addict. Their importance is maintained, their need is felt, only during the pressure of some fires.

A prisoner, who becomes too comfortable with the living conditions of the prison, or who enjoys the pride of being a model prisoner, has little desire of being set free. He fears that after his release he will have to "work" to readjust to the life of the free world. He will have to make his own decisions. He will have to "think", at least occasionally. If he is suddenly released, he may even suffer some depression.

Some people take pride in being labelled a "Professional Fire Fighter". There is nothing wrong in being a professional. But, most such people suffer from an illusion. Doing something perpetually is not the same as doing it professionally.

Practice does not always make one perfect. Only the right practice can make one perfect. The person who does not learn from every practice, who does not keep improving from practice to practice, will never become a true professional in that field.

The person, who has been fighting the same kind of fires, day after day, for years, can be hardly called a Professional Fire Fighter.

If you are in a similar situation, and if you are looking for some help, here are some suggestions.

1. Be willing to put out the fires.

Unless you are truly willing, you can never get out of it, and no one can help you.

2. Tell yourself that you are going to put them out gradually.

If you try to put them all out immediately, your subconscious will revolt and you will fail in your endeavour.

3. Take an aerial view. Back up. See the whole picture.

If you are serious about getting to the root of the problem, you must try to take a dispassionate look at it. Slow down. Relax. Think. Plan your strategy peacefully. Try assessing the relative value of all your activities, and putting them in the order of value.

4. Allocate some Regular Review Time

Fifteen minutes every day, plus one hour every week, plus three hours every month, for three months will bring unbelievable change in your life. During the Review Session ask yourself some questions similar to those listed below.

"What did I do today, this week, this month?"

"Why did I do it?"

"Could I have done something differently? In what ways?"

"What would happen if I had not done some of the tasks to the perfection that I thought I had to achieve?"

"Did I devote some time for "Planning" today, this week, this month? If not, why not?"

"Did I rush to the call of a new fire? Why? Why could I not take a moment to think of the best strategy for fighting that fire?"

It is natural to jump at the call of a fire. But almost always it has been found that the fire could have been dealt with more effectively if people would have maintained a cool mind and taken some time to review the options available to them.

Investigations of hotel fires reveal that the majority of deaths could have been avoided, if the people did not panic and instead had taken a few minutes to think and organize their escape.

If you can't find time for these regular reviews during your normal working hours, for your own benefit, you should do them on your own time.

The three month program, suggested above, will take about forty hours of your total time but will repay you with many more hours of peace of mind, and an increased life.

Yes, you can stop fighting your fires. Find out your unique pay off, and see it in the light of the total damage. A quick but regular review can locate the real cause. With some self-discipline and perseverance, you can prevent their recurrence.

"When a man does not know what harbour
he is heading for, no wind is the right one."
                                    - Lucius A. Seneca

62

Labels Govern Our Lives

Our mind is highly analytical. It expresses all its thoughts in terms of labels such as good, bad, big, small, black, white etc.. The same label generally carries different meanings to different people. This is one of the important reasons for most communication problems.

This essay points out that we are often limited by the labels that we attach to our potentials. By developing our awareness of the roles of labels, and by using them properly, we can alter our lives.

Read also essay numbers 7 and 69.

W hether we like it or not, we live in a world of labels. All our activities are influenced by some kind of labels. Even the limits that we can reach are controlled by them. In some respect, our entire lives are governed by them.

What are labels?

Labels are names. But they are much more than simply names. They represent some unique characteristics, and all the characteristics of one label are simultaneously and immediately identified with that label.

Our mind is highly analytical. It works relentlessly to put everything in some order. Nature, on the other hand, wants variety in everything. Look at the weather. No two days are identical. There are five billion people on this planet. Yet, no two persons, not even Siamese twins, are exactly identical. What a marvel of variety!

Look at any tree. It may have thousands of leaves. From a distance they may appear to be identical. But if you examine them closely, you will definitely find differences between every two leaves.

Our mind is capable of noticing all such differences, but if it tries to point them out to us, we would go insane, in a matter of minutes. Therefore, it tries to create some order out of the apparent chaos.

Imagine a huge library full of shelves. On each shelf there are a number of sections. Most of them carry labels such as: male, female, good, bad, tall, short, white, dark, rich, poor etc.

When we come across something new, our mind, through our senses, receives a great deal of information. Within a fraction of a second, it looks for the proper section to file the new information. The variety of information always exceeds the number of sections available to the mind. For some pieces it may not find an exact location, and therefore, it places that information in the section that it finds to be the closest match.

When we see a black or a white ball, our mind stores this information in the appropriate section labelled "black" or "white", assuming that we already have such sections in our library.

Now, suppose that we see a ball which is neither white nor black, and that we do not find any existing place that can adequately accommodate the new information. What does our mind do?

It has two options: to create a new section labelled, say, "Gray" or to put the new information in either the "White" or the "Black" section, whichever it thinks to come closest to that new shade.

Although our mind is very efficient, it is basically lazy in taking initiative for opening new files. Unless we make the extra effort, it prefers to avoid the additional work. Once it feels comfortable accepting the new shade as a black (or as a white), in all future cases, a similar shade will always be placed in the same category, without feeling any remorse.

Suppose that our mind was not comfortable in placing that shade into either white or black, and that it decided to create a new category called "Gray". In that case, it would try to sort all future shades in the categories of "White", "Black" or "Gray". It does not matter whether the shade is light gray or dark gray; it must be placed in one of the known categories. Once filed, the originality of the shade is lost. Our mind treats all the pieces of information in one section as if they all complied perfectly with the label of that section.

The same process is used to sort out every piece of information that reaches our mind. We use a variety of labels in our everyday transactions. Since the labels are personal, those of the sender cannot totally match those of the receiver. This is the root cause of most communication problems.

Our labels create our mental glasses, or the filters, through which we perceive our world. It is in this way that they influence our behaviours and thereby govern our lives.

The labels also influence our self-image. As we assess our own image, we need to file the resulting information in some appropriate categories. When we come across a gray area, we must decide whether to file it under the white or the black. In case of doubt, we tend to undervalue ourselves. This results in some lowering of our self-image. If this cycle is allowed to continue, it may have devastating influence on our lives.

Others may label us as capable or incapable, strong or weak, intelligent or dumb. Even their casual labels may have a profound influence on our ability to cultivate our true potential.

The ordering characteristic of the mind is very valuable. In its absence we would go crazy in no time. However, we must guard ourselves against being its victim.

The cure is to recognize the presence and the influence of labels in our lives. Just the awareness can make an instant improvement in the degree of our transactions. We may be able to understand others more accurately. We may start realizing why we react in certain ways. We may be able to discern the controlling forces behind most of our behaviours.

We must be careful when using labels. We must be willing to open new categories when the old ones cannot adequately accommodate a new piece of information.

Just like Frankenstein, we first create the labels for our own convenience, and very soon they start controlling us. If we want to regain our control, we must review the labels that we use. We must discard those that are useless or harmful. We must take the initiative of creating additional ones where required.

"Reading maketh a full man; conference a ready man; and writing an exact man."
                                        - Francis Bacon

63

Adversities Strengthen Us

This essay was written following a severe winter storm in Alberta.

Every adversity brings some advantage. If we can stay cool, in the face of the adversity, we can see the advantage and benefit from it. By teaching some valuable lesson, the adversity enables us to cope better, with a similar future adversity. In that way it strengthens us.

This essay provides several practical tips for staying cool, even in the face of an adversity.

Read also essay numbers 39 and 92.

L ast week we were hit by one of the most severe winter storms of this century. I need not describe it - almost every Albertan has experienced it personally. Local, and even National, newspapers, radios and televisions, have covered it extensively.

The issue that I want to address is whether this storm was harmful or beneficial to us.

You may call it a mockery to even think of this storm as being beneficial to us. But let's look at it in a slightly different perspective.

I do not know how much you suffered from this storm, but if you faced another similar storm, would your suffering be the same, a little more or a little less?

With a few rare exceptions, another similar storm would create less suffering, because we learn from our experiences. In other words, we become a bit stronger after facing every adversity.

Thousands of Albertans were amazed by their own ability to cope with extraordinary situations. This proves that they have more strength - better capability - than they had believed.

This storm has enhanced our awareness of several facilities that we can call upon for help. Hundreds of people have discovered that their neighbours, or colleagues, have more "heart" than they had imagined.

Through the media, many "experts" shared valuable advice to help us deal with different kinds of emergency situations and to avoid being victimized. This "free education" would not have been possible without the storm.

The storm has taken its toll. Eleven people died of heart attacks and several others suffered severe frost bites. But perhaps, the blame for this rests less with the storm and more with the victimized persons, because they had not realized the possible consequences of such a storm. One cannot solely blame the storm for these losses.

No one can predict death. A single event, such as shovelling snow, may precipitate heart failure, but there are numerous prior events that lead to the eventual heart attack.

A doctor friend of mine, in his late thirties, experienced some chest pains while playing tennis one day near Halifax, Nova Scotia. He was rushed to the hospital where he and his wife (also a doctor) were employed. Although he was a doctor, an athletic person, and under forty, he did not recover. From this, can we conclude that playing tennis during summer can be fatal? We have heard of many who had heart attacks while swimming, walking, or even sitting in their living room!

The main reason for a casualty is rarely the magnitude of the adversity, but our lack of training in coping with it, and our actual reaction to it. We fear the "unknown", anything that we have not encountered or experienced before.

Last summer, directly after one of my talks, I went shopping. As I got out of my car, I felt very hot. I took off my jacket, placed it on the seat and closed the door. Suddenly I realized that my keys and my wallet were in my jacket pockets.

Trying to keep myself calm, I asked a store manager to allow me to use her phone for an emergency. I called my daughter and asked her to bring the duplicate key, which she did within half an hour.

After having retrieved my own keys, I noticed that my car had been parked just next to the office of Alberta Motor Association. Since I am a member of AMA, I should have approached them right away for help!

In the face of heavy pressures we panic, and under panic we do not think clearly. This is the main cause of our being victimized.

If we remember to maintain a cool mind, consciously as well as unconsciously, we would fight the adversity and thereby enhance our strength. In that case the adversity would prove to be beneficial.

You may say, "Well, it's easy to preach but difficult to practise." You are right. We all tend to succumb to our adversity. I myself was blinded to the fact that my car was parked just next to the AMA. However, I am going to share a few ideas that may reduce the chances of your losing your cool in the face of some extraordinary adversity.

1. In the Book of Mormons we frequently encounter the expression, "It came to pass ...". In the same light we can think that our adversity shall also come to pass. Every mountain has a peak. We have been able to scale all our mountains until now and we can scale this one too. Let's hang on, and this also shall come to pass. Once it passes, it will leave us a bit wiser than we were before its arrival.

2. Let's not lose our confidence in our ability to cope with new adversities. We actually have far greater ability than we think we have. Instead of saying, "Why me?", let's cultivate the habit of saying, "Try me". If we change our attitude toward our adversity, we will discover that it is not as potent as we had assumed it to be.

3. Let's have faith in God and His plan. Every act of God is aimed at some overall benefit. In the absence of adversities, we relax so much that we tend to fall asleep. God sends us new adversities simply to wake us up.

4. Let's be ready to face whatever comes. Let's refuse to worry about it. Ralph Waldo Emerson once said, 'For every minute you worry, you lose sixty seconds of your peace of mind.' Let's stay calm and take a moment to think. Let's do the best we can and leave the rest to God, for He helps those who do their share of the task first.

We can never know our real strengths until we test them and adversities provide us with opportunities to do this.

Despite all the damages and the casualties, most adversities are beneficial to us, because they teach us valuable lessons. They build our strengths and help us discover some of our latent potential.

64

You Can Eliminate
One-Third Of Your Problems

Do you feel swamped by too many problems?

By following the simple technique described in this essay you can not only eliminate approximately one-third of all your problems almost immediately, but also cut down the magnitude (the severity) of the remaining two-thirds.

You don't believe it? Well, just read the essay and check it out for yourself.

Read also essay number 61.

Would you like to eliminate one-third of your current problems? Well, it's possible and it's simple. First, be willing to part with some of your problems, and then apply a simple technique described herein.

It may appear paradoxical, but most people are reluctant to part with their problems, no matter how distressful the problems may be. They see them as their security blanket.

Unless you are willing to part with problems, no one can really help you.

The other factor is our perception of problems in general.

We treat our problems in the same way that we treat a stranger. Not knowing his intention, we become defensive. But we forget that we are also strangers to other people and that strangers can also have loving and caring hearts.

Although we may perceive most of our problems to be a "drag", a "headache" or a "necessary pain of life", not every problem is bad. Some of them sustain our basic life. Some provide us with the opportunity to grow. Some even provide us, when necessary, with the jolt to kick us out of a rut.

But by habit, or due to laziness, we lump all our problems into one file called "trouble".

One day a farmer asked his son to sort out a bushel of apples according to size - big and small. When the boy had finished sorting them, the farmer thanked his son and then mixed the two piles of apples.

Bewildered, the son asked, "Dad, why did you ask me to sort when you were going to mix them again?" The father replied, "The main idea, my son, was to pick out the rotten ones. You see, as you were examining the size of each apple, you automatically identified, and threw away, the rotten ones!"

The main reason of feeling overwhelmed by our problems is that we mix the good, the bad and the rotten ones together.

If we had more than one file into which to divide our problems, we would be forced to examine them more closely.

We would then discover that some of them are not as bad as we had assumed them to be and that many in fact are not even our own problems. It is estimated that about one-third of all our problems fall into this last category.

By nature we like to assume the role of "the General Manager of the Universe". We worry not only about our own problems but also about those of many other people - our children, our employees, our neighbours and so on.

By providing "guidance" to others for handling their problems, we feel that we help them. But, in fact, we hurt them. Unless we allow others the opportunity to test their wings, we prevent them from learning how to fly.

Technology, and the resulting lifestyle, is changing so rapidly that it is unfair to compare today's living conditions to those of twenty-five years ago. Yet, we tend to treat our children in almost the same way that our parents treated us.

It is likely that our own parents failed to allow us the optimum opportunity for our growth. Moreover, in most cases, for their age, the children are more capable than their parents. Then why should we prevent them from assuming full responsibility for their own problems?

Problems may be compared to illness. It is ironic, but not every illness is harmful. Minor cases of illness help us take some preventive measures, or build our immunity to some disease.

The pain of appendicitis is not pleasant, but this pain itself is actually a blessing, because it draws our attention to some serious problem. Had that pain been "tolerable", many of the victims of appendicitis would ignore it, and the result would be disastrous.

At the age of fifty-three, John D. Rockefeller Sr. was dying of a cancerous disease called "worry". All he could eat was some crackers and acidulated milk. But the jolt of this sickness injected new life into him. He started donating to charitable causes. He donated millions of dollars to build "The Rockefeller

Foundation", for research to fight diseases. Consequently, he lived for another forty-five years!

Your "troublesome" problems may outnumber your "beneficial" problems, but you still have some of each kind. The main reason why you do not notice them is that you have not really looked for them.

But how can one identify the problem?

Your beneficial problems are those over which you have full control. These are the tasks that you want to do. No one is really forcing you to work on them.

Your harmful problems are the ones which are controlled by someone else. You feel that you have no choice but to deal with them. You work on them because you are afraid of the consequences of neglecting them.

The tasks that you feel you should do, but which you do not really have to do, are really not your problems. You may feel that you should teach your child how to organize his or her time, but you do not have to. The child has better knowledge of the relative values of his or her different tasks. You may worry and fuss and yet make little headway.

I think it was Lee Iacocca who once said, "The main task of a good executive is to find the right person for the job and then to leave him alone to do the job."

By identifying the problems that are really not yours, and by disciplining yourself not to meddle with them, you can eliminate one-third of all your problems.

"It is not enough to be busy.
The question is, 'What are we busy about?'"
- Henry David Thoreau

65

Walls Block
Both Good And Bad

Would you like to protect yourself against all external dangers or threats? Would you like to build a wall that could fully secure you?

It is relatively easy to design and build walls that could secure us. But we must be careful in choosing the right kind of wall, because the very wall that protects us also acts as a barrier against some good things that could otherwise freely flow to us.

Starting with the issue of the closure of one of the local streets, this essay presents a profound philosophy of love, openness and growth.

Read also essay numbers 69 and 73.

Life is full of events and influences which contain some good and some bad elements, generally intricately mixed. Every rose bush has some thorns. Every light casts a shadow.

Most of us go through our entire lives trying to identify, and separate, the good from the bad. This is perhaps the greatest challenge of productive, worthwhile living.

As we gain experience and feel that we have acquired the wisdom to identify the good and the bad, we start building walls that would keep all the good on our side and all the bad on the other side.

Unfortunately, the same wall that protects us against some "bad" influences can, and generally does, prevent some good influences from reaching us. For example, the wall that protects us against bad weather can prevent some healthy sunshine, gentle breeze or refreshing fragrance from reaching us. In fact, some walls harm more than they help.

Hitler built a wall for protecting himself against negative arguments and influences. He did not want anything to deter him from his main goal. He shielded himself against the bearers of bad news. The result? He lost touch with reality. This was perhaps the main cause of his demise.

The Great Wall of China was designed and built to protect its citizens from the invasions from the north. At the time, China was rich in culture and wisdom. It made perfect sense for them to protect themselves against the "paupers" and the "robbers". The wall served its purpose, but it also kept China out of contact with the rest of the world. Consequently, China has remained in the dark for ages. It is only recently that the negative impact of that wall is being realized, and some doors are being opened.

Every wall is proof of the presence of some inner weakness. Unless we have something to hide, we don't need walls. The greater the need to hide, the bigger and the stronger are the walls that are required.

Some walls serve as our masks. We nurture them; we cling to them, because we know that in their absence our real self will be exposed.

In the North West Frontier of India (which is now a portion of Pakistan, bordering with Afghanistan), there lived some extremely violent people. The government had tried every means within their power to talk to them. Finally, Mahatma Gandhi decided to try.

He went to the hills, alone and without arms and shouted, "You are really not strong men as I had been told. In fact, you are very weak. That's why you are hiding and carrying guns. If you are truly strong, then drop your guns. Come out in the open and let me see you." They dropped their guns, came out of hiding and their leader, Abdul Gaffar Khan, became a lifelong disciple of Gandhi.

Walls separate us from other people.

Jesus said, "He who will serve the most shall become the ruler of all". Life is fulfilled only through the service of others. The more we are able to serve, the greater the happiness we experience in our lives. But if we keep hiding ourselves in some ivory tower, then, towards the end of our journey, we would experience a great deal of repentance. Walls prevent us from reaching out and serving people.

About ten years ago, the Shah of Iran was forced to leave Iran. Although he had plenty of money, he could find no place to live peacefully. He died a very unhappy man, because during his reign he had built huge walls around himself.

During the 1987 tornado in Edmonton, soon after leaving work for home, two people in a car encountered some violent wind. They decided to wait for a few minutes until the wind subsided. To protect themselves against the wind, they parked their car by the side of a "strong" wall. Within minutes that strong wall crumbled and crushed one of them to death.

Although this was an isolated incident, the fact remains that every wall that protects us also deprives us of something useful. If we are careful in the designing, the deprivation can be small compared to the benefit of the protection.

Yes, it is wise to build suitable walls for our essential protection, but before erecting them, we must take a few moments to think of the obstructions that they would create. If we are not careful, then we may imprison ourselves with walls that we ourselves erect. By trying to handcuff someone else, we may end up handcuffing ourselves too.

Being greedy by nature, we have a tendency to build stronger and stronger, and higher and higher walls around our castles. The very walls that protect us from external, harmful forces, also prevent us from savouring the spice of life - the experiences of variety, the thrills, the opportunities to serve others and to make the optimum use of our talents.

Our present society has already erected enough walls. Let's not build additional ones. Let's work on opening our hearts, on demolishing some of the existing walls.

Life is too short to be spent erecting walls. Let's make the maximum use of whatever life we have left, in reaching out and serving.

As flowers require openness for full blossoming, so we need openness, freedom and absence of walls for the proper expression of our souls.

Yes, the very walls that protect us from some bad things obstruct some good things from reaching us.

"A loving heart is the truest wisdom."
- Charles Dickens

66

Don't Abdicate
Your Democratic Right

This essay was written during an election. It suggests that exercising democratic right is a duty. By abdicating this duty we give up a portion of our control over our life. In the long run this creates a sense of guilt and, therefore, unhappiness.

The essay points out that it does not take a great deal of energy to go out and vote, or to attend a few forums to hear the candidate's views. Therefore, we should be an active participant, exercise our democratic right and thereby take charge of our life.

Read also essay number 25.

A lmost everyday we hear someone complaining about something that the government failed to do, or something that it did against the interest of an innocent group of people.

Is it fair for us to criticize the government? After all, we were the ones who elected them and gave them the mandate to govern us for the duration of the term.

You may say that you disagree with the issues, or with the candidates from your constituency, or that he or she was elected in spite of your opposition. This is often the case. However, we must remember that democracy demands that we accept and learn to live with the wishes of the majority.

The major part of the problem is created not by those who act, but by those who fail to act - those who are too negligent to exercise their democratic right. Someone once said that a bad government is elected by the good citizens who fail to vote.

It has been found that less than forty per cent of the eligible voters actually cast their vote, and that less than forty-five per cent of all votes that are cast determine the formation of the government. This means that less than eighteen per cent of the eligible voters determine the make-up of the government.

Because of the multiple party system, it is unlikely that the actual government would be voted in by more than fifty per cent of the eligible voters. But there is no reason why over forty per cent of eligible voters should abdicate their democratic right.

Why do the majority remain uninterested in elections? Some rationalize their indifference by arguing that "My one vote is not going to make any difference".

Yes, one vote generally does not make any dent in the actual result, but there are cases where just one vote has made all the difference. Consider, for example, that Hitler had been elected the leader of his party by the majority of just one vote!

There is another reason why we must exercise our right, even if it makes no difference. We must perform our share of the task to satisfy our own conscience.

The central message of Bhagwad Gita, the Hindu Scripture, is, "You do your duty and don't worry the least about the outcome".

Every time that we fail to do our share of the duty, we build a little feeling of guilt. A tiny piece may appear to be inconsequential, but if we let it build , it could, and generally does, exert significant pressure over us. Drips can turn into trickles, trickles into streams, streams into rivulets and rivulets into mighty rivers.

Failing to perform our duty even once sows a seed for future failures. It can become a habit which could control us for the rest of our life.

I have mentioned that exercising our democratic right is a duty. Yes, it is our duty, because it affects the quality of our life as well as that of our neighbours and our children.

Some people rationalize their indifference by saying that they don't like to align themselves with any one political party. You may not like to reveal your particular alliance, but the fact is that everyone is aligned to one party or the other.

We have a strong need to belong. Throughout our life, we constantly strive to belong to some group. The main attraction of peer pressure is to satisfy the need to belong. Some teenagers run away from their homes when they find it difficult to identify themselves as belonging to their family.

The root cause of most morale problems is some conflict in "belonging", when a person is forced to belong to a group of which his own conscience does not approve.

Whether you accept it or not, you are already aligned to one of the political parties. Shed off your shyness, and voice your likes or dislikes of the issues of the campaign. Raise some issues that have not been already addressed. But at least get to the polls and exercise your democratic right.

There is another very important reason why we must get out and vote. We experience happiness when we feel a sense of internal control over our life. Some control over our living environment is essential for our happiness. The three levels of government play a paramount role in deciding the type of our living environment.

Recently I saw a cartoon in which a man is begging for money, although money is falling from the sky all around him. Someone rebukes him, 'For God's sake, pick up your own damn money.'

At the moment, the three major political parties are making great promises in terms of the money that they would spend for our benefit. Let's open our eyes, examine their money, and pick the one that we feel to be the most credible.

An election is the only occasion in which every citizen holds equal power. Whether you are rich or poor, old or young, educated or uneducated, employed or unemployed, male or female, black or white or brown, as long as you are a citizen of this country, and resident in this province, you have as much influence as anyone else.

It is your duty to take charge of your life. You can do this by playing your part by supporting the candidate that you consider to be the most suitable. Please get out and vote.

I would like to make a small suggestion to the government. As an incentive to bring all the eligible voters to the polls, I suggest that the government offer some reward such as a draw or a prize open only to those who have taken the time to come out and vote.. Every trade show exhibitor knows that large number of visitors can be drawn by offering some kind of a draw. This suggestion is not intended to insult the responsible citizens, but to mobilize the indolent ones. In our society a free draw has far more power than most government regulations.

> "Those who know how to think
> need no teachers."
> - Mahatma Gandhi

67

Only The Problem Solvers Can Survive The Future

Would you like to survive, and possibly grow, in the next decade(s)? If yes, then you must learn to welcome problems.

A brief review of the rate of the recent technological advancements, and a projection of their advancement in the near future, suggests that we are in for greater and greater free, global, competitions. This will result in the survival of the fittest - not in the biological sense, but in the sense of our ability to solve new and complex problems.

This essay suggests that we must learn to welcome and solve problems, because only the problem solvers can survive the future.

Read also essay numbers 1, 63, 68 and 100.

W ould you be interested in knowing what the future has in store for you? Will it help you to plan your business, if you had a slightly more accurate idea of what to expect in the next five years?

One way of predicting the future is to review the past, to analyze the current trends and then to project them into the future. Therefore, let's start with a quick look at our past.

Although man has been on this planet for roughly five million years, it was only about five thousand years ago that he learned how to grow food. This means that it took mankind approximately four million nine hundred ninety-five thousand years to learn how to grow food. Isn't that incredible?

Having learned how to grow food, mankind settled down, built shelters, started living in groups and developed some communication codes. Spared of the time lost in wandering (in the search of food and shelter), they found some time to think.

Within the next four and a half thousand years, they discovered how to start and control fire, invented the wheel, invented some devices for travelling on rivers and developed some language system, for mutual communication.

Then came the Industrial Revolution and man invented machines for almost every work that he had been doing manually. Consequently, the standard of living suddenly soared to unprecedented heights.

Although, in mankind's eyes, the progress had been phenomenal, the actual rate of progress was very slow, compared to today's standards. This is evident from the fact that about ninety-five per cent of all our inventions have taken place in the last five hundred years, and that about eighty per cent of all of them have happened within the last one hundred and twenty-five years. Approximately eighty per cent of all pharmaceutical drugs available today did not exist sixty years ago!

There has been more progress in our standard of living in the last thirty years than had occurred in the previous five thousand years! Today, an average person can afford a personal computer, home video, microwave oven, jet travel, car telephone and even a Fax machine. Only about fifty or sixty years ago such luxuries were not available to even kings or queens!

Computers and telecommunication have literally caused our world to shrink into one intricately interwoven society. Within minutes the news of any change in the conditions of one corner of the world is disseminated to every other corner. If you develop a new product or a new technique, it can be duplicated, or even improved, by someone else within a matter of days. Today, especially because of television, people have become quite knowledgeable and aware of their own rights, privileges and accessibilities.

All this has been leading us to global free-trade and privatization. This is going to create more and more competition. We have just begun to see the tip of the iceberg of mergers and acquisitions. In the years to come, many weak businesses will be either finished or merged with strong ones.

About a century ago, Charles Darwin prophesized the theory of "the survival of the fittest". This theory is as true today as it was during his time. However, Darwin talked about survival in the biological sense. Today, with the help of various kinds of social assistance programs, our government takes care of our basic biological survival. But, we must take our own initiative if we want to enjoy something more than basic biological survival.

Today, we are struggling for another kind of survival; survival against keen competition. We must remember that there is a solution to every problem. He who can quickly detect the root of the problem, and then suggest its solution, will move ahead. He who is slow in this, will lag behind and may soon be out of the game.

President Harry Truman used to remark, "If you can't stand the heat, get out of the kitchen." In a similar way, if you can't stand the pressure of new problems, you must get out of the way of others. If you don't step aside voluntarily, you will be over-run by those who love the excitement of new problems.

Problems are the very essence of our lives. They sustain, strengthen and renew us. It is only in the presence of problems that we can verify our worthiness, or that of others. It is only when faced with a seemingly insurmountable problem that we discover potentials that we did not really know we possessed.

The nature of most problems can be compared to that of a thistle. From a distance it appears to be strong and menacing. If you approach it timidly it will prick you and hurt you. But if you approach it boldly, you will discover that only a slight force can crumble its spine.

The ability to effectively deal with problems is a skill which can be acquired, just like any other skill. The first requirement is the eagerness to learn it. The more we can appreciate the importance of detecting and solving problems, the more willing we would become to learn it.

Every solution raises another problem which is more complex than the previous one. Our growth and advancement is directly related to our willingness to seek new problems, and to solve them.

We can control our future, if we cultivate a liking for our problems. God gives us problems to strengthen us. Let's be happy for them. We are alive, and in business, simply because of the problems around us.

Become a professional problem solver, discover the acres of diamonds in your future and prepare yourself for survival and growth, because only the problem solvers can survive the future.

"Genius is one per cent inspiration
and ninety-nine per cent perspiration."
                                    - Thomas Edison

68

Every Solution Engenders New Problems

Some people postpone dealing with their problem because they have the unconscious feeling that once they solve this problem, they will have nothing else to do. But this is a shear myth. The human mind is extremely creative. Before the current problem is solved, it easily thinks of ten additional, even more complex, problems to work on.

Computers have solved many problems, but they have also generated many new problems for us to work on. It is the same story in every other facet of our life.

Read also essay number 79.

It is true that every problem has a solution. But we often ignore the fact that every solution engenders some new problems.

A friend of mine, who strongly believes in the power of positive thinking, was invited to speak to hospital staff members. Throughout the day he kept on emphasizing the importance of a friendly, caring and loving atmosphere and suggested that this would speed up the healing of the patients. Excited by this idea, the participants got busy, trying to put the principle into practice.

From that day on, the patients of that hospital did definitely heal faster, but in less than three months, that hospital was facing another problem, "How to fill the twenty per cent empty beds?"

Let me give you some more examples.

The invention of the telephone has definitely enhanced communication, but it has also engendered several new problems. For example, it has invaded our privacy. It often robs us of our thinking and meditating time. Often we seem to give more value to the caller on the telephone, than the caller in person. Sometimes it exposes information about us that should have remained private.

The field of medicine is full of examples where the solution to one problem may lead to some other problem. An x-ray provides us with important information about the bones or tissues below the surface, but it may also damage some healthy tissues which are exposed to it. An antibiotic controls the bacteria that cause one disease, but it may also cause some side effects. The latter, at times, may be worse than the original disease.

The computer is an excellent example of solving one problem and creating another at the same time. We have become so dependent upon it that if it goes down, it literally paralyses us. It is often used as a scapegoat for poor service. In that way, it prevents us from building a strong, integral personality. We can fool others, but not our own conscience.

The computer creates problems even when it is functioning flawlessly. We seem to treat it like a godly power. Anything produced by a computer is generally accepted as gospel. But we forget that behind every computer-produced document, there is a human mind that programmed it. Except for the speed, there is nothing that a computer can do which a human being cannot. Even its phenomenal speed creates many problems for us.

Since a computer works very rapidly, it demands that we keep supplying it with an adequate number of problems. As such, we have to keep finding, or inventing, the next problem for it to work on. Fifty years ago, most reports were fifty pages in length, and their content was generally simple. Today, because of the computers, most reports are several hundred pages long, and contain charts and graphs of a complex nature.

Had a company like the Principal Group collapsed fifty years ago, the evidence of its entire enquiry would have hardly exceeded a thousand pages. Today, it has swelled into hundreds of thousands of pages and yet many persons feel that the enquiry has not been covered adequately!

The automobile is another good example. The shortage of fuel was, at one time, a serious problem. This was alleviated by the design of lighter cars. That led to the problem of "reduction of crash-worthiness" and thereby of "more injuries and deaths".

Despite some grievances about freedom of choice, of personal right, the seat-belt legislation has saved many lives and prevented serious injuries. This again has created another problem. There is now a shortage of organ donors.

One solution to the fuel shortage problem is fuel-efficient cars. But the more we solve this problem, the more we run into the problem of parking facilities. The more we solve the latter, the more we will have the problem of traffic jams. The chain is virtually endless. The solution to one problem almost always gives rise to another.

One reason of this is the fact that life is a game of "working on solving some problems". As long as we are alive, we must have some problems to work on. The moment we run out of problems, the game will be over and our life would come to its end. Fortunately, we never run out of problems. We simply give up playing the game, because we get tired of it.

Some people are reluctant to work on their problem, because they fear that once they have solved it, they would have nothing to work on.

To sustain our lives, nature has provided us with an extremely curious mind which keeps looking for, and generally finds, new problems for us to work on. If it can't find problems, it invents them.

If you suffer from "the nothing to do" problem, remember the advice, "Go as far as you can see, and when you will be there, you will see some more." Get working on whatever you can find. Before you are through with it, you will discover much more to keep yourself occupied.

The vast majority of people suffer from "too many problems to handle". Don't be disheartened. Pick up the one problem that you find most interesting (or the least threatening). For the moment, forget all other problems. Simply concentrate on this one until you solve it to your satisfaction. Then look for the next one that interests you.

As long as we are alive, our life will require us to find some exciting problems to work on. Let's be thankful for our problems. Let's do our best in dealing with the immediate one. As we succeed, nature will find the next one for us to wrestle with.

We can prolong our life by remaining interested in the game of "working with new problems". The game can last as long as we refuse to quit. We can never run out of problems because the solution to every problem engenders new problems.

6 9

Take A Look
At Your Mental Looking Glasses

Our mind receives information about its environment with the help of the five sensory organs. But before reaching the mind, the incoming data is fil tered, on the basis of the mind's past experience. This is equivalent to seeing through some special lens, or mental looking glasses.

This essay discusses how our mental looking glasses are formed, and some technique of modifying them so as to minimize the distortion of the incoming data.

Read also essay numbers 15, 65 and 97.

H ow would you feel if someone told you that what you are seeing is not reality but simply your imagination? Well, there is more validity in this than what you may accept.

We are generally so preoccupied with our own thoughts, interests and concerns that we miss noticing a good portion of the things which are around us. Even the one that we notice, we do not really notice objectively. Our observation is almost always distorted by our dominant thoughts at the moment.

It is common knowledge that the eyewitness account of the same accident, reported by a number of different witnesses, often turns out to be radically different. In some cases they may even appear to be describing entirely different accidents.

There is a classic example of a picture in which two men, one white and one black, are standing face to face. The white man has a knife in his hand. After being shown this picture for a few seconds, the viewers have been asked to describe the outfit of the two persons in that picture. The great majority have said that it was the black man, and not the white man, who was carrying the knife!

Why does this happen?

We see everything in the light of our experiences, values and beliefs. They appear to constitute some kind of spectacles, or glasses for us to view. All incoming information to our mind is affected by the nature of our spectacles, or looking glasses. What we perceive as reality, is in fact only our view of reality.

While a man was taking a nap one afternoon, his mischievous grandson sprinkled some Limburger cheese on his moustache. Within seconds the man woke up, sniffed around and said, "This room stinks". He then went sniffing in the other rooms and remarked, "The whole house stinks". Finally, he went to the back-yard, for some fresh air and, in disgust, yelled, "The whole neighbourhood stinks".

As the problem was not with his house or his surrounding, but with the cheese on his moustache, there may be little or nothing wrong with our circumstances but rather the fault cold be with the glasses that we are using to view those circumstances.

We react and behave in exact accordance with our perceived reality. It is therefore important that we pay some attention to the make up of our looking glasses. We should know their common characteristics and pitfalls.

Our looking glasses have a definite pattern of distortion. They magnify our weaknesses and play down our strengths.

We ignore the features of our own personality and admire those of others. We see others as being happier, or luckier than we are. But we forget that everyone wears some kind of a mask. They have their own conflicts and turmoils, but they hide them under their mask.

When you ask someone, "How are you today?", the most common response is, "Very well, thank you". But you can bet that there is a great deal of storm behind every "very well". The person may be hiding his financial tension, family problem or job pressure.

But what can we do?

We have no choice but to live with our looking glasses. However, it is within our power to modify them in such a way that they create the minimum distortion. We can develop the awareness that we are more capable than we think we are. We can stop placing everybody else on a pedestal. We can try to see people without their masks.

We can modify the make-up of our own looking glasses by changing our reaction to our past experiences, and by changing our beliefs and values. A complete turn around may not happen over night, but any change in the right direction will be helpful. As we move, we gain momentum.

It is sheer folly to ruminate over past experiences. We should look for the advantage in each negative experience and thank God that it did not get any worse.

I remember one person who suffered badly from stagefright. No matter how much he tried, he could not speak in front of an audience. Then I suggested that he imagine everyone in the audience to be in their pyjamas. The moment he could visualize that, he was able to speak. I have helped others by asking them to imagine that the person they are talking to is dressed as a clown.

A friend of mine once told me that whenever he had problems relaxing, he would imagine that he was visiting and eating with his grandpa, who did not enforce strict table manners, and who said that it was all right to make mistakes in his house.

We can change our beliefs by regular positive affirmations and by surrounding ourselves with positive people. We can refine our values by regular introspection. Some regular time invested on meditation or solitude is very beneficial.

Stop censuring yourself for every mistake that you have made. It is all right to make some mistakes. Everyone makes mistakes, but only fools advertise theirs. It is not only perfectly all right, but also essential to make some mistakes occasionally, because it is only through our mistakes that we truly learn a lasting lesson.

Occasionally, and deliberately, doing a few things wrong immunizes us against our fear of making mistakes. The damage of doing something deliberately wrong is never as severe as we fear.

What you see or experience is seldom the actual reality. It is always tainted and distorted by your unique looking glasses. If you wish to change your experience, take a look at the looking glasses that you have been using. Know how they are formed and modified, and take the initiative to modify them as you wish. As you modify them, you will experience a corresponding change in the world around you.

70

What You Have Today,
Is Just What You Asked For

Are you happy with the tasks that have ended up in your lap? If not, then would you like to find out who is responsible for this?

This essay suggests that it is not some external circumstances but we ourselves, that are responsible for every single task that we have ended up with.

The essay further suggests that one can easily change the make-up of one's tasks, if one wishes. Read this essay to find out how.

Read also essay numbers 15, 31 and 61.

A re you happy with the tasks that you are handling today? Or, do you wish that you did not have to do some (or maybe most) of your current tasks?

There is hardly a moment when we do not find someone complaining about some of the tasks that he or she has to do. This includes everyone, even you and me.

Why is it that almost everyone feels caught up in some kind of a grind? Is there no way of getting out of it, or of at least improving the situation?

To answer these questions, let's examine how a certain task happens to fall into our lap.

Recall a task that you performed recently, and which you thought you had to do. Then ask yourself, 'Was there someone else who could have handled it to the same degree of perfection or reliability that you did?

It is unlikely that you are the only person capable of handling any particular task. If it relates to the duty of a parent, both parents could qualify. If it is a task for a group, more than one member of that group could qualify.

Now, here is an important question. "If someone else also could have handled it, then why is it that you ended up assuming the responsibility for it?"

There is a saying that, "Had the fish not opened its mouth, it would not have ended up on the platter." Whether we agree with it or not, every single task that has ever ended up in our lap, ended up there because at some point or the other we had opened our mouth.

It is natural for every task we volunteer for to fit this rule. But amazingly, a great deal of our regular tasks fall into a similar category as well.

"Opening the mouth" does not simply mean expressing ourselves verbally. It can, and generally does, take place non-verbally.

'Who should put out the garbage? Who should come up a few minutes earlier to set up the room? Who should stay behind for the clean up?' Such questions are being raised all the time and some volunteers "open their mouth" mostly unconsciously, and generally non-verbally.

There is no job description that spells out every detail of the position. A great deal is left for interpretation by the persons dealing with the related position. Consequently, the actual function of any given position is highly affected by a change in the persons in and around that position.

Let me ask you a question. "If a new fire-fighting task suddenly was presented to your group or organization, to whom would it normally go?" Of course, it would go to the person who has, somehow, indicated his liking for fighting fires.

Most people who complain about having to fight fires, actually take pride in the fact that they are asked to fight fires, because they are good in that skill. They would suffer from depression if most of their fire-fighting tasks were suddenly taken away from them.

Our actions send out signals about our likes and dislikes. These are being received, monitored and interpreted continually by the people around us. It is based upon their interpretations of our messages that we finally end up with our unique pile of tasks.

A person who is perceived as being aggressive, ends up with the tasks that demand an aggressive approach. A person who likes to work within his own shell, soon ends up with the tasks that require minimum outside contact. It is only in this way that our unique tasks have slowly trickled down to us.

Is there something that we can do about it?

Yes, we can actually play an important role in deciding the make-up of our tasks. Here are some suggestions.

1. Realize and accept the fact that you have got only that for which you have asked.

2. **Acknowledge that it is unfair and futile to complain about the make-up of your bag of tasks.**

3. **Try to enhance your awareness of the messages that you have been communicating to others.**

4. **Endeavour to modify your messages in such a way that they bring you the kind of tasks that you would enjoy working on.**

The non-verbal component of our communication signals dominate their verbal counterpart. Not only do they constitute over ninety per cent of the total signal, but they also outweigh the verbal component in case of a conflict between the two.

You may say that you hate working on a certain task, but if you stay awake half the night for it, you actually communicate that you can tolerate it or that you may perhaps enjoy it.

Ralph Waldo Emerson once said, "What you are speaks so loudly, I can't hear a word that you are saying."

Yes, we may keep our mouth shut but it is impossible for us to shut out all non-verbal communication. Let's remember that "no answer" is often a "clear answer".

We are the captain of our ship. We are the master of our soul. Through our thoughts, beliefs, attitudes and actions, we paint the world that we would like to have. Slowly and positively, that kind of world becomes our reality. We literally attract people, resources, and circumstances that harmonize with our inner world. We not only have the control, but we are also constantly creating our own world.

Let's stop complaining about the tasks that we don't like. Let's do something about them. Let's focus our attention on the ones that we do like. According to the law of attraction, what we focus upon, grows.

Today you have exactly what you have been asking for up to this moment. If you want to see something different in your bag, all you need to do is stop complaining about what you don't want and start asking what you do want. For, as the Bible says, "Ask and ye shall receive."

71

"Not Too Bad"

Is Very Treacherous

Do you sometimes use the phrase, "not too bad"?
If so, do you realize what influence it has on your life?

This essay suggests that a small inconvenience,
that we can tolerate, is the most treacherous thing in
life, because we soon get used to it, and therefore, we
do nothing to alleviate it. Bit by bit, by tolerating the
little inconveniences, we end up tolerating even the
huge ones. This smoulders, and may ultimately extin
guish the fire of our life.

Read also essay number 28.

In our life, we encounter many kinds of problems: some we enjoy working with, some we hate, and like to get rid of as quickly as possible. Some problems make us revolt, or demonstrate our strong disapproval.

The type of problem which is perhaps the most insidious is the one that can be classified as "Not too bad". These are treacherous because they damage us very subtly. Often we don't even recognize their presence.

Many people stumble over little pebbles, but hardly anyone stumbles over a hill. A watch which is four hours slow or fast, hardly creates a major problem, because we immediately recognize its fault and decide not to depend upon it. But a watch which is four minutes slow or fast can, and often does, create many problems for us.

A friend of mine often says, "Elephants don't bite, only mosquitoes do." The same principle applies to our problems. The little things that we keep ignoring, add up and create huge problems later.

Saying, "It's not too bad", implies that we can tolerate the situation. We do absolutely nothing to alleviate the problem because we don't feel it necessary. Soon we become used to it and we don't even feel its presence.

When another problem of a slightly greater magnitude later comes to us, we compare it with our last experience and discover that "It's not too bad" after all. Therefore, we decide to tolerate it. The chain continues.

Bit by bit, we keep tolerating problems of even greater magnitudes. We literally become insensitive to them. We cultivate a habit of inaction, and later we become a slave of this habit.

Let's look at a couple of examples illustrating this point.

Not too long ago, the postage rate for a first class letter within Canada was thirty-two cents. When we became used to that, Canada Post decided to raise it to thirty-four cents. We groaned for a while but accepted it by saying, "It's not too bad".

What happened then?

A few months later Canada Post raised it to thirty-six cents, then to thirty-seven cents and then to thirty-eight cents. Had they decided to raise it straight from thirty-two cents to thirty-eight cents, there would have been far stronger reactions - demonstrations, questions in the Parliament, outcries in the media etc. But how is a slow increase different from a drastic increase? The answer is simple: the former is insidious.

Another example is taxes. To finance the expenses of World War I, the United States Government proposed a ten per cent Income Tax. Opposing it violently, one Senator said, "If we allow the government to tax the public by even one per cent today, soon the day will come when they would be taxing us as high as fifty per cent."

To this the proposing member replied, "This is absolute nonsense. The people of the United States will never tolerate any government that would try to impose a tax of fifty per cent." Today, the top bracket for Income Tax, in the United States, is well over eighty per cent!! There is some similar story for every other tax that we are paying today.

Psychologists have done an interesting experiment with frogs. They put one frog in a glass jar half-filled with water and they left the big mouth of the jar uncovered. They lighted a Bunsen burner underneath to raise the temperature of the water very slowly.

As the water warmed up, the frog felt a little uncomfortable. But, by tolerating a little more inconvenience each time, the frog ended up being stewed in the jar. But if someone thumped the jar, the frog could have easily leap out of that jar. The frog was free, and had the capability of getting out of that fatal situation, but could not overcome the insidious enemy, "not too bad".

But why do we tolerate an inconvenience?

We tolerate it, because we are basically lazy. We act only when we perceive the benefit to be substantially greater than the corresponding effort, in trying to solve, or to alleviate the problem. If the perceived benefit is not attractive enough, we elect to tolerate it and justify our decision by saying, "Well, that's a part of life."

Complacency, or lack of ambition, is another cause. We fear the unknown and prefer to accept the current situation. We often surrender ourselves to the mercy of our current condition, and hope that it will improve all by itself.

In some respect, we are asleep. Every new problem tries to disturb our sleep. But if it lacks the necessary force to awaken us, we continue to sleep.

When a reporter asked Mahatma Gandhi about his main strategy for attaining the independence of India, he said, "By awakening the masses." As more and more people of India awoke from their slumber, the country found itself closer, and closer to independence. The main reason why an average person uses less than ten per cent of his total potential, is that he stays asleep during most of his life. The more awake he can stay, the more he can use his potential.

Many years ago, the philosopher Pogo said, "We have found our enemy, it is us." How true! We are our main enemy. We are slaves of our habits. Our habits are formed, piece by piece, through little actions or inactions. Every habit, including that of "It's not too bad", is cultivated very slowly, and then starts ruling our lives. Every time that we say, think or accept 'It's not too bad', we enhance its power over us. This is our most insidious enemy.

But what can we do?

Waking ourselves up from our slumber is the main solution. Here is how I feel we can do it:

1. Start paying attention to the situations that fall in the category of "Not too bad".

2. Take a moment to think about the long term effect of such situations, if you ignored them or allowed them to grow.

3. Start developing your awareness of the poisonous effects of the seed, "It's not too bad."

4. Stop ignoring such problems. Take the trouble of uprooting them while they are still in their infancy stage.

"You may not realize it when it happens, but a kick in the teeth may be the best thing in the world for you."

                                        - Walt Disney

72

Voluntary Service Brings Many Rewards

This essay was written for "Volunteer Week".
Since volunteer work carries no cash reward, it has often been looked down upon.

The essay suggests that volunteer work provides many rewards, including an opportunity of discovering one's natural talents, and of discovering one's real purpose in life.

Read also essay numbers 38, 42 and 74.

T his week we are celebrating the contributions of volunteers in helping the growth of our community. Let's take a moment to reflect upon volunteerism. What does it mean? What values, if any, does it carry?

The dictionary meaning of the word "voluntary" is "doing or being ready to do things willingly, without being compelled".

Suppose you divided all your activities in the categories of "voluntary" or "involuntary" and had the option of choosing either, which would you rather choose? My guess is that you would choose the "voluntary" one. Then why is it that people look down upon voluntary tasks?

The word "voluntary" also implies doing something for free. But is there anything that is really free?

A king who wished to leave a legacy of wisdom for the future generations asked his wisest subjects to record all the wisdom that they possessed. After a great deal of work, they produced twelve huge volumes. The king was impressed, but knowing that people are basically lazy, feared that very few people would read it. Therefore he asked them to condense it.

The faithful subjects worked hard to condense it into a single volume of about five hundred pages. Although he was impressed by their remarkable job, the king felt that it was still too voluminous for an ordinary person to read. He asked them to condense it even further. They condensed it from five hundred pages to fifty pages, to five pages, and finally to one sentence. The king was elated, until he read the sentence, "There is no free lunch."

There is no free lunch in life. We cannot get anything totally free. Fortunately, there is a corollary to this philosophy. If you cannot get something for free, then nobody else can get something for free from you either. That means that there is nothing like a truly "free" service, including volunteer services.

There are two important reasons why we perceive ourselves as offering free services:

1. Our society measures every transaction by the yardstick of money.

But nature does not work that way at all. It compensates us for our services in a variety of different ways. We plant a seed and get back fruits!

Every work provides us an opportunity of acquiring a new skill. Whether we get paid for it or not, the acquired skill is ours to keep. That is the main gain for the effort.

2. We expect every transaction to be concluded immediately and completely. In other words, we look for instant gratification.

But in nature, there is always a definite time lag between the rendering of the service, and the reaping of the harvest. Often, the greater the lag, the greater is the return on the investment.

There is another interesting phenomenon that we should note. No species can survive alone. Each is dependent upon the other. Consequently, the return of our service generally comes from an entirely different direction.

In September, 1966, I came from India to Hamilton, Ontario. I really did not know anyone on this continent. There was one student in Hamilton whose name I had heard in India. He helped me get adjusted to the new land. But, soon after that, he disappeared.

The next September, I started helping a new foreign student on the campus. When he asked how he could return my favour, I asked him to extend a similar service to some other foreign student the next year. I did not bother checking how he fared, but am confident that he returned more favours than he had received from me.

God created every one of us for a specific purpose. But He left it up to us to discover our purpose. Unfortunately, most of us go through our entire life without knowing our unique purpose.

The moment we discover our unique purpose, we experience a restless urge to work towards fulfilling it. We get so engrossed in it that we literally forget ourselves. We lose our sense of time, location or an awareness of our physical needs. I have read that while working on some of their paintings, Leonardo da Vinci and Michelangelo forgot to eat for several days.

The root of every discovery of "one's unique purpose" lies in some kind of volunteer service.

Mahatma Gandhi came from a family of "grocers". His grandfather and father became advisers to the local princely state. Gandhi himself was drafted to become a lawyer. But noticing that most of his clients could not afford the fee of a lawyer, he started serving them unconditionally, and without fee.

But the more he tried to serve them for free, the more money he received from some other sources. Slowly he discovered that his main niche was not in the practice of law, but in the nursing of the sick and the wounded, and in the helping of the helpless. Had he continued working as a lawyer, perhaps he would have died a very wealthy man, but he would not have become even a fraction of the man that he became through his volunteer service.

Albert Schweitzer came from a family of musicians. He earned doctorate degrees in music, theology and philosophy. Then he felt the urge of studying medicine, which he did. He had many options for working and earning a decent living in Austria, but he volunteered to go to Africa, and to open a hospital in the middle of the jungle. Could any amount of money buy the enrichment of life that he received in his volunteer service?

7 3

Always Remember
The Silent Third Party

If you knew that you were being followed and watched, every second of your life, would you make any change in your current way of living?

This essay suggests that you may fool every single person in the world, but you cannot fool your silent third party. Being silent, he does not say a word, but he is always alert. He observes every single detail, makes notes and draws your attention to relevant facts. For every good deed that you have done he pats your back and for every bad deed, he haunts you.

The essay further suggests that if you recognize the presence, and the influence, of the silent third party, and act accordingly, you would not have to fear anybody else.

Read also essay numbers 57 and 65.

 L ife consists of a series of games. Almost every moment we are involved in transactions with people. Like any game, we feel that the main objective is to win. Often we use unfair means to win the game, or to gain a favourable situation for a future move. If we are successful, we pride ourselves for having outsmarted the other person.

But how does the other person feel, when he discovers that he has been outsmarted? And is it always necessary that one loses so that someone else wins?

Let's recognize the fact that no one likes to lose a game. Fortunately, the games of life are of a different nature than those of sports. We can win while helping others to win at the same time. This is commonly known as the win-win situation.

Win-win is not an exception, but the general rule, for all life-games. Every time that you do something to make someone happy, you raise your own happiness as well; and whenever you cause someone to feel a little down, depressed, humiliated or miserable, you also lose some of your own happiness or the peace of your mind.

The best way to build your own self-esteem is to do something to raise the self-esteem of a few persons. Simply try it for a day, or even an hour, and verify the effect yourself. Like the bread cast on water, everything comes back to us.

But what about the so-called smart people?

I have purposely used the expression "so-called" because those who consider themselves to be smart today, will discover someday that they were not smart at all.

The word "smart" connotes that one takes advantage of someone's weakness. This generally happens when the other person is taken by surprise. If he is fore-warned, he could not be out-smarted so easily.

Imagine for a moment, that in every transaction there is a silent third party present. He is fully aware of everything. He hears everything that you say, and even knows what you think but don't say. He is able to see not only what is open and visible, but also what is hidden deep down in your heart. He makes an accurate record of your every act and thought. He observes everything, but never makes one comment. Occasionally he shows you a few pages of his notes.

If such a person followed you everywhere, day and night, would you be still trying to outsmart others? Perhaps you would not. At least you would give it a second thought.

You may think that I am talking of a fictitious person. You are partly right. I am not talking about a real person but something which is equivalent to a person.

I am talking about our conscience. It follows us every single moment of our life. It doesn't say a word, but it haunts us, and forces us to recall our past deeds and thoughts. For every "good" of our past, we feel good today, and for every "wrong", we experience some hollowness in our heart. Occasionally we do not recognize the cause of this hollow feeling. We just feel its presence.

It is impossible to win the game of life by outsmarting others. It is impossible to cheat or to deceive others, because the silent third party would know that we did not play a fair game. The scoreboard may declare us to be the winners, but we will be unable to experience the ecstasy of winning.

Sometimes we dislike a person but mask our true feelings by using diplomatic words. We feel proud of our "smartness", but in the long run we fool no one but ourselves. It is difficult to pretend to be one kind of a person on the surface and a distinctly different kind in reality. This creates an inner conflict and eventually results in some form of psychosomatic illness.

Entertaining a negative thought inside ourselves is more harmful than letting it out. Inside, it works like a slow poison.

Every harsh language or cruel thought boomerangs on us. We are bound to be confronted by circumstances where we have to pay for every thought and deed with our own coins.

It is impossible to injure someone without injuring yourself, or without paying some price for it. The price is often dearer than money, it could be peace of mind, or even your sanity.

In the same way, it is impossible to help someone without receiving some benefits ourselves. By helping our neighbour row his boat across the river we find that we ourselves have been able to cross the river.

According to the law of the universe, you must keep a piece of what you give away. Give away hate and you keep a piece of hate. Give away love, or happiness, and you will keep a piece of love, or happiness. Remember, the hand that gives away roses, retains some fragrance of that rose.

Reminding ourselves of the silent third party encourages us to be fair and just in every transaction and brings us lasting happiness.

By nature we like to help others and to be fair and just. But a problem arises when we notice that the other person is not fair and just to us. The only right solution to this problem is to refrain from "striking back", especially in your thoughts.

It is said that he who lives by the sword, dies by the sword. Let's try to forgive the other person. Let him be responsible for his acts and thoughts. Let's take control of ours.

I admit that this is not easy. But one of the challenges of life is to discipline ourselves to do what is right, even when it's not easy to do.

It is especially important to forgive the other person when he deserves it the least. Anyone can forgive when the forgiveness is deserved but it requires a strong, disciplined character, to forgive when it is not deserved.

Let's recognize the presence of the silent third party in our every transaction. If we fear and obey him, we will not have to fear or obey anybody else in life.

"Character is what you are in the dark."
- Dwight L. Moody

74

Whatever You Do,
Do It Lovingly

Are you happy with what you are doing, or do you feel that a lot of tasks have simply been dumped on you?

This essay suggests that very few tasks are truly thrust upon us. The rest we choose to accept ourselves. The essay describes how the "choosing" takes place.

Since there is a tremendous difference in the psychological impact of a task that we feel we have to do and the one that we choose to do, we should be careful in the use, or the lack of use, of the "choosing" process. This essay further suggests that once you choose to do a certain task, you should put your whole heart into it, and do it willingly and lovingly.

The essay also makes a reference to the role of "perception" in determining the nature of a task, and how it could be altered.

Read also essay numbers 17, 31, 70 and 72.

Do you find some of your work to be a drag on your life? Would you like to learn how to alleviate some of this?

We can divide all our work into two simple categories: things that we love to do, and things that we resent doing, generally known as "the chores". A balance of the two would be acceptable, but the tragedy is that most of us get bogged down by our chores.

Working on a task that we like is similar to driving a well-tuned car. We cover a distance quickly and enjoy the ride at the same time.

Carrying out an activity that we resent is similar to driving a car which is either poorly tuned, or whose brakes are jammed. The car poses the threat of breaking down any time. It drags, wears down quickly and makes us feel tired.

By nature we cannot sit idle. We must have something to keep our mind and body occupied. The work that we like rejuvenates us. While the work that we dislike, drains us. No one who keeps on working on "chores" all the time can expect to live long.

It is a myth to assume that "chores" are essential elements of life. No, life does not require us to spend most of our time doing chores. There is no task that we are literally forced to do. We have several choices. We can choose not to do it at all. We can choose to change our perception, and thereby not see it as a chore. We can modify it in such a way that it would not remain a chore any longer.

To reduce some of the drag, we must find a way of interspersing our chores with some work that we love to do. The more we can do this, the better we can improve the quality of our life.

A study of the lives of the great achievers reveals that they spend very little time working on their chores. I believe that this is not only characteristic but also an essential requirement for high achievement in any field.

But what do we do when we have so many chores to handle?

The answer lies partly in our perception of our tasks and partly in deciding what we want to get out of our lives. Here are some suggestions:

1. Stop being the slave of "Perfectionism".

We often find that many new tasks accumulate in our lap, before we have finished some of the old ones. One reason why we find ourselves unable to finish them quickly enough, is that we don't seem to attain the perfection that we feel is required.

The standard of the perfection needed to finish a particular task is rarely set by someone else. Generally we ourselves set it too high. If we lowered our standard just by a small amount, in most cases we would not lose much, and save a lot of time and energy.

2. Stop demanding too much order from your children.

Children find themselves under too many pressures - school assignments, peer pressure, home discipline etc. By being more demanding on them, we simply make their lives, as well as our own, more difficult. Tolerate some mess in their rooms. They will catch up with this later. After all, our rooms were not very organized during our childhood and notice how quickly we caught up, when we had to depend on ourselves!

3. Stop thinking that you are doing a favour for somebody else.

According to the law of sowing and reaping, as we sow so shall we reap. No one can sow for us and likewise, we cannot sow for someone else. Never nurture the feeling that you are doing a favour. Every deed of yours will be rewarded. But don't expect the reward to come from the person that you are serving. Trust God. He will compensate you.

After having rendered a service, simply forget it. Making reference to it, or trying to use it as a bargaining tool, would work against you. The more you try to forget it, the more others will remember it.

4. Use self-talk to change your perception of the task.

Keep telling yourself that you are doing it purely because you want to do it. Never let any feeling of compulsion creep into your mind. It is surprising, but we can tolerate most of the hardships that are caused by the activities that we want to do.

5. Cultivate the habit of being thankful for every condition that life presents to you.

There is some benefit in everything. Look for the benefit and thank God for giving you the opportunity of serving.

The greatest, and the most lasting, satisfaction in life comes from the feeling of being useful to others. Start seeing every "chore" as an opportunity to be useful and it will evaporate like morning dew in spring.

It is not the actual conditions, but our perception of the conditions, that really matters. By changing our perception, we can convert most of our chores into activities that we love to do.

Hundreds of thousands of people went to work for Mahatma Gandhi. Before assigning any task, he advised them, "You either do it willingly and whole-heartedly, or don't do it at all".

Let's heed Gandhi's advice. Let's take a closer look at our chores. Are they really so distasteful? If they are, let's drop them. No one will force us, at gunpoint, to work at them. But if they are tolerable, and if we choose to do them, let's do them with pleasure.

> "Laugh and the world laughs with you,
>   Weep and you weep alone,
> For the sad old earth must borrow its mirth,
>   But has trouble enough of its own."
>   - Ella Wheeler Wilcox

75

For Affirmations,
"Good" Is Better Than "The Best"

Are you familiar with some affirmations of the type, "I am the best"? Do you practice some yourself? If so, do they work?

This essay discusses why the affirmations of the type, "I am the best" rarely bring the expected result, and suggests that the affirmations of the type, 'I am good' are actually more effective.

"I am the best" sets up many opposing forces, while "I am good" creates nothing but harmony, cooperation and good will of everyone around you.

Read also essay numbers 24 and 99.

It may appear strange but as far as affirmations are concerned, "good" is better than "the best".

An affirmation is based on the theory that our subconscious mind is impressed by continually repeated instructions, and then it helps us to move, and slowly actualize the image of the particular affirmation. Obviously, the ideal image should be "the best" image conceivable.

In principle this theory is perfectly valid. However, in practice it seldom works. I am not saying that it doesn't ever work. I am only saying that the success of this technique is the exception rather than the rule.

It is true that Mohammed Ali became the World Heavyweight Boxing Champion because he kept on saying, "I am the greatest". But we must understand that for an affirmation to work, many other factors must be considered, and followed.

To achieve anything in life we need the support and cooperation of other people. We need the support of our family members, customers, clients, colleagues, superiors and subordinates. We need the support of the innumerable people who participate in the making and the implementation of the various regulations that affect our life in one way or another. We need the support of the countless others who contribute in making our life easy, so that we can concentrate on the "important" things.

Saying "I am the best", implies that you consider yourself to be superior to others. This creates a psychological rift.

No one likes to be considered inferior. Therefore no one will give you any assistance that will make you superior to him or her. It is true that you could move ahead with your own drive, but it would be very difficult. A number of little forces working against you can soon wear you out.

Every time that you use the statement, "I am the best", you create the thoughts of jealousy, envy and hatred in some others. This builds a psychological force against you. Very soon you notice that your affirmation does not really work.

"I am the best" has a negative influence, because it alienates us from most of the people whose support we would need to achieve what we want to achieve.

Mohammed Ali is an exceptional person. He did not mind being labeled as "crazy" and he literally drowned himself in his own world of 'I am the greatest'. Are you willing to go to that extent?

There is an easier and, in my opinion, better way.

Rather than affirming, "I am the best", try affirming, "I am good". For example, you can say, "I am a good athlete", or, "I am a good sales person", or, "I am well-organized", or, "I have good memory".

Saying that you are good, takes you out of the game of competing with others. Every one will support you to be "good", and to remain "good", as long as you allow them the same right. It will build an atmosphere of peace and harmony.

It is estimated that a normal person uses less than ten per cent of his potential capability. This means that over ninety per cent of our capability remains untapped. The main challenge in life is to develop the awareness of our untapped capability and to endeavour to use it as much as possible.

By remaining involved in competing with others, we limit ourselves, because the most that we could aim for would be those ten percent of our real capability. But by competing with ourselves we can open ourselves to the full range of one hundred per cent.

If you aim for a hundred, and fail miserably, you may still attain a twenty. But if you aim for a ten, and succeed triumphantly, you are unlikely to attain anything greater than the ten. You can never attain something beyond your dream.

Thus you can see that "I am good" is more effective than "I am the best".

Some people think that "I am the best" is still a better affirmation, provided that you affirm it silently. But I disagree. I believe that it is impossible for us to hide our real thoughts.

We reveal them, through a variety of non-verbal signals such as voice tones, body language and innocent remarks. These thought vibrations are picked up, largely unconsciously, by the minds that it may affect. Thus, even the silent affirmation, "I am the best" generates some psychological opposing forces.

One of the main reasons why we are limited to about ten per cent of our full potential is that we are too busy trying to behave differently from our real thoughts. The moment we free ourselves from playing that game, and assent to remaining just one, person in both our thought and behaviour, we start activating our unused potentials.

There can be only one "best" in any given group. By trying to become the best, we begin ostracizing ourselves from the group. This makes us feel very uneasy. But everyone can be "good". Everyone can be healthy and happy, and we can achieve that by affirming, "I am good".

The best affirmation that I have ever encountered is, "Day by day, in every way, I am becoming more successful". It contains no element of external competition and it is true that compared to yesterday, we are going to be more successful today, because yesterday's experience has made us slightly wiser today. I urge you to repeat this statement few times each morning and to notice a marked improvement in your own success rate.

We become what we think about most of the time. Our success is determined by the support of hundreds and thousands of people. We cannot afford to alienate them, and expect to live a happy prosperous life. I believe that affirmations of the type, "I am the best" work against us. There is no need to compete with others. Our main task is to make the best use of what we have been blessed with. We can do this by affirming, "I am good".

76

"Being Busy"
Can Be Underproductive

Do you feel guilty if you waste a minute here, or a minute there, doing nothing?

This essay suggests that being busy does not necessarily mean being productive.

You can be most productive only if you give full attention to your most important task at the moment. This requires that you frequently review your entire list of tasks, identify the most important one on the list and then discipline yourself to work on it until it is done. The discipline of "frequent reviews" and "single minded attention" to one task at a time, is the most valuable skill.

The essay also suggests that the only way to think, or to review clearly, is to relax occasionally.

Read also essay number 45.

332

L iving in a fast society, we seem to be always on the run. We have been trained to use every second of our time. We are always thinking of some ways of making use of our time. Often we look for more than one activity that we could handle concurrently.

Eating and watching television, or listening to the radio, is very common. Another example is that of listening to the radio or a cassette player, while driving or taking a bath.

I am sure you can cite numerous situations, where people try to cram in more than one activity at the same time. In fact, the more activities that you can cram in, the smarter you are considered to be.

But how advantageous is it to handle more than one activity at the same time?

With some exceptions, I believe that it is not advantageous and even under-productive, or a poor use of our time.

Remember, our mind can entertain only one thought at a time. When we get involved in more than one activity simultaneously, our mind has to keep switching from the thoughts of one activity to that of the other. This results in a mediocre performance in each of the activities.

Even the simple combination of eating and watching television at the same time, greatly affects the level of our performance, in the two activities. We are likely to miss a good deal of the information presented on the program, and we would find it difficult to digest and to assimilate all the nutritive values contained in that food.

Every external stimulus creates some tension within our system. This affects the normal function of the various glands. An exciting television program can significantly alter the production of the enzymes necessary for the proper digestion of the food.

You can verify this by devoting, for a few days, your full attention to the "eating", while eating, and then noticing the changes in your ability to digest the food.

In almost every case, it is much more productive to concentrate on one activity at a time, until we have completed that activity to our satisfaction, and then to drop it, at least temporarily, from our mind.

Listening to light instrumental music, or to some light natural sounds such as the sound of ocean waves, birds chirping, waterfalls, natural streams or wind blowing through trees or meadows, are some exceptions. Light natural sounds tend to stimulate our right brain and to calm our left brain. This enhances our overall creativity.

Being busy does not necessarily result in being effective. The latter demands that we remain busy working on the right activity. This requires thinking, and we cannot clearly think when our mind is being bombarded by thoughts of two or more interests.

We often find ourselves so busy mopping the floor that we have no time left to repair the leaky faucet, or even to question ourselves about the source of that water.

Recently I read a story of two teen-age boys who were fishing by a stream one day when they noticed someone floating down the stream. The boys jumped in, pulled the person out of the water, gave mouth-to-mouth resuscitation and saved his life.

The next day they were fishing in the same spot, and noticed another person floating down the stream. Again they jumped in and saved that person's life. From then on, people floated downstream quite consistently and many died en route to the hospital, which was about eighty miles away. The city council then decided to build a hospital on that very spot.

Soon the hospital became very busy and well-known across the country. Many interns went there to serve their residency. One day, one of the interns approached the administrator and said, "There is one thing that bothers me. Has anyone ever gone upstream to see why people are jumping into the river?"

"No", answered the administrator, "we just don't have the time. We are too busy treating the victims."

Sometimes it is more productive to stop fighting the immediate fire and to take a moment to think of the cause of the fire.

For clear thinking it is essential that we focus our attention for some definite duration, on only one task at a time. As a "pause" before and after a word emphasizes that word, so a brief mental silence, or a lull before and after the handling of an important task, enhances our ability to think clearly on that task.

Being busy and being productive are generally not the same. Productivity demands thinking. We must know where we want to go and why we want to go there. We must think of all the possible ways of getting there, choose the most suitable way for us, and only then get busy working on it.

There are one thousand four hundred and forty minutes in every day. Let's devote one per cent of our total time, or fifteen minutes a day, to thinking and planning. It is best to allocate the fifteen minutes in one block, but if you can't, then choose three blocks of five minutes each.

"The best cure for the body
is a quiet mind."
- Napoleon Bonaparte

7 7

Full Moon Increases

Mind Activities

This essay discusses the influence of the lunar cycle on the activities of our mind.

With the lunar cycle there is a change in the amount of the sun's rays reaching our planet. This creates a definite change in the magnetic field around us. The latter affects the reaction rate of the mind. A change in the amount of the light around us also makes a corresponding change in the rate of the mind activity. Thus full moon causes our mind to be most active (and thereby restless) while the new moon produces a cool, relaxed mind.

Read also essay number 16.

"Why are more crimes committed on a full-moon than on any other day of the lunar cycle?", someone asked me just a few days ago.

This question has been haunting me since that day.

Statistics indicate more suicides and more baby births on a full moon than on any other day. People who suffer from hysteria, or some other mental sickness, are more prone to experiencing an attack on a full moon day. Many animals behave quite differently during the full moon. For example, crickets sing louder and much longer; mad dogs howl much more; many dogs bark at the full moon and so on.

What is the cause of all this?

There appears to be two likely reasons.

The first is the presence of the extra light during a full moon night.

Light has a profound influence on our behaviour. We feel exhilarated in the presence of light, and depressed in its absence. Long winter nights create depression in many people. Several cloudy days in a row make us feel a bit depressed. As the cloud clears, the depression decreases.

Because of the reflection by the moon, we receive an additional amount of light, during the light period of the lunar cycle. Moreover, since the duration and the size of the visible moon increases with the approach of the full moon, the amount of additional light increases rapidly, reaching its peak during the full moon.

The extra light has not only direct but also many indirect influences. The people and the animals that get excited create some noise or some commotion, which, in turn, excites others. This generally sets up a chain reaction.

The second reason is related to the influence of magnetic waves on the activity of our mind.

We literally live in an ocean of the earth's magnetic field. We receive and transmit thoughts to each other, mostly unconsciously, through the medium of this magnetic field. With any change in the make-up of our surrounding magnetic field, our ability to transmit and to receive thoughts changes too. With the change of this ability, our mood and our behaviour changes.

The sun rays, originated by some nuclear reactions on the sun's surface, are highly radioactive and influence the earth's magnetic field. This is clearly seen in the creation, and the changes in the patterns of, the Northern lights. Any change in the activity on the solar surface, or in the amount of the sun rays reaching us, makes a corresponding change in the make-up of the magnetic field around us.

There are three distinct cyclical patterns which influence the magnetic field around us. These are: seasonal, nocturnal and lunar. The seasonal change is caused by the change in the distance of the sun, and the tilting of the earth relative to the sun. The nocturnal change is caused by the earth's facing or not facing the sun. And the lunar change is due to the changes in the sunlight reflected to us by the moon.

In addition to the three regular cyclic changes, there are many local variations, depending upon the local weather conditions. These variations in the magnetic field around us make a definite corresponding change in our moods and our behaviour. Within one lunar cycle, these changes reach a peak on the full moon day.

If we understand the influence of the lunar cycle, we can better understand the cause of the fluctuations in our own moods and behaviour as well as those of the persons around us. We can then become more tolerant of others' "odd" behaviour and be able to express more love for them.

There is a saying that 'Fore warned is fore armed'. By becoming more conscious of the influence of the sunlight and the magnetic field around us, we can control our mood and our behaviour. For example, if you notice that you are becoming more restless, and if you wish to control it, you can do so by cutting down the amount of the sunlight (or the moonlight) that is reaching you. You can also help cut down the noise that is reaching your mind by reducing the intake of some stimulating foods for a few days around the full moon.

It is claimed that sleeping parallel to the magnetic lines provides most relaxation to the mind. Since the earth's magnetic lines originate from the North pole and terminate in the South,, sleeping in the north-south direction, with the head towards the north, is the most soothing position for the mind. Sleeping east-west is least soothing, and causes us to dream more. Such dreams make us feel exhausted by the morning.

I do not know any certain way of checking the validity of this hypothesis, but I have tried several positions and have found the north-south position, with the head towards the north, to be the most relaxing. Is this is simply my belief? I don't know.

The extra light of the full moon and the corresponding altered magnetic field of our environment significantly increases the activity of our minds. This is the main reason why there are greater number of crimes committed during a full moon.

From the above discussions one may conclude that the full moon is harmful for our minds. This is not always true. Yes, a full moon does increase the activity of our mind. If you are striving for a quieter mind a full moon is going to be a hurdle to you. But if you are looking for an environment of greater creativity, the full moon will be very conducive.

"Man's greatness lies in the power of his thought."

- Blaise Pascal

78

With Age You Can Become More Valuable

Do you feel that you are becoming less and less valuable as you get older?

This essay suggests that the usefulness of a person is not related to age, but to his or her willingness to serve. As the experience builds up, one can become more useful during his or her senior years, as compared to the middle years.

The essay also suggests that "Having a cause to live for" is the most important force behind anyone's life.

Read also essay numbers 10, 18 and 49.

A nyone who has reached the age of sixty-five is labeled a "senior". There is nothing wrong with that. But, our society generally implies that a senior is good only for a few, relatively unimportant, tasks. Are we justified in attaching such labels to the senior members of our society?

The retirement age of sixty-five was adopted by the Railroad Retirement System of the United States, in 1870! This was subsequently adopted by the Security System of the United States in 1937. In the past fifty years, our life expectancy has increased by nearly fifteen years. Are we justified, today, in presuming that every person loses his or her ability to contribute to the society, or the company, as soon as he or she reaches the age of sixty-five?

History is full of examples, of men and women who made outstanding contributions to mankind, while they were in their seventies and eighties. George Bernard Shaw wrote several good plays in his eighties.

Grandma Moses picked up the brush when she was seventy-eight and produced over fifteen hundred paintings during the next twenty-three years. Golda Meir founded a new political party when she was sixty-eight, and became the Prime Minister of Israel two years later.

At the age of eighty, Sir Winston Churchill stepped down as the Prime Minister of England, but remained in the House of Commons to become the "Father of the House". Four years later, he fought and won another election.

At the age of sixty-nine, Ronald Reagan became President of the United States of America, and held that office successfully for eight years.

Where would our world be if people like Mahatma Gandhi, Thomas Edison or Pope Paul II had decided to retire at the age of sixty-five?

It is however also true, that the vast majority of the so-called "seniors" appear to just pass their time. What is the cause of this tremendous disparity?

One reason of our seniors' becoming less productive is the general conditioning process of our society. We are told, over and over, that when we reach the age of sixty-five, we will not be able to retain our productivity, and that we will become dependent. With time, we start believing this, and then we react, or perform, accordingly.

The second reason perhaps is the fear of the total evaporation of the market for our services.

Since our youth we are used to serving our immediate family members. When they become totally self-dependent, we are left with no one else to serve.

Moreover, we have an unconscious feeling that we won't be able to compete with the younger generation, and therefore, we keep talking about "the good old days". The new generation cannot relate to our old days. They are more interested in the days to come. This creates a generation gap. The young prefer to depend on themselves, rather than dwell on the past.

The people who have been very productive in their seventies and eighties did not waste any moment thinking, or talking, about their good old days. They considered the whole community as their family, and thereby broadened the market of their services.

It is a mistake to think that we become less productive with age. In fact, with age, we can, and should, become more productive. The main productivity comes from the mind, which can stay young even when the body starts to get old. Let me share with you a couple of interesting, related stories.

An accident paralysed Milo C. Jones and left him confined to bed for the rest of his life. He did not give up and decided to use his mind. He came up with a plan and explained it to his family. Under his guidance, they planted their entire farm with corn. Then they raised pigs by feeding them the corn. Then they slaughtered the young pigs and manufactured delicious little pig sausages. In less than ten years, the bed-ridden Jones, and his family, had become millionaires.

In 1883, John Roebling and his son Washington, were inspired by the idea of building a bridge connecting Brooklyn and Manhattan. However, in the early months of the project, an accident killed the father and left the son badly paralysed. Washington could neither talk nor walk. All he could do was move one finger. Using his mind, he developed a code system, and with the help of his wife, communicated his ideas and plans for the building of the bridge. For thirteen years, he tapped out his instructions, and that is how the Brooklyn Bridge was built.

I sincerely believe that we can live as long as we can maintain our will to live and the latter is directly dependent upon our feeling of being useful to others.

The older you become, the more experience you accumulate, and therefore the greater wisdom you possess. Don't let that wisdom go to waste. You owe it to mankind to share what you have. The more you share a piece of what you have, the more you receive a piece of what you lack.

Forget your age. Forget those old good days. Forget your personal needs. Pick up a new cause, or a new project, and get involved. The new challenge will rejuvenate your mind and your body.

If you are a "senior", let the world know that you feel proud of it. I am definitely proud of you. I look forward to consulting you and receiving some wisdom from you. I salute you.

"I will study and get ready, and then maybe my chance will come."

- Abraham Lincoln

79

Problems Are The Food
For The Mind

Are you nourishing both your body and your mind adequately?

For sustenance, both our body and mind must receive a continuous supply of appropriate food.

If you fail to nourish your body, it will immediately draw your attention, through signals such as illness or weakness. But if you fail to nourish your mind, it will not complain, it will suffer silently, will atrophy and may even die. Therefore, it is up to you to nourish your mind adequately.

This essay suggests that the main food for the mind is "problems" or "challenges". It advises us to be thankful for every problem that comes our way and to use it to stimulate, and thereby nourish our mind.

Read also essay numbers 1, 67 and 68.

W e possess a body and a mind. To sustain life, we must nourish both. One cannot survive without the other.

For their sustenance and growth, they must be fed regularly and properly. We must also realize that different kinds of life require different kinds of food. For example, I love ice cream, but a fish loves earthworms instead! What is food for one, may turn out to be a poison for another.

Most bookstores these days are replete with health books. In the sale of books, the category that surpasses all other categories is that of health and cooking. It is obvious that people are very interested in knowing about the right kind of food. But almost all of these books talk about the food for the body, and very few talk about the food for the mind.

The food that we eat at the dining table is not the food for the mind. Mind works on thoughts, and only thoughts can be its food.

Everything that grows is not a food for our body. Some are food, some are poison and some are purely junk. In the same way, not all thoughts are food for the mind, in the true sense.

The thoughts related to regrets of the past are totally useless, harmful, and therefore poisonous for the mind. Some poisons are so mild that they work insidiously, and harm us very quietly. In fact, slow poisons are far more lethal than the potent ones, because we recognize, and take immediate preventive measures against the potent ones. But the mild ones escape our attention and our defence mechanism.

Only the thoughts that can stretch our imagination are good and healthy food for our mind. The ideal thoughts are those related to overcoming the hurdles, or solving the problems, which prevent us from reaching our worthy life goals. When we know the purpose behind our effort, the work appears to be less painful, or at least becomes more tolerable.

When a child hears, "You need a good supply of protein to build your muscles" or "Spinach will make you strong like Popeye", he is more apt to eat those foods.

As too much food is unhealthy for the body, so too many problems can be harmful for the mind. At the same time, too little food, or too few problems, will fail to sustain the mind. The question is, 'How many problems are too much or too little for the mind?'

There is no universal answer for this question. What is "problem" for one person may very well be "child's play" for another. It's all relative to the person's ability, or his past experience, in handling problems.

Unfortunately, we underestimate our own abilities and therefore see far too many tasks as "problems". Moreover, fearing the unknown, we imagine the problem to be of a far greater magnitude than it really is.

Our attitude plays an important role in deciding what is healthy or unhealthy for us.

When confronted with a new task, we first check our library of past experience. We look for an experience that was similar. If we do not find one, we look for the one whose extension, extrapolation or projection would come close to this problem and then try to assess if we have the needed capability for handling the current problem. If we feel that we have the capability, then we do not see it as a "problem". But if we do not, then we try to assess its magnitude. The latter is often tainted by our perception of the difference between the current problem and our related experience.

It should be noted that the influence of any food on our body is also highly affected by our current attitude to that particular food. If we sit down at the dinner table and say, "Oh, no. not the same crap again", that food, no matter how nutritious it might be, is not not going to nourish our body.

According to the Hindu philosophy, the same dish can produce different results in different people. The difference depends upon how one   obtains the dish. If we work hard, earn our labour, and buy that dish, it will prove to be highly fruitful for our body. But if we rob someone to obtain that dish, it will work as a poison. This is so because our conscience knows everything. If the means is not fair, it bugs us. If the means is fair and generous, it praises and blesses us.

There is one major difference between the characteristics of the food for the body and that of the mind.

The same dish can sustain our body day after day, but the same problem cannot. What was a problem for us yesterday, may cease to stretch our imagination today. The mind must continually be fed with new problems.

In some respect this is also true of the food for our body. We get bored eating the same food. The problem here is not with the body, but with the mind, which demands new stimulations all the time.

Our problems are the food for our mind. We need them in order to sustain our mind, and thereby to survive. Let's be thankful for our problems. It is true that too many huge problems may break us, but the reality is that no problems are as huge as we imagine them to be. If we maintain a positive attitude to our problems, we will be able to see them in the right perspective. Even large problems can be broken down into small, manageable pieces, and then tackled relatively easily.

"Problems are the price of progress.
Don't bring me anything but trouble.
Good news weakens me."
- Charles F. Kettering

80

You Can Make

All The Difference

Have you ever down-played the value of your own contribution? Do you sometimes think that your role is too insignificant to make any noticeable dent in the whole system?

This essay suggest that our contribution may appear to be small, but it is not insignificant. You may be only a drop, but remember that just one drop of ink can change the colour of a jug of water. Every leader is proof of the fact that a single individual can mobilize huge forces.

You may feel alone, but don't worry. Keep performing your share of the task, and you will discover that you can make all the difference

Read also essay numbers 47 and 69..

We often feel that our contribution to society is too small to make any difference. As such, we find little enthusiasm for our share of the task. We put in just a little or no effort and end up proving that we were right all along.

How about you? Do you sometimes feel that you are just a drop of water in the vast ocean of society? Do you feel that your contribution is of almost no importance? If so, I believe that you are wrong.

Whatever the type, or the degree of your contribution, it is valuable and at times it could make a tremendous difference.

Adolph Hitler won the leadership of his party by the margin of one vote. Mahatma Gandhi was often the only person to believe and act on the premise of "non-violence". Christopher Columbus was perhaps the only person on his ship to believe that land could be found by going farther west. One seed, properly cultivated, can produce thousands, and ultimately millions, of fruits. Talk of little contributions!

Our universe works on the basis of a multitude of tiny contributions. Let's just look at how our body functions.

The physiological function within a cell is ridiculously simple. Each cell focuses on its own function. Individually the contribution of any cell is negligible. But collectively they perform miracles.

In our head there is only one bone, the lower jaw, that moves. What a difference this one bone makes! It enables us to eat, and thereby to keep the body alive. It enables us to talk and thereby to communicate with each other.

There is a story that once some parts of the body complained that they had to do more work than others. The hands had to pick objects, chop wood etc. The legs had to do the walking. The eyes had to be watchful, and to point out directions, and so on. They noticed that the lazy stomach did nothing. So they made an agreement, to stop feeding the stomach. It was not long when they realized the important contribution that the stomach was making.

A certain Austrian town once hired a mountain dweller to clear the debris from the pools of water up in the mountain crevices that fed the lovely spring flowing through their town. With faithful, silent regularity, the old man patrolled the hills, removed the leaves and branches, and wiped away the silt that would otherwise have choked and contaminated the flow of water. Soon the town became a popular attraction for vacationers. But, hardly anyone saw that man. No one knew exactly what he did or if he did anything.

Several years later one member of the Town Council questioned the salary paid to this unknown man. Since no-one could really explain why he had been receiving the salary, the Council decided to lay him off.

The next Fall those mountain springs began to get clogged by the debris of leaves and tree branches and by the following Spring they were badly contaminated. The town was no longer an attraction for the vacationers and then the Town Council realized the value of the little contribution made by that invisible, strange, keeper of the spring.

In the olden days, playing an organ required two persons - one to play the keys, and the other to operate the bellow. While performing one evening, a renowned organ player received applause after applause. During the intermission he told his assistant, "I am doing very well this evening, am I not?" His assistant simply nodded his head. After the intermission the player played the same keys but his performance was not the same, because his assistant was not operating the bellow properly.

Whether you are the stage performer, or an assistant working behind the stage, your contribution is important for the overall success of the show.

People often say, "I am only a cog in the big wheel". There is nothing wrong, or unfair about that.

A nail may be a poor little thing. No one gives it the same respect that one gives to a piece of diamond. But at times the poor nail can become more valuable than any piece of diamond.

It is said that once a war was lost for the want of one nail. (See essay number 47 for the detail.) Think of the value of that one nail.

We have the potential of doing, or achieving, much more than we actually do. Let's stop undervaluing the importance of our "little" contribution. Let's focus on our share. We are responsible only for that.

We will never receive the opportunity of handling a million dollar task, until we have demonstrated our ability of adequately handling some of the one dollar, the ten dollar, and the hundred dollar tasks.

You may be just one, and your contribution may be just "one little" contribution, but let's remember that, like the invisible keeper of the spring, or the bellow operator, you can make a significant difference. In fact, you can make all the difference, if you want.

> "The greatest things are accomplished by individual people, not by committees or companies."
> - Alfred A. Montapert

81

Worry is the Chewing Gum of the Mind

Without any doubt, worry is the most futile act. It saps our energy and gives us no worthwhile fruit in return.

If you are troubled by some worry, read this essay, and learn some simple techniques for getting out of that vicious cycle.

Read also essay number 45.

A chewing gum helps to keep our mouth occupied and thereby to keep our mind off a pressing thought or tension. But it provides no nourishment to the body. At best it can act as a mouth freshener, provided that it has been supplemented with some refreshing element.

In the same way, worry may help us keep our mind off a more important, and generally more difficult, task. But it does not help us solve any problem. It provides absolutely no nourishment, or meaningful benefit to our mind.

Life cannot remain idle. It demands some activity, every single moment. It prefers to go round and round, on a treadmill, rather than to remain sitting inactively. For a while, even a treadmill provides some exercise to the body, but beyond that it proves to be a sheer waste of time for the body, and dull and boring for the mind.

Chewing gum is good for a little while, but then it starts sapping energy for no concrete result.

Worry, or thinking in circles, is helpful provided that it is limited and is used as a tension producing mechanism. But we must learn to get off the treadmill of worry and to use the same time and energy in thinking something more constructive.

Our mind must be used every second, twenty-four hours a day. If we fail to use it for some definite purpose, it picks up the first thought that it encounters, and then wanders along that direction. If we do not consciously control its direction, it generally starts going in circles.

We have a great deal of control over the activity of our mind. But if we have not exercised this control for a long time, then taking back that control would require conscious effort and time.

It is impossible to throw away a thought from our mind. We cannot create a vacuum there. Jesus said that if you try to remove one evil from your mind soon you will find nine others in its place. The only way to get rid of one evil thought is to replace it with some other good one.

It is said that an idle mind is an evil's workshop. Our main challenge lies in keeping it occupied with the right thoughts.

There are two distinct ways of keeping our mind occupied constructively. One is to keep ourselves occupied in some physical activity - any activity, including the chewing, but preferably in an activity which is productive.

While our hands and feet are busy, our mind must pay attention to their activities. During those moments it cannot find the time to worry.

The other method is to suspend all physical activities and to focus the mind, deliberately and consciously, on one simple but calming thought. Meditation, progressive relaxation, visualization etc. can be used.

A simple thought such as "I like myself", "Thank you, Lord", "I am glad to be alive", "I am at peace" or "I am surrounded by love and beauty" can calm the mind and keep the worry thought out.

There are two physical phenomena, namely seeing and breathing, which deserve special mention here.

The external signals coming from our five senses stimulate our mind. These stimulations aggravate our mind if it has already been worrying. Cutting down the amount of these external signals can reduce our worry proportionately.

It is estimated that about seventy per cent of all external sensory signals find their way through our eyes. Thus, by simply shutting off our eyes and keeping them closed for a moment, we can remove some of the worry thoughts almost instantly. If you doubt the power of this simple activity, I ask you to try it whenever you catch yourself worrying.

If sight-stimulus acts like the fuel to the fire of worry, breathing acts like the supply of oxygen reaching the fire. Any reduction in the amount of the oxygen can cut down the intensity of the fire and may even extinguish it. Try consciously to slow down the rate of your breathing and notice a significant drop in your worrying.

It is suggested that we rehearse the fire escape before the onset of an actual fire. In the same way, we should rehearse replacing our worry thoughts by some peaceful thoughts, before the arrival of an emergency. Take a few moments every day, preferably two or three times during the day, to sit down comfortably and to breathe slowly with your eyes closed. Those few moments will boost the battery of your life and enable you to successfully combat the struggles of the rest of the day.

Worrying is an insidious disease. We have become so used to it that we are unable to detect its presence. Let me suggest a simple game.

On the back of a business card, or any small card, write the word CYT, (which stands for, 'Check Your Thought'), and put it in a place where you can see it occasionally. Whenever you happen to glance at it, ask yourself, 'What am I thinking at this moment?' You will be amazed, how often you would find yourself worrying.

This simple game can enhance your awareness of the influence of worry on your life and can help you in getting rid of it.

Keep reminding yourself that worry is the chewing gum of the mind. It's all right to chew for a few moments, but foolish to substitute it for regular meals.

> "When I look back on all these worries, I remember the story of the old man who said, on his death bed, that he had a lot of trouble in his life, most of which never happened."
> - Sir Winston Churchill

8 2

Death   Means

Going   Out   of   Sight

This essay pays tribute to the accidental death of eighteen year old Jason Catchpaugh.

What does death really mean? Jason passed away, but his memory and his influence will stay with us for a long time. In some respect his life is influencing us more now than it did before.

This essay suggests that life really means making some contribution to society. Since we can keep making some useful contribution, even after the end of our bodily life, death does not mean that we are finished and forgotten.

Death simply means going out of sight.

Read also essay number 88.

In the last eight months, I have attended the funerals of three persons who were very close to me and whose death was a complete surprise.

Last October, Gurmit Rai, the Chemistry teacher at Salisbury High School, passed away at the age of fifty-two. He was in perfect health, exercised regularly, coached badminton and had revealed no sign of any illness, until the moment of his death.

A few weeks ago, George Rossborough, the General Manager and Past-President of the Sherwood Park Chamber of Commerce, died. He had successfully quit smoking last Fall. He might have been under stress but no one had noticed it. He had just finished a nice supper, in the company of his loved ones, and had dozed off, as usual, in an easy chair, when he suffered a fatal heart attack. He was sixty-two years old.

A few days ago, Jason Catchpaugh died in an automobile accident. The weather conditions at the time were ideal. Jason was a mature, responsible citizen. He was of sound body and mind. He had just been sworn in as a member of the Canadian Military Police. He was only eighteen years old.

My youngest sister died two years ago of a sudden, minor illness. Since it was "minor", the illness had been ignored, until it became uncontrollable. She was twenty-five years old.

There are thousands of examples of death's unexpected arrival. We hear about others, we talk about others, but we never think that it could happen to us.

Life is like a clock that has been wound once and no one knows when its hands will stop moving. When life is over, the clock remains the same in all respects, except that its winding has run out.

Sir William Osler, a great surgeon and philosopher, often said,'The best way to prepare for tomorrow is to live today superbly well'. Living superbly may mean different things to different people. I feel that it means carrying out our individual assigned tasks and enjoying life at the same time.

The two may appear to be contradictory, but in reality they are not. They complement each other extremely well. We experience true happiness only when we feel that we have been able to make some meaningful use of our life.

To play any game well, one must first learn the rules and limitations of that particular game. Life is a game with its own unique rules. During the course of the average life we learn some rules but don't learn others. Often God sends us a calamity or a misfortune to teach us a needed rule of life. Nothing happens without His will and everything is planned by Him for our ultimate good.

About twenty years ago, Art Linkletter's daughter Diane jumped out of her apartment balcony and died. It was later learned that she had been experimenting with drugs. She was sixteen years old, and the baby of the family.

For a while, Art was extremely bitter. Then one day Dr. Norman Vincent Peale called Art and discussed that God must have a reason for taking away Diane's life. As Art thought it over, he started seeing some light and direction. Soon he decided to dedicate his life to the teaching of the danger of drug abuse. Since Diane's death, Art has made more contribution to the welfare of mankind than he had done up to that incident. The world has become a safer place for teenagers to live, because of Diane Linkletter's death.

Jason's death is a tremendous loss for all of us, especially his immediate family. But like Diane, Jason's life has served mankind much more than what we may at first envision.

It is wrong to think that death means losing a person completely.

As a ship moves away, it disappears from the sight of those who watch it from the shore. But in reality the ship does not vanish. It just goes out of sight of those viewers.

Life is like that ship. It is constantly moving away, at some unknown speed. Different ships will disappear at different times from the sight of the viewers. But not one will truly vanish. It will still be there, somewhere beyond the horizon. Its influence will be felt by us as long as we live.

It is tragic, and extremely sad, to lose sight of our lovely ship. But it is unwise to cry over it forever. We must trust God's plan. We must get back to our individual, assigned, tasks. We should pray for the life that has gone beyond our sight, but we must not forget that the hands of the clock of our own life may stop at any time.

Life may be unfair, but we were not given any power in the bargain, when our life was being allotted to us. We accepted it unconditionally and must live it unconditionally too. In the game of life we are not to reason why; we are just to live every moment to the best of our ability.

Gurmit Rai, George Rossborough and Jason Catchpaugh are now not within our sight. But they have not left us entirely. Their souls, their spirits, are just around the corner. They will continue to influence our lives in the same way, and sometimes even more than if they were still living.

> "There is no sense in crying over spilt milk. Why bewail what is done and cannot be recalled."
>
>   - Sophocles

83

Dissatisfaction

Can Be Healthy

Do you sometimes feel dissatisfied with what you have, or with what you do? If so, you should consider yourself fortunate.

According to this essay, dissatisfaction is the mother of every single progress in our civilization. The more dissatisfied a person, the greater his motivation to act. The more he acts, the more he discovers his own capabilities. Only a mild dissatisfaction is harmful, because it lacks the power to move the person, and soon one loses whatever dissatisfaction one had before.

The essay points out that if you find yourself totally satisfied with everything around you, you may have lost your will to live.

Read also essay numbers 52 and 71.

There is not a day when we do not meet someone who is dissatisfied with something - his job, his relationships with family members or just the weather. Is it a misfortune to find oneself dissatisfied?

The answer depends upon the individual situation and the attitude of the person encountering the dissatisfaction.

In most cases, dissatisfaction is healthy and beneficial. Dissatisfaction has been the main cause of every progressive step in our civilization. The greater the degree of dissatisfaction, the faster has been the progress. When a person feels that he can no longer tolerate a certain condition, he is willing to move mountains in order to change it, and often comes up with a big invention.

The only exception is the case of mild dissatisfaction. When we encounter a condition that we feel we can tolerate, we do nothing to resolve it. Soon we get used to it. Bit by bit, we keep tolerating worse and worse conditions. In that way, a mild dissatisfaction is unhealthy and harmful to us.

Dissatisfaction is a positive sign of life. As long as we live, we will be dissatisfied with something. Only robots can be totally satisfied with what they have, or what they do.

Our mind craves for that which it does not possess. As soon as it possesses something, it loses interest in that. It continues to seek things outside its known frontiers. When you are satisfied with all that you have, you have actually lost your will to live.

A young person is energetic and ambitious. He loves to go for higher stakes, ignoring anything that creates mild dissatisfaction. As he grows old, he seems to lose his drive and gives up many of his ambitions. To fulfil his need of dissatisfaction, he becomes annoyed with little things like the weather, or petty communication problems with the people around him. In that way, he scatters his life-force and gains nothing in return.

Being dissatisfied with the weather is futile. The weather will not listen to our complaints. It will keep on doing what it wants to do. Complaining about the weather is like a dog barking at the moon.

No weather is all bad. Every type of weather is beneficial for someone. When we complain about the weather, we simply prove that we are being ridiculously selfish.

If you want to save your life force for constructive works, refuse to complain about the weather. Nature can be controlled only by obeying it. Obey it by accepting what comes and control it by making the best use of it. It's like playing Martial arts - you don't fight the momentum of your opponent, you just redirect it and take advantage of that momentum.

Being dissatisfied with another person is generally futile too. Every person is unique. It is impossible to find another with the exact likes and dislikes as you. God put us with dissimilar persons so we could learn tolerance. If we cannot learn to adjust within our petty differences, how can we adjust ourselves with Nature?

The people around us keep changing all the time. With the exception of your spouse, no one is going to stay with you for long. Then why not tolerate some differences for the little sojourn together and enjoy life?

You may say that not all differences or dissatisfactions are really little. Well, it's just a matter of perspective. If you separate your bias, your unnecessary feelings, and start seeing things from the other person's point of view, you will find the difference to be much smaller.

It is normal to feel miserable about our own conditions but let's remember that every alive person occasionally feels miserable. If you were to compare your conditions with that of every other person on the planet, you would feel ashamed to even mention yours.

After a certain exam, I was feeling extremely miserable. I was literally crying. Soon a number of students joined me. Everyone was complaining about how badly he had done. Suddenly I lost my control and cried, "Now I don't think I have any chance of earning the distinction."

There was a lull. My sympathizers were concerned about passing that subject, while I was concerned about losing the top positions. Our problems are relative.

If you feel miserable about your job, or your financial position, think of the people in Argentina. The government is on the verge of raising the gasoline price by five hundred per cent. A similar raise is expected on a number of other basic commodities!

In India gasoline is one dollar a litre and that is the average daily wage of about one fourth of Indians!

If you find yourself to be dissatisfied, know that you are alive and kicking. If that does not help you, I suggest that you go to any public library, browse through different newspapers and learn a bit about the living conditions in the other parts of the world. You may be complaining about your worn out shoe, but there are millions who would like to grab yours.

"A gem cannot be polished without friction,
nor a man perfected without trials."
                                    - Chinese proverb

84

Nothing Happens
"All Of A Sudden"

Do you sometimes find yourself caught by surprise?

According to this essay, no crisis in life comes all of a sudden. Through a variety of signals, each crisis gives us ample warning. But unfortunately we either overlook, or ignore those signals.

This essay discusses the need, and some ways, of enhancing our awareness, so we could notice, and understand, those signals readily.

Read also essay numbers 76 and 86.

W ithin two weeks of the fatal accident of Jason Catchpaugh Alberta Transportation came up with some ideas for improving the traffic flow at the intersection of Highway 14 and 23rd Street. Traffic ,problems resulting in accidents had been noticed at that intersection for almost seven years. Why hadn't someone suggested the improvement before? Does it take the loss of a life to move the government?

The intersections of Highway 21 and Wye Road, and Highway 21 and Baseline also had many accidents. The government decided to install traffic lights on those intersections only after there had been some fatal accident!

Most traffic developments have taken place following the incident of some loss of life. Why is it so? The department employs "experts". It has access to every Accident Enquiry Report. It can get reports of similar problems and their eventual solutions in other provinces, states or countries. They have computer programs to predict trends. Still they wait for the final trigger; a fatal accident.

Nothing happens "all of a sudden". No crisis occurs "all of a sudden". Every crisis develops gradually and keeps giving ample signals of its onset. If we are awake and willing to observe those signals, we would have plenty of time to take preventive measures and save the loss in most cases.

The gas tank in our car never runs dry "all of a sudden". The gauge keeps showing the gradual drop in the gasoline level. In most cars the reserve light comes on to give us ample warning. But does that mean that we never run dry?

A few years ago, I was returning from Calgary. My gas tank level was low. Near Ponoka the reserve light came on, but I "knew" that I could still reach Edmonton. As we approached Leduc, my wife suggested that we pull out and fill up, but I thought that to be a pure waste of time. Two miles past Leduc, the tank ran dry. I ended up walking back to Leduc for the gas.

Our body is a good example. In a variety of forms it gives us signals of any upcoming sickness. But in most cases, we either fail to observe those signals, or decide to ignore them, because they are too insignificant   to be bothered with.

Mild   fever, mild headache, some loss of sleep, burps, gas, unusual sweating, itching, slight pain in some parts of the body, are the little   signals. Many serious diseases occur, simply because some similar little   signals are not observed in time.

But why have we lost our power of observation?

Anything that we fail to use, we lose. We are so inundated by external suggestions that we have little   need for using our own senses. We hear and notice only that which we are told or shown by the media.

Did you watch the televised federal debate of the leaders of the three political parties, in October, 1988?   Even if you did watch every second of that three hour debate, you were not expected to understand what the candidates had said, because immediately following the debate, a team of "experts" came to tell you what each candidate had actually said! In some respect, they tainted your original observation, did they not?

In the Bible there is a story that once the Lord   gave one virtue to one of His men, two virtues to another and four virtues to a third one. Some time later, He called these three men and asked what they had done with their respective virtues.

The one who had two virtues said that he had used them and thus turned them into four. The one who had four virtues said that he also had used his   and had turned them into eight. But the one who had only one virtue to start with did not feel like parting with his. So he just saved it   and still   had only one virtue. The Lord became very angry with him and decided to take away   even the one that he had This is a universal law. We always lose that which we fail to use.

To revive our senses we need to recognize the   external stimuli which are killing them. Any stimulus which does not help enhance our senses, hurts us. One of the greatest killers is noise. It is   like a weed. It chokes our senses. It prevents them from growing.

If you want to test the impact of noise, try isolating yourself from all kinds of sound for a period of thirty to forty minutes. You will experience a tickling feeling. Some of your sensory nerves, which have almost been atrophied, will start getting rejuvenated.

We have allowed our life to become unnecessarily too fast. We need to slow down. We need to take time to cultivate our lost senses, so as to be able to listen and to observe the little signals within and around us. On the surface we seem to do it, but in depth I think that we are missing the mark.

I know several people who go camping with a portable television. Of course they always carry their stereo and their walkman. To me that is not going away to the country.

"There are no tragedies,
just facts not recognized in time."
- William D. Montapert

85

Keep Counting Your Blessings

Would you like to have a few more blessings? According to this essay, to have more blessings, you should pay more attention to the blessings that you already possess, because what we pay attention to, grows.

If you feel that you do not have any blessings that you could count, this essay suggests that you may not be looking in the right places. For example, you may be overlooking your healthy body, a family, or your ability to sleep when you lie down. Without any doubt, you possess many more blessings than you are aware of. You generally find only that which you look for.

Read also essay numbers 46 and 95.

W e have many   more blessings than we think we have. We generally overlook most of them because we take them for granted and pay attention to only those things that we lack.

Do you remember a day when you were not feeling well - when you had a cold, an upset stomach or just a hangover? Can you recall how miserable you felt that day?   Did you go to see a doctor? How did you   get through the day? Perhaps   you can describe that day in great detail.

Now think of a day when you were not sick at all.   You may have some difficulty recalling such a day. Although we all have many healthy days, we   have difficulty recalling them. Why?

We treat the healthy days as normal and therefore pay little attention to them. For every hundred healthy days we may have one sick day, and yet   we focus all our attention on that one day. A similar situation exists in every facet of our life. We overlook all our blessings and ruminate over the few things that we lack.

Ten good deeds of a child will go unnoticed, but one wrong can hardly escape our attention. Ten good events may be overlooked, but one bad one will pester us all day and night.

The main trouble is that we attach little   value to what we already have and crave for what we lack. Unless we become sick,   good health appears to be of   little importance.

It is a known fact that we alienate ourselves from those things that we keep denouncing. We cannot attract riches as long as we keep cursing the rich people. The only way to attract riches is to praise riches, to admire those who have acquired it.

According to the law of the universe, we attract what we pay attention to, what we praise in our mind.

Some people feel that they have nothing to be thankful for. This is not true.   They have many riches, but they   have completely blinded themselves from   seeing what they already have.

Everything is relative. What may be riches for one may be just dirt for somebody else. But there is some richness even in dirt. Once we start being thankful for the "dirt", more valuable things start coming our way.

There is a   story of a farmer who faced drought after drought. But he never cursed nature. After every harvest he prayed, "Thank you Lord. You have at least returned our seeds." Think of that. He could have easily lost his seeds, his initial investment. But since his original investment had been returned year after year, he had the potential for harvesting a good crop.

How many of us thank the Lord for "returning at least our original investment"?

Riches are relative. When Mark Spitz returned from the Munich Olympics, he was a very frustrated athlete. He considered himself to be poor, because he returned with only two Gold Medals. Can you imagine someone returning from an Olympic Games with only two Gold Medals? Instead of cursing the Games, he expressed his gratitude for those two medals and resolved to win seven Gold Medals at the next Olympics. He did.

We have been blessed with a lot of riches in terms of our families, social conditions, educational facilities, communication systems etc. But since those are readily available, we attach almost no value to them.

Some people consider themselves unfortunate because they were born in the wrong family, wrong society, wrong time, wrong order etc. Let's briefly compare our average conditions with those of Abraham Lincoln and see how we fare.

Abraham Lincoln's mother was an illegitimate child. She was brought up by her uncle and aunt and was totally illiterate. At the age of twenty-two, she married a man who was not only totally illiterate but also savage in many ways. He built a shack - worse than that for any animal built today, in the bush. They had no bed, no door, no windows, no floor. They slept on leaves which were spread over logs. The nearest neighbour was half a mile away. These were the conditions under which Abraham Lincoln was born.

The Lincolns had no milk, no eggs, no chicken, no vegetables - not even potatoes. They ate what they could hunt. There was no doctor for miles. By the age of fifteen, Abraham Lincoln had learned the alphabets. He could read some, but he could not write. Then a priest came to the nearby village and started a "Blab" school. Lincoln had about twelve months of schooling there.

We are a million times better blessed than what Lincoln had been. Or is that a fair statement?

Some experts say that Lincoln became such a great President only because he had been brought up under such great hardships. If these experts are right, then even hardships should be treated as blessings.

It's not what we have that really matters. How we use what we already have makes all the difference in our life. The more we use what we have, the more we are going to increase the chances of being blessed with that which we lack at the moment.

Let's stop overlooking our blessings. Let's focus our attention on what we already have because that's the only way of getting more.

> "Always keep that happy attitude.
> Pretend that you are holding a
> beautiful fragrant bouquet."
> - Candice M. Pope

86

Don't Ignore "Common Sense" During Storms

Have you ever had the experience where the advice given by the media did not apply, or did not make sense, to your unique situation? If so, how did you feel?

This essay suggests that it is all right to take advantage of the service, and the advice provided by the media, especially during the time of crisis, but it may prove to be foolish to depend on it, or to remain glued to it, for every manoeuvre.

The essay draws our attention to some situations where it would be silly to depend upon the media. On such occasions our own common sense should be our best guide.Let's not ignore it.

This essay was written when a secon tornado, within two years hit Edmonton.

Read also essay numbers 34 and 84.

Two years ago Edmonton was hit by a tornado. Since that time we have become very conscious of tornadoes and the media has been playing a role in alerting us of any possible tornado formation. There have been several close calls but none a real threat. Some people even started taking the tornado alert as a joke.

But last week another tornado did hit the West End of the City. Luckily the damage was small compared to that of 1987.

Have we learned a lesson from the 1987 tornado? Why is it that so many people ignore the tornado warning?

I have found some advice to be ridiculous. For example, almost every television station suggested that their viewers go to their basement and stay there until the warning had been lifted. They also asked them to stay tuned to their channel. Do they assume that every viewer has a television set in the basement? Or, do they advise their viewers to move their set to the basement for the duration of the tornado alert?

Several stations, televisions as well as radio, advised their audience to move to a central room such as a bathroom which does not have an outside window, and to stay there until advised. Is it practical to crowd a whole family inside a windowless room for a couple of hours?

I also feel that the media oversteps its jurisdiction. Its role is to alert the public, not to run their lives. Their approach appears to claim that they, and only they, can save the life of their audience. They treat them as robots, having no brain of their own, waiting for the next instruction. They talk like the pilot, "Sit back, relax and let me take care of the plane and your life."

While one is flying, it is sensible to let the pilot control the plane. But once the plane is on the ground, we are totally responsible for our actions (or lack of actions). If we get hurt, we cannot sue a particular station, just because we were tuned in and waiting for the next instruction.

The media advised those on the road, to get out of their car, go to the nearest ditch, and to hang on to a tree etc., (until the time that they heard from the station). Isn't that ridiculous? They did not advise them to use their own senses and to check if the danger was over. They expected every one on the road to be equipped with a walkman!!

During the alert my daughter was working at MacDonald's. I tried to call her but the telephone line was dead. Against the advice of the media, I got out of the house. As I drove, I found many cars on the road, and not one person in any ditch. When I reached MacDonald's, it was pouring so heavily that I sat inside my car - again, contrary to the advice of the media - for nearly twenty minutes. Finally, I went inside and discovered that my daughter was not free to go home. She was working at the drive through which was extremely busy.

I asked her if she had heard of the tornado warning. She told me that every fifteen minutes she was being updated, but she was too busy to worry about it. Imagine, someone serving an endless line of cars, at a window, while the media was advising people to stay as far away from windows as possible!

As far as a tornado is concerned, I don't believe that ignorance is bliss. During the 1987 tornado I was extremely lucky to have escaped injury. I was driving parallel to the path of the tornado and was not even aware of it. My car sustained hail damage worth over two thousand dollars, while I was busy talking to my friends in the car.

I believe that the media is doing a marvellous job of alerting and teaching us tornado safety. But we should not give up our own responsibility. The media alert should be used only as a guideline and we should supplement it with our own common sense. There is a time lag between an occurrence and its reporting by the media. In addition, the weather radar generally covers a broad area. It cannot accurately predict what could happen over one house or a car. During the 1987 tornado, the Ostrem Chemical building was badly damaged, while the Alberta Glass building, only a hundred yards away, was not affected at all.

Nothing happens all of a sudden. Even a tornado takes a few minutes to develop. If we use our own senses, and remain alert to the changes in conditions around us, we can sense the actual touch down of a tornado near us. We should use the media alert to perk up our own ears and eyes. We may notice such a thing as a dark funnel cloud moving towards us, a sudden increase in the debris flying around or a sharp increase in the wind around our location.

If we know what to do in different situations, even a one minute warning can be plenty to take the necessary action. We can rush to our basement, to a central room without windows, or get out of our car and run to the nearest ditch. But we must learn to depend on ourselves and not on the media to tell us when we should start running for the shelter.The ultimate responsibility rests on us and we can hone this skill only by exercising it.

Life and death are controlled by God. Our duty is only to perform our tasks to the best of our ability. We can enjoy our life to the fullest, only by performing our duty, by not depending totally on the media, but by assuming our own responsibilities of using our senses and the common sense that the Lord has blessed us with.

"I sometimes wish that people would put a little more emphasis on the observance of the law than they do upon its enforcement."
                                             - Calvin Coolidge

87

Barefoot

From Africa To America?

Here is the story of a young African boy who dreamed of going to America, for his college education. He had no idea where America was. He was too poor to even buy a pair of shoes.

With nothing but his dream in his heart, he started walking barefoot to America. In two years he walked about two thousand five hundred miles. Moved by his determination and perseverance, other people started helping him and he did reach America.

Is your dream loftier than his? You can realize your dream, if you possess half as much determination and persistence, as he did.

Read also essay number 2.

A mong all the stories that I have read about the extraordinary achievement by ordinary people, the one of Legson Kayira has touched my heart the most. Kayira, a teenage boy, living in a tiny village of Nyasaland, East Africa, dreamed of going to the United States, even though he did not know how far, or in which direction, the United States was. He had no one to guide him. He had no map. His only resource was his belief that his dream would come true. This story appeared in "Guide Post", a monthly magazine published by Dr. Norman Vincent Peale. Here is the story in brief.

One day Legson Kayira told his mother, "I want to go to America to go to college. Will you give me your permission?"

She gave him the permission and prepared some maize for him to eat on the way. She had no idea how far America was. Even the boy did not know. All that he knew was that "it was far".

The next day he left home wearing his khaki shirt and shorts. He carried the only treasures that he owned: a Bible and a copy of Pilgrim's Progress. He also carried the maize, wrapped in banana leaves, that his mother had given him.

He had no idea how old he was. Such things meant little in a land where time was always the same. He was between sixteen and eighteen years old. His father had died, when he was very young. From the local missionaries he had learned about America and a little about the life of Abraham Lincoln. He had also read the biography of Brooker T. Washington, who had been born a slave and who had risen in dignity and honour to become a benefactor of his people and his country.

His intention was to make his way to Cairo where he hoped to get passage to America. Cairo was three thousand miles away, a distance that he could not comprehend. He thought that he could walk this distance in four or five days. But in four or five days he had covered only about twenty-five miles. His food was gone. He had no money.

But he would not give up his dream. He decided to walk as long as it took him to reach Cairo.

He developed a pattern for his travelling. Villages were about five or six miles apart, on forest paths. He would walk to the next village reaching there in the afternoon and would ask if he could work to earn food, water and a place to sleep. When this was possible, he would spend the night there then move on to the next village, early in the morning. Occasionally he encountered some wild animals but they did not bother him. He was occasionally sick with malaria, but resumed his walk as soon as he was well enough.

By the end of a year he had walked one thousand miles and had reached Uganda, where a family took him in and gave him a job of making bricks. He stayed there for about six months and sent most of his earnings to his mother.

In Kampala, the capital of Uganda, he unexpectedly came across a directory of American universities. Opening it at random, he saw the name of Skagit Valley College, Mount Vernon, Washington. Having heard that American universities sometimes gave scholarships to deserving young students, he wrote and applied for one.

He was granted a scholarship and assured that the college would help him find a job. Overjoyed, he went to the United States authorities who asked for his passport and the round trip fare in order to give him the visa.

He wrote to his government for a passport, but the request was refused because he could not tell them when he was born. Then he wrote to the missionaries, who had taught him during his childhood. With their effort he was granted a passport. But he still could not get the visa, because he did not have the fare.

He then resumed his walk. His faith was so strong that he spent his last money to buy a pair of shoes which he would wear when he would reach the college of his dream. He carried the shoes, to preserve them, and continued his barefoot walk.

When he reached Sudan, he found the villages to be farther apart and the people to be less friendly. Sometimes he had to walk twenty or thirty miles in a day to find a place to sleep, or to work to earn his food. At last he reached Khartoum, where he went to see the American Consulate.

Being highly impressed by his story, the Consulate wrote to the college asking if they could pay for his fare. The students of Skagit Valley College, after hearing the plight of this boy, raised seventeen hundred dollars for his fare and so he obtained the visa.

He had walked for over two years and covered a distance of about two thousand five hundred miles, on barefoot.

We often hear about someone having an unrealistic dream. In many instances we become our own worst enemy by telling ourselves that what we want is unrealistic. But what can be more unrealistic than for an African teen-age boy, living in one of the most underdeveloped villages of the world, to dream of going to America, by walking. He was aware of the vastness of the Atlantic ocean that separated his country from America, but he had no idea of the vast land mass that he also needed to cover.

He later became a Professor of Political Science at Cambridge University, England. He authored a novel, "The Looming Shadow" and a nonfiction book based on African life.

It has been claimed that nothing is really impossible. I do not know if I can make the same statement. I have no qualms however, in saying that what we feel to be impossible is far less impossible that we believe it to be.

> "Every great achievement is the story of a flaming heart."
>
> - Ralph Waldo Emerson

88

Life Is

Like A Train Journey

Using the simile of a train journey, this essay describes how some people come in, while others move out, of our lives.

Since every person must pursue his or her own journey, we must learn to ultimately depend upon ourselves. We have little awareness of where the journey started and have no knowledge of when it will terminate. Our task is to make the best use of each single moment.

Read also essay numbers 32 and 82.

L ife is like a journey on a train. Every one of us is riding a separate train, running on its own track and at its own speed.

During our journey we come close to some other trains whose tracks seem to be almost touching ours. If two nearby trains happen to be travelling at almost the same speed, we get the illusion that the passengers of the other trains are actually riding on our own train. But after a while, owing to the different tracks and the different speeds, those passengers move away from us. But failing to understand the true reason, we feel frustrated, and often depressed.

Life is dynamic. There are no two identical days, hours or minutes. Everything is in a constant state of change. The speed, the track, and even the direction of the train, is changing from moment to moment. This is the main reason why we discover that some of our dearest friends suddenly move out of our life.

We board the train of our life at birth, at which time we have almost no consciousness. When we do gain the consciousness, we are so used to the ride that we fail to notice it. Death marks the termination, in this world, of the journey of the particular person.

The people around us are simply fellow travellers. They are on their own journeys. For a while they may stay with us but sooner or later they leave us, because their journeys are different.

Our first fellow passengers are the members of the family in which we are born. Then we get some friends, colleagues, neighbours etc. After our marriage we generally have a little family of our own. But each person, irrespective of the way that he or she comes into our life, is similar to a fellow passenger, who may ride very closely, but will not stay with us throughout our journey. This is a law of life. We must be willing and ready to separate from others, often at a very short notice.

Some passengers, who separate from us today, may rejoin us some other day, but many never meet again. Those whose journey has terminated simply cannot meet again. But there are some who do not meet because of the difference in their tracks and speed.

We mourn the separation from some fellow riders because we cannot see why his or her journey has suddenly ended. We think that we are wise and knowledgeable, and therefore should know when the purpose of one's life has been fulfilled. But in reality we are just pawns in the overall game of God's plan.

We believe that we give birth, or that we have the capability of giving birth, but we only play an instrumental part in the process. When it comes to giving or taking away life, we are but a puppet in the hands of God.

Man thinks that he has acquired tremendous knowledge. He feels that he can control his environment. To some extent this is true. It is a miracle that man has been able to obtain pictures and other information about the planets and stars which are billions of miles away. But then he also finds that he has still to learn and to grow. He is terrified by the powers of a tornado,a hurricane or many similar acts of nature.

No matter how much science advances, man will never be able to create life. But for Nature this appears to be an extremely easy job. Just see how easily weeds grow out of some tiny cracks within a driveway or a sidewalk. It is fascinating how mosquitoes survive the harsh winter and the annual efforts of man to eradicate them.

We never had, and we will never have, control over life and death. This is totally in God's hands. We have to be thankful to Him for whatever He grants us. Our task is to make the best use of every single moment that we are alive.

Some people think that they perform favours for others, especially for their own children. In reality everyone is responsible for their own favours. What we sow, we reap ourselves. If we do good deeds, we reap some good rewards and vice-versa.

It is a myth to measure the value of a life by its length. Perhaps we do so to console ourselves that we still have time to make some contribution. But who knows when the hands of the clock of life will stop moving?

Life is like a train journey. We are responsible for our own journey. The people around us are busy caring for their own journeys. We can use their companionship to enhance the pleasure, or to lessen the burden, of our journey, but we cannot and should not abdicate our own responsibility.

Every journey has a beginning and an end.It is all right to briefly grieve the loss of some company, but we should not allow that to cloud our mind to such an extent that we forget our own task. We should carry the memory of the departed fellow passengers, but should not allow it to overshadow, or darken the train of our own journey.

It is nice to help our neighbours clean their yard, but it is unwise to let our own house run down at the same time.

> "Finish each day and be done with it. You have done what you could. Some blunders and absurdities no doubt crept in; forget them as soon as you can. Tomorrow is a new day; begin it well and serenely and with too high a spirit to be encumbered with your old nonsense."
> - Ralph Waldo Emerson

89

Exercise

Your "Power to Choose"

How much control do you feel you have on your life?

This essay suggests that you have far more freedom to choose the course of your life, than you may be aware.

The essay further suggests that by becoming aware of, and exercising, your "power to choose", you can increase your control over your own life, and that choosing proper affirmations, and appropriate role models, also helps a great deal.

The essay draws our attention to the fact that at every single moment we are making choices, and we are free, to a large extent, to choose what we like and that this is the road to lasting happiness.

Read also essay number 17.

E veryone craves happiness and is relentlessly working to acquire it. But unfortunately very few people seem to know the path to happiness.

Thinking that another fellow is happy, we copy his methods. However, soon we discover that what we thought to be happiness was only an illusion. We then look for some other, happier, person. The process goes on and we generally reach the end of our life without finding the happiness.

Recently I saw a weak man outfight a mighty bull. The bull kept charging a red cloth and the man simply moved it slightly, just before the bull could strike it. Soon the bull was totally exhausted. The man then walked close to the bull, but it withdrew and walked backwards, away from the red cloth and the man, and fell to the ground.

Not everyone goes after happiness as the bull goes for a red cloth. Many feel that they lack the necessary strength to even get into the game. Among the few who do participate, a great majority end up like that bull, exhausted and having accomplished nothing.

But what is the solution to this problem?

The first step is to find the right path.

There is a story that one day a country lady visited a nearby city. At one place she needed to cross a busy street. Having never seen such fast traffic, she was terrified and therefore hesitated for a long time Finally a man came near her and said, "Do you mind if I cross the street with you?" She was relieved and felt that God had finally answered her prayer.

The man held her hand and started walking across. Traffic was coming from every direction. Some drivers honked, some screamed and others stopped with terrible screeches. Several times the two pedestrians had to stop completely, but slowly they continued.

When they reached the other side, the lady said, "You almost got us killed. The way you were walking it seemed that you were blind." The man replied, "Lady, I am blind. That is why I needed to cross the street with somebody."

This story has a parallel in our daily life. Assuming that the other fellow is more knowledgeable and competent, we seek his guidance, instead of exercising our own faculty.

For lasting happiness we must have a feeling of control over our own life.

It is rare to have total control over one's life. Living in a social environment we must subjugate some of our controls for the overall good of the community. But we have much more control than what we believe, or are aware of. The degree of our happiness is directly proportional to the degree of our feeling of having control over our life's affairs.

The average person finds more than eighty percent of his or her activities to be of an obligatory nature. If you doubt this number, just pay attention to the frequency of the use of the phrase, "I have to". This phrase gives one the feeling that his life is controlled by some outside condition or force.This creates a psychological drain on his system and saps his inner strength.

The opposite of "I have to" is "I want to", which implies a sense of power. The "I want to" feeling revitalizes us. It recharges the battery of our life.

If you can reduce the number of your "have to" activities by just ten per cent, you will experience a surge of energy that you would not believe. This is equivalent to removing a twenty-five pound load from the back of a marathon runner.

There are several ways of getting rid of the "have to" activities. One technique, which has been described in essay number 17, is to amend the "have to" activity in such a way that it turns out to be a "want to" activity. Another technique is to replace the "have to" with "choose to".

God has given us full freedom in choosing what we like to do. In fact, every single action of yours is ultimately your own choosing. You may feel morally or socially obliged to act in a certain way, but whether or not you obey it, is your own choice. There are few instances when you truly act against your own choosing. Often we use our social or moral obligation as a cop-out for doing what we ourselves like to do.

For the next few days pay attention to the phrase "I have to" and replace it with "I choose to". Saying "I choose to", is tantamount to expressing that you have the control.

You can use this even when you are not engaged in something fruitful. If you are watching a soap opera, just tell yourself, "I choose to watch this program for the next hour or so." The important thing is to maintain awareness that you are in control.

We were born with the ability of having a great deal of control over our life. We have lost it because we have failed to exercise it. By continually telling ourselves that we have to live the way that we are living, we have made ourselves the miserable beings that we are today. We can change this and regain control over ourselves. From now, instead of saying, "I have to" say , "I choose to".

According to the law of inertia, once a wheel starts rolling, it gains momentum. Using this system you can slowly and positively attain real happiness in your life.

> "Man's power of choice enables him to think like an angel or a devil, a king or a slave. Whatever he chooses, mind will create and manifest."
>
> - Frederick Bailes

90

Young And Old,
Go Back To School

Do you feel that you are too old to go back to school?

This essay suggests that no one is too old to go back to school. In fact, by going back to school you can rejuvenate yourself and thereby cut down some of your aging.

This essay discusses the formal and informal types of learning and advises us to keep our mind stimulatedand active.

You either move up or slide down. As long as you keep learning, you keep moving up. But the moment you stop learning, you start sliding down.

Read also essay numbers 18, 22 and 44.

September is the traditional time for going back to school. While some students dread it, others look forward to it as a new and exciting experience.

There are two kinds of learning. One is formal in which we enrol ourselves in some kind of a structured program. The other is informal in which we learn something at our own speed and with our own interest.

Although "Going Back to School" connotes joining a formal learning program, it does not exclude joining other programs where we may learn some craft or trade.

Life demands that we keep learning. When we learn we grow. When we stop learning, we stop growing. We start slipping or moving towards our death. There is no middle ground. We either move forward or slide backward.

A lady was once given a rocking chair as a gift on her seventieth birthday. She declined to accept the gift, saying that she could not use it because she did not have the time for rocking. Through her years she had learned that the only way to maintain life was to keep busy by learning something new.

There is a story of a girl who had been ill for a long time. Everyone, including her doctors, had given up hope of her ever leaving the hospital. Rumours spread that she was to die within weeks. At that moment, one of her relatives presented her a beautiful dress and said, "I made this dress specially for you to wear on your first day of school." The girl was very delighted and looked forward to the day when she could wear that dress. Within a short time she recovered enough to go to school. Of course, she wore the special dress on her first day. As she became occupied in learning new things at the school, she recovered more and more and soon was fully cured.

We experience new vitality only when we are absorbed in learning something new.

Some of us feel that our main duty is to be the background support for our school-going children, grandchildren, nephews etc. This is not true. We may have some obligations to our family members, but we cannot abdicate our responsibility to ourselves. No one can perform a task which is ours. No one can learn or grow for us.

We can best serve others by making ourselves better human beings. We can accomplish this through increased knowledge, skill and wisdom. If our example is worth emulating, others will copy us to the degree that they find it valuable. It is only in this way that we can provide a lasting and valuable service to others. We should direct at least ten per cent of our life towards our personal development by learning and thereby growing mentally and spiritually. One hour every day, devoted to growing and developing, is the bare minimum. It is necessary for our survival.

Some people consider themselves to be too old to go back to school. Well, anyone who has not gone to school for some time is definitely getting old, not because of his age, but because he has let himself grow old by neglecting to keep his mind active and sharp.

Some people feel that they have learned enough and that there is nothing more worth learning. I earned my Ph.D. degree seventeen years ago and yet I do not remember one week, when I did not feel the urge to learn something even more important. The more I learn the more I realize how little I know.

Going back to school does not only mean taking up new courses. You can learn a great deal by teaching others what you know. In the process of trying to teach others, you learn how people learn. This itself is a fascinating lesson. You also learn many facets of the subject or the skill that you had previously overlooked. Each mind has its own way of looking at things. Every interaction with some other mind creates some new growth in us.

Unfortunately the vast majority of us believe that we do not know anything worth teaching.In one survey people were asked to rank themselves as below average, average or above average. It was found that about ninety-five per cent of the people surveyed considered themselves to be below average.

Isn't that shocking? Mathematically only fifty per cent could fall below the average line!

You have more skills than you are aware of. You possess more gems than you give yourself credit for. Don't hide your gem. Take it out and display it with pride. No one can rob it from you. On the contrary, the more you display it, the shinier it will become, because what we use, grows.

Weeks, months and years will pass either way. If you do not employ them in some premeditated learning by going back to school you will waste them in other less fruitful activities such as sitting in front of the tube. I realize that life should not be all work, but squandering all our time is equivalent to writing our life off.

Wisdom lies in not spending any time repenting over what we did not do yesterday, but on taking charge of this day. Let's join our young ones in going back to school.

"The minute a man ceases to grow,
no matter what his years,
that minute he begins to be old."
- William James

91

Today's Trails Will Make Tomorrow's Roads

Have you ever thought about the origin of most of the current roads?

According to this essay, the origin of most of our current roads lies in the trails used by animals, especially cows and horses. Primitive men followed animal trails. As civilization progressed, the trails that were used more widened and ended up becoming the paved roads.

The essay suggests that our character or personality is formed in a similar way. What appears to be a casual thought (a casual footstep) today, may turn out to be the root of our character (the paved road) tomorrow. Therefore, we should be extremely vigilant about the thoughts that we entertain today.

Read also essay number 4.

H ave you given some thought to the development of the roads around your neighbourhood? If you trace diligently, you will find that the starting point of every road has been some simple footsteps taken by animals and later followed by primitive men. These men had absolutely no idea of the importance that their casual steps would gain over time.

The very land on which we live today was roamed by wild animals only a few centuries ago. In fact, man himself, in those days, wandered around like Gypsies. The animals, as well as men, moved from place to place in search of food, water and protection from enemies and bad weather. Their instinct was their only guide. In most cases they gathered around some source of water, such as rivers, lakes or seashores.

Since water can accumulate only at a spot which is surrounded by some high grounds, the gathering place almost always included hills or mountains. To move towards and away from the source of the water, the animals advanced one foot in a direction that appeared to be the easiest to walk, and which offered the least danger to their survival. Thus, using their instinct and repeating the same process for every step, they discovered, generally through a series of trials and errors, a safe trail for themselves.

Primitive men followed the animal trails. Slowly, through repeated use, those trails became more prominent. When they settled down, they used those trails as their guides for building roads.

It should be noted that everything in nature follows the path of least resistance. Rivers and streams appear to be crooked, but every inch of their way has followed the path of least resistance.

Every time I pass through the Rockies I marvel at the lay out of the roads and the railway tracks. Whenever I have asked some experts, they have given me the same answer, "We followed the Indians' trails". But how did the Indians discover those trails? The answer is, "They followed the animals' trails".

So it is.   Yesterday's trails have led to today's roads and highways.   Even the impressive Trans-Canada Highway was developed using the process of combining numerous little trails, each of which might have looked ridiculously simple and unimportant.

If yesterday's trails were responsible for today's roads and highways, then today's trails should   contribute towards the building of tomorrow's roads and highways. This means that we are carrying an important responsibility. We must ensure that we leave the right trails to guide future generations in building their efficient roadways.

There is a striking parallel between the building of the highways and the formation of a personality. If the origin of every highway lies in some casual tiny steps, the seed of every personality lies in some casual thoughts that roam in the mind of that personality. One tiny step may appear to be of little significance, but the same tiny step, repeated many times, can leave a lasting impression.

Our personality has been formed by many simple, single thoughts that have wandered into the atlas of our mind. We also follow the path of least resistance. We repeat familiar thoughts. We fear that new thoughts may require more energy or that they may take us to new, unfamiliar and possibly dangerous grounds.

Repeated use of any thought creates some kind of a trail in our mind. Some of those trails do not survive long. But others keep taking stronger shape with time. Our total personality may be compared to a set of thought-highways, going criss-cross through the atlas of our mind.

The knowledge that, through our thoughts, we have been the creator of our own personality, may be nerve wracking, but it is indisputable. By letting our thoughts run smock we create a poor personality, of little   help to our community. On the other hand, if we want, we can assume control over our thoughts and employ them to build a powerful personality which can move mountains.

Let's increase our awareness of the role that our thoughts play in controlling our lives. Let's pay attention to the thoughts that roam through our mind. A thought that looks tiny, casual or of little significance, may, like the casual steps of those wandering animals, prove to be an important brick in the final mansion of our personality, and therefore of our life.

Remember, the quality of a final product depends upon the quality of its ingredients. Therefore, let's pay some attention to the quality of thoughts that we are entertaining today. We cannot transform ourselves overnight. But we can initiate the thousand-mile march by taking our first step at this very moment. Let's move right now and think a nice, healthy thought, which may prove to be the gateway to the Supreme Personality.

"Every revolution was first a thought in one man's mind."
- Ralph Waldo Emerson

92

What Made Terry Fox
A Hero?

> *This essay was written on the occasion of the annual Terry Fox Run Day. It provides a brief account of how the Terry Fox Run started and which factors raised him to the status of a national hero.*
>
> *This essay suggests that the loss of Terry's leg was the main driving force behind all his accomplishments, and that only an adversity can propel a person towards some greatness.*
>
> *Rather than shying away from our own adversity, we should accept it and combat it so as to rise to a higher level.*
>
> *Read also essay numbers 1, 51, 63 and 100.*

This week, across Canada, we are celebrating the Terry Fox run. Let's take a moment to review who Terry Fox was. Where did he come from, how did he become the man that he became and how did the Terry Fox run start?

On April 12, 1980, Terry Fox, the one-legged man, started a "Marathon of Hope" run across Canada. By the end of August, when he was just a few miles away from Thunder Bay, he had to stop because he was unable to breathe normally. By that time he had run 3339 miles and raised 1.7 million dollars for the Cancer Research Fund.

Terry was flown to Vancouver. The doctors diagnosed that his cancer had spread to his lung.

While Terry was fighting with his cancer, the rest of Canada was praying for his recovery and feeling sorry that, although the Fund Raising had gained momentum, Terry was far shy of his goal of 22 million dollars, one dollar for each Canadian.

Suddenly CTV came up with an idea. Within 48 hours, on Sunday, September 9, 1980, they organized a four hour telethon and raised a total of 10.5 million dollars.

On the next anniversary, a Terry Fox Run Day was organized across Canada which raised 3.2 million dollars and a similar one in September, 1982 raised 2.3 million dollars. The annual one day fund raising, through sponsorship running, has been supplemented by many other fund raising programs. Terry Fox has been mentioned in the 1983 Guinness Book of Records, as the top charity fund raiser - raising 24.7 million dollars in 143 days.

The Terry Fox Run has not only raised funds for cancer research, but has also fostered Canadian unity. That is why it has been a popular event every September.

Terry Fox was born in Winnipeg. His parents were not high school graduates. They had four children. His father worked as a switchman for Canadian National Railways. In 1966, to get away from the Manitoba cold, he moved to Vancouver at a loss of 12 years of his seniority. Terry was 8 years old at that time.

Terry was an average student. He loved competitive sports and was very fond of basketball. His ambition was to become a physical education teacher.

Terry enjoyed good health. He was very disciplined and never missed any practice or training session.

On November 12, 1976, he was involved in a car accident but was not hurt. A month later he experienced some pain in his right knee. Thinking that it was related to his accident and fearing that he may not be allowed to participate in the basketball games, he did not tell anyone.

One day, in the beginning of March, 1977, he limped back home from his regular jogging. After a series of tests he was diagnosed as having Osteogenic Sarcoma, a cancer of the bone. On March 9, 1977 his right leg was amputated, six inches above the knee. He had hardly reached full maturity.He was only 18 years and 8 months old.

The night before the amputation, one of his coaches, Terri Flemming, gave Terry a recent issue of "Runners' World" which featured a story about Dick Traum, an above-the-knee amputee, who had run in the New York Marathon. That story inflamed Terry's imagination. He realized that losing a leg was not the end of the world. He decided to accept his fate and to fight against the adversity. That night he resolved to run across Canada. He was not a "runner" while he possessed both his legs. He became a runner only after he lost one of his legs!

Terry's uniqueness included persistence, vision and spiritual thinking. Such characteristics are generally found in people of deep religious beliefs. But Terry's family did not go to church. It was after his amputation that he came in contact with a Japanese-Canadian girl named Rika Noda, who influenced him to read the Bible. In his later life Terry had so much faith in God that he even defied his doctors' orders.

What would Terry Fox have become if he had not lost one leg? Perhaps he would have become a great physical education teacher, earned a decent salary and lived a peaceful life.

What would Mahatma Gandhi have become if he had found a decent job in India after returning from England? Perhaps he would not have gone to South Africa and discovered "None-violence".

What would Demosthenes have become if he had not stuttered in his childhood? Perhaps he would have inherited all the money that his forefathers had left, but he would not have become one of the greatest orators of the world.

What would Abraham Lincoln have become if he had married Anne Rutledge instead of Mary Todd? Perhaps he would have lived a very happy life, but he would not have become one of the greatest emancipators of slavery.

The list is endless. In every case we find that some great adversity turned an ordinary man into an extraordinary one. It was the loss of his leg that made Terry Fox the man that he became.

If you are afflicted with some adversity, stop cursing it. Accept it. Confront it and it can turn into a blessing.

> "Great things are done when men and mountain meet.
> This is not done by jostling in the street.
> - William Blake

93

Ask For More Skills,
Not For Fewer Problems

Do you feel that you have too many problems?
Would you like to get rid of some, or maybe all, of your
problems?

Using an imaginary character, this essay shows
what would happen to us if all our problems were
suddenly solved or taken away from us.

Normally we keep complaining about the
responsibilities that "we have" to shoulder, but in the
total absence of all our responsibilities, we would feel
very restless.

This essay suggests that the solution does not lie
in getting rid of "the tasks beyond our current
capability", but in our willingness to learn the
additional skills needed to handle those tasks.

Read also essay numbers 1, 61, 70 and 90.

J ohn had an unusually rough day at work. He was used to the pressures of fighting fires, but this was too much. He seemed to have reached the end of his wits and patience.

In the evening he hardly talked with his wife or children. Feeling totally drained, he sat down in front of the television, but did not know what was going on. Frequently he dozed or recalled some of the activities of that horrible day.

"Why do I always end up with the fire fighting tasks? Why does the boss pick only on me? I am doing far more than my share. In fact I am doing three times as much as an average guy in the same position. Where is the justice? I wish my telephone would stop ringing. This gadget is supposed to increase productivity, but it hardly allows me any time to work peacefully on one project. And the visitors? I wish I had a place where I could hide myself once in a while, so as to get some work done." He had many questions, but no suitable answer.

John had a restless night. He even contemplated running away from that jungle. But his hands were tied. He was the bread winner of the family. His children needed his support, and so on.

That night John dreamed that an angel visited him and granted him one wish. Without any hesitation he said, "I wish that no one bothered me with their problems."

The next morning he was anxious to find out if his wish had really been granted.

When he reached work he was astonished to find that not a single telephone message was waiting for him. His work space had been thoroughly cleaned and every item had been put away. His "In" and "Out" baskets were empty and the "Pending" basket, which used to be overflowing, had been removed. His secretary informed him of the company policy. From that moment, he was to be left alone to work peacefully on his own projects. No one was to visit him or to call him unless he wanted. He could come and leave at any hour that he liked. He would not be called to attend any meeting and no one would bother him with a rush consultation.

John pinched his left arm to check if he was still dreaming. But this was no dream. This was really happening!

He thanked his angel and slumped down in his chair.

He enjoyed the day immensely. He found plenty of time to think about his major projects and to reflect upon the course of life that he was planning.

The second day he felt that he was not needed as much as he had been. But he enjoyed the quietness. For the first time he was his own boss.

By the end of that week he felt a bit uneasy and wished that someone would call, or just drop in. He longed to be consulted. He wanted to know what was happening in the other parts of the company. He felt anxious to find out how his past suggestions were working out. In short, he felt left out or "out of touch" with the real world.

Although he enjoyed the new liberty, soon he started dreading it. He feared that it may turn out to be the blessing, or the curse, of the Midas' touch.

By the end of the second week, he was convinced that he was no happier than before. The solution had to be something in between the two extremes. It was vital to be needed, but at the same time there must be a way of escaping at least once in a while.

The more he reflected upon his situation, before and after that dream, the more he realized that, given the choice of the two, he would prefer to be run down by too many demands than not to be needed at all.

Since he had been given the liberty of talking to others whenever he liked, he started visiting his old friends and finding out how they were doing. Soon, he was deluged with demands for consultations. But now he was careful not to let people run over him. He discovered that if he exercised his rights properly he could determine when to be bothered and when to be left alone.

"What if everyone in the company had been given the same liberty?" he thought. In that case it would be almost impossible to run any business successfully.

Instead of wishing for the extreme, now he wished to have an hour every morning in which to think peacefully, review past work and to plan the activities of the upcoming day, the week and even the month.

Within a month John found the new arrangement to be very effective. He was getting much more done and even found the time to help his colleagues. He was able to return home with a feeling of worthwhile accomplishment and could enjoy the evening with his family.

John felt very proud of the new skill that he had learned. His close friends and associates also tried the technique and reaped the benefit. Thus John concluded that it was foolish to wish for fewer problems and that wisdom lay in wishing for more skills for solving problems. "After all, it is only through combating some problems that we gain strength in life."

"Education is the ability to listen to almost anything without losing your temper or your self-confidence."

- Robert Frost

94

It's All Right
To Change Your Mind

How do you feel when you have to change your mind, or alter one of your earlier decisions?

You will never have every possible piece of information needed for making a decision. Yesterday's decision was based on the best information that you had received to that date. If you keep growing then today you should have acquired some additional wisdom. In the light of this new wisdom you may find your previous decision to be wrong. In that case you should not feel ashamed of changing your decision, or of changing your mind, today.

This essay suggests that it is not a weakness, but a strength, to change your previous decision based upon additional knowledge.

Read also essay numbers 15, 20, 33 and 53.

W e have often heard comments such as, 'It's all right for you to change your mind because you are a woman. I can't, because I am a man.' The other day I heard one person say, 'Is your mind working any better, after you changed it?'

Such remarks are obviously derogatory. Changing one's mind implies weakness in the character of the person involved. But is this a valid conclusion?

The quality of any decision is dependent upon the quantity and the quality of the related, pertinent, facts.

When Mahatma Gandhi had become one of the most successful lawyers in South Africa, someone asked him the main secret of his success. He replied, "Facts constitute two-thirds of the law. I concentrate my efforts on gathering as many pertinent facts as possible and then the law takes care of itself."

If you were provided with all the related data, and if every piece of that data was accurate, you would have no problem making the necessary decision. In that case, it would be silly to change your mind at some later date. Unfortunately, we cannot wait forever to gather all the pertinent data.

Even the information that is available to us is generally not accurate in the strict sense.

Our senses feed our brain with information about the world around us. We then take that information to generate new data related to the problem at hand.

The information supplied by our senses does not directly reach our brain. It is censored. Our brain acts as a kind of filter which allows only that information to pass which it considers to be favourable for our ultimate welfare. This is the main reason why we generally see only what we want to see. The Bible says, "There are people who have eyes but who don't see and there are people who have ears but who don't hear." I believe that this applies not only to some, but to every person. Every person is blind. The difference is only in the degree of blindness.

Computers, no matter how sophisticated, cannot make any decision until every single piece of required information has been supplied. But human beings have to always work with incomplete data. As we grow in our personal or business life, we are required to make more and more decisions based on fewer and fewer facts and less accurate data.

Yesterday's decisions were based on the best information that we had received to that time. Just a little piece of new information can sometimes alter the entire picture and therefore require that the old decision be changed.

A decision based on insufficient and inaccurate data, cannot be perfect. It would be silly to stick to our past decisions, when we receive additional, relevant, information, which could affect the initial decision.

Mahatma Gandhi was famous for making speeches without any notes. He maintained that he spoke from his heart. Consequently, many of his comments were found to be inconsistent with his past remarks. But he did not feel the necessity of justifying any of his past statements. He said, "At that particular moment, that appeared to me to be the truth. Since then my understanding of the subject matter has changed considerably. Today I see a different truth. I have never tried to be consistent with my past remarks or actions. I have always moved from truth to truth".

We can plan only as far as we can see or envision. It is foolish to plan into the dark area and to be adamant in not modifying the plan.

Technology is changing our living conditions so rapidly that forecasting is extremely difficult. Why not leave the task of planning the crossing of the river until we get close to it?

No, it is not a weakness, but a strength of character to admit that we are wrong, that our past decision was based on incomplete and distorted information. Changing our mind, when necessary, indicates that we have grown, that we have acquired some additional wisdom, that we have gathered and assimilated more and better information related to the matter.

It is only our ego that is hurt or threatened when we try to change our stand. Our society is partly responsible because it interprets every change as a weakness. Some people try to manipulate others by taking advantage of this. But our main obligation is to be true to ourselves. There is nothing wrong with changing our mind whenever we receive some new, significantly different, information.

You can never please everyone. No matter what you do, some people will scoff at you. If you feel that your newly acquired wisdom suggests that you change your past decision, just go ahead. It is perfectly all right for you to change your mind under these circumstances.

> "The man who never alters his opinion
> is like standing water, and
> breeds reptiles of the mind."
>   - William Blake

95

To Have A Tank-full, Be Thankful

Would you like a tank full of blessings?

This essay suggests that to have more, you must first show your thankfulness for that which you already have.

The essay compares our memory with a perfectly dark warehouse which one enters with a flashlight in hand. As one can see only the item on which one happens to direct the light, one recalls only that experience on which one happens to direct his attention.

According to this essay, the objects of this warehouse keep growing in the presence of light, and keep shrinking in the absence of light. Thus, the thought that gets more attention, takes bigger shape.

With the simple analogy of the warehouse, this essay advises us to be very careful in deciding which thoughts we should concentrate upon.

Read also essay numbers 45, 46 and 85.

W ould you like to have a tank full of good things in your life? You can have it, if you first cultivate the habit of being thankful for every good thing that you already have. Let me illustrate the technique by way of a simple analogy.

Imagine a warehouse which contains everything that you can think of. It is totally dark and has no light of its own. You enter this room with a flashlight which projects a narrow beam. You are free to direct this light in any direction you like. There is absolutely no restriction on you. You may wander to any part of this warehouse, if you like. You are free to pick up any object that you find interesting.

Since the room is perfectly dark, at any one time you can see only the object on which you have your light pointed. The objects which are close to the lighted object may receive some reflected light, but you cannot clearly identify them, unless you choose to point the light directly on them.

As soon as it is lighted, the object starts increasing in size and continues to grow as long as the light is maintained. The moment the light is withdrawn, its growth ceases and it starts to shrink. If left in the dark for a long time, an object may become too small to be noticed.

Each object in the warehouse has the power to attract similar outside objects. The power of attraction of an object is proportional to its current size and the degree of similarity. Naturally, the bigger it gets the more outside objects it can attract.

Thus, if you could choose the right objects and keep the light focussed on them for sufficient duration, you could possess the most valuable objects, both inside and outside of the warehouse. In that way, you could get anything that you want.

The warehouse represents our memory. The inside objects represent our past experiences. The outside objects represent the external resources. Our past experience lies imbedded in the dark memory warehouse. The flashlight represents our current attention. Any past experience can be lighted, or brought to the forefront, by the simple act of paying attention to that experience. The longer we dwell upon one particular experience, the more powerful it becomes, and the more external resources - of its own kind - it can attract. But, if we decide to forget an experience, it can immediately be put back in the dark room.

God has given us full control and freedom over the choice of our thoughts. We are free to wander to any part of the warehouse of our memory and pay attention to any experience, or thought that we like.

Remember,the warehouse contains all kinds of objects, both good and bad. However, we remain unaware of all, except the ones on which we direct our attention. Whatever thought we pay attention to, grows in magnitude and attracts many other thoughts of a similar nature. Once we start looking for the bad ones, we are likely to run into a vicious cycle which would make us see nothing but the bad things. But if we could control our attention and concentrate on good thoughts for a while, we would be in a position to see a lot of good things. Both good and bad are always present around us.

Unfortunately, we have been trained to look for the negatives.

A man may enjoy good health for three hundred and sixty-two days of the year and be ill for the other three days. But the average person recalls the three lousy days instead of the three hundred and sixty-two healthy ones. By paying more attention to those three miserable days, he multiplies his misery and is likely to attract more misery in the future.

It is quite possible that your current life contains more miseries than blessings. But, irrespective of the situation, the only way to get your blessings to increase, to multiply, is to focus your attention on them, and not on your miseries.

Maintaining the spirit of thankfulness has many advantages.

It prepares our mind for accepting the inevitable. It quiets our mind and thereby enables it to see what is still available. It promotes good spirit. By letting the other person know that you recognize his "good deed or intention", you encourage him to repeat the "good" or to look for some other good deed in some other area.

It conveys the message that you forgive the other person for any harmful deed that he might have, consciously or unconsciously, done. This makes him drop his guard and become more supportive.

If we fail to recognize what we already have, we will lose it. The only way to hold on to it, is to recognize it and to be thankful for it.

The average person has trouble finding anything good in his current life. The main problem is not the lack of blessings, but the lack of his ability to focus his attention on his current blessings.

If you want a tank full of good things to come your way, start focusing your attention only on good things. Be thankful for the good things that are already present in your life. The more you do this, the more good things will be added to your life.

"Our attitudes control our lives. Attitudes are a secret power working twenty-four hours a day, for good or bad. It is of paramount importance that we know how to harness and control this great force."

                                        - Tom Blandi

96

Change

Is Generally Good

Do you fear change?

This essay suggests that change is the very essence of life. Where no change is allowed, life ceases. Therefore, instead of dreading change, we should welcome it.

We fear a change in the same way that we fear a stranger. But as not every stranger is going to hurt us, not every change is going to harm us. On the contrary, change is beneficial to us, because it keeps our mind alert, active and therefore young.

Read also articles 1, 25 and 83.

O ur life has been changing very rapidly. There have been more technological developments in the last twenty-five years than during the entire nineteenth century. For a person born before World War II, the first Trans Atlantic flight was a great thrill, but for someone born within the last two decades the same flight is boring because it is too long and too slow.

The day man landed on the moon, we were glued to our television to watch the landing. Although we witnessed it, we found it difficult to believe. A few months ago, when the television station replayed some of this footage, we remembered the details of our initial thrills. At this instance, a friend of mine called his daughter to watch those pictures. But she was busy doing some "important work". When he implored her to come quickly she said, "Daddy, I have been seeing people walk on the moon all my life." How true! By the time she was born, space travel had become almost routine.

In many social gatherings, the most popular topic of discussion is, "The influence of the rapid technological change on our lives". The general consensus is that we just do not know where we are going, or what kind of life-style we can expect ten years from today.

Most people seem to dread change. But is "change" really dreadful or harmful for us?

Change is life. There can be no life where there is absolutely no change. In our body thousands of cells are dying, and are being replaced every single second of our life. Every single cell of our body, including the cells of our bones, are totally replaced every ten months.

Change keeps things fresh. Stop moving water and notice how quickly it becomes stale. Let the same water flow, and it becomes fresh again, very quickly.

How long would you enjoy seeing the same picture in a kaleidoscope? No matter how brilliant or interesting a picture, very soon you will feel bored with it. You would wish to see some other pattern that you have not seen before. If the picture is not changed, you would become restless in a short time.

A nudist couple applied for a divorce. When the judge asked for the main reason, they said, "Because we have been seeing too much of each other."

Change provides variety. It is the "oxygen" of our mind. Stop feeding "change" to your mind and notice how quickly it dies. The mind craves for that which it does not possess at the moment and the moment it possesses it, it loses its interest in it. Then it craves for something else. Change enables us to keep feeding our mind with something new at all times.

Imagine driving on a perfectly flat, straight highway through a barren land which does not present any change in the view for hours. How long could you drive on it without getting bored or tired? Imagine another highway that passes though the Rocky mountains, which presents many twists and turns, climbs and descents, peaks and valleys. It is more work to drive through the mountain than it is to drive on that flat, straight highway, but which one is more pleasant?

There are as many, and perhaps more, accidents on a flat, straight highway than there are on the mountainous ones. On every straight highway, we find some sign or notice, placed at least every mile, to keep the drivers' mind occupied and interested!

Every change carries some element of surprise. This makes it an interesting and healthy diet for our curious mind. Each turn in the road brings some surprise. There is no such thing as ennui while travelling a new road. Even maps, charts or guideposts cannot reveal everything about a new road. It is only change that can keep us alert and alive, on the road of life.

Change enhances longevity. It is true that current medical science has been able to control many diseases that used to cause early deaths, but "change" has helped us pass our time, and our life, rapidly, without paying too much attention to the clock.

Recently I asked a little boy, "How come you are growing so quickly?" He said, "I don't know. The birthday keeps coming." When we are engaged in dealing with some change, the years pass mostly unnoticed. In the complete absence of "change" time appears to stand still and we experience a lack of life.

It is true that change always carries some risk. But we thrive on risks. An athlete who successfully lands a single axle strives for the double and as soon as he is successful at this, he strives for the triple and so on. Take away all the risk from any game and you kill all the fun of that game. In the same way, take away every risk from a community or a corporation and you have figuratively killed every member of that community or that corporation.

But all change is not progress. We must learn to separate the wheat from the chaff. We should be thankful for every change that comes our way, but take a moment to look at it calmly and to decide what we should do with it. Every change brings some advantage. Let's look for the advantage and think how we can wrestle with it, overcome it and build our mental muscles at the same time. It is foolish to jump into the ring without thinking,planning and preparation, but it is more foolish to keep away from every ring forever. It is only by fighting gradually, according to some regimen, that we can build strength.

Let's welcome change, because generally it is good for us.

"A victory without danger
is a triumph without glory."
- Pierre Corneille

97

Mistakes

Can Be Profitable

Are you afraid of making mistakes? Do you feel bad every time you make a mistake? If so, you need to re-examine your perception of "mistakes'.

This essay points out that no matter how much you try to learn from other people's experience, you must also be willing to make mistakes and learn from them.

Mistakes have often led to some important inventions and discoveries. In fact, every mistake can be turned into a profitable experience if we make a sincere effort to learn a lesson from that mistake and resolve never to make the same mistake twice.

Read also essay numbers 11, 46 and 51.

H ave you made some mistakes recently? If so, how do you feel about them?

An average person considers himself inferior for having made any mistake. But is it really harmful, or disgraceful, to make mistakes?

Someone asked a man, "How did you become so wise?" He replied, "From my good experiences." He was then asked, "And how did you have the good experiences?" To this he replied, "By learning from my bad experiences."

It is said that experience is the only teacher. We learn by doing.

Our mind tries to analyze and sort out the positive and the negative elements of every experience. It learns a little from the positive, and mostly from the negative. A person who is afraid of making mistakes is preventing himself from learning and improving himself. There is no shame in making mistakes. The shame lies only in failing to learn from the mistakes.

Many "mistakes" have resulted in some important discoveries and inventions.

A man was trying to build a glass pot that could meet certain special needs. He had tried many ideas, but had not truly succeeded. One day he brought one of his pots home.

By mistake his wife used that pot to warm some food in her oven, and to the great surprise of the man, that pot did not crack. His wife's mistake actually led to the discovery of Pyrex!

Using Galileo's calculations, related to the size of the Earth, Christopher Columbus estimated the distance from Spain to India to be roughly six thousand miles, sailing straight west. Since this was considerably less than the distance from Spain to India , by sailing around South Africa, he became very excited. He desperately wanted to sail straight west to prove it.

Many people doubted the accuracy of his calculation. But Columbus was too confident to listen to anyone. Later it was discovered that Columbus was grossly in error. The radius of the Earth was actually three times larger than what Galileo had suggested.

Had Columbus known the correct radius of the Earth, he would never have attempted the voyage. In those days men had no means of sailing for eighteen thousand miles, and no one knew of the existence of a huge land mass to the west between Spain and India. It was because of Columbus' serious mistake that America was discovered!

In a certain soap factory, one day a man forgot to switch off his machine during his lunch break. When he returned, he found the entire room full of soap foam. It took him and his colleagues several days to clean up the mess. That mistake led to the discovery of shaving cream!

Another man, while trying to invent a special kind of glue, ended up inventing a substance which was so useless that it could not hold any two objects together. He tried using the "non-sticking-glue" for keeping little pieces of paper, as book markers. Soon he discovered that he could move the marker from one page to another, without damaging the page. This led to the discovery of the "Post-it" notes.

"Mistakes" also provided the root of the discoveries of X-ray, photographic plate, uranium and insulin.

Researchers have discovered a unique communication system used by bees.

After picking up some pollen from a flower, the bee flies straight to its hive (thus the expression "bee line"). Immediately after its arrival, it dances in a triangular pattern and makes some intermittent sounds, in such a way that the apex of that triangle points to the source of the pollen and the gap between the sounds indicates the distance of that source.

Other bees watch this dance, understand the signal and fly to the source of the pollen. However, the researchers estimate that only about eighty-two per cent of the bees are intelligent enough to understand that signal. The remaining eighteen per cent fly out and get lost.

While trying to return to their hive, these bees generally stumble upon some other source of pollen. Then they themselves perform the dance and signal the location of the new source.

Had every bee been intelligent enough to understand the original signals, they would all go only to the known source, which would soon be depleted. Thanks to the unintelligent eighteen per cent, new sources are continually discovered.

It is wise to learn from the mistakes of others and to avoid making similar mistakes. But it is nonsense to expect to learn everything from others' mistakes. It is impossible to learn so much from others' mistakes that you would never make any mistake of your own.

Every mistake carries some useful lesson. If you look for a lesson, you will find one. And if you consciously try to take advantage of that lesson, you will discover that you have actually benefited from the mistake.

Mistakes teach us lessons. Stop regretting having made a mistake. Analyze it just long enough to extract the lesson from it and then drop it from your mind forever.

You and I are wiser today, only because of the lessons that we have learned from our mistakes.

"All men make mistakes, but only wise men learn from their mistakes."
- Sir Winston Churchill

98

"I am sorry"

Is A Cop-out

The phrase, "I am sorry", is used extensively in our society. We use it without paying any attention to its influence on us.

This essay suggests that, although this expression is considered to be a sign of humility, it should be avoided, because indirectly it relieves us from the responsibility, and opportunity, of learning some lesson from our mistakes.

Rather than saying "I am sorry", this essay advises us to think of what we would do if we found ourselves in a similar situation again.

Read also essay numbers 25 and 97.

Have you noticed how often we use the expression, "I am sorry"?

Since our early childhood, this phrase has been drilled into us. Generally we use it automatically, and mostly unconsciously.

On the surface this phrase appears to convey a sign of humility. But in reality, it is nothing more than a cliche. It is almost like the expression, 'How do you do?', when the person asking that question rarely means to find out how you are. Often he is in such a rush that he disappears before he has uttered the last word of that phrase.

Many parents consider it their foremost duty to train their children to say "I am sorry". Often the child is compelled to say so, even when he is not at fault. As he grows, the phrase unconsciously pops out of his mouth, without realizing that he is apologizing.

But how wise is it to say, "I am sorry"?

Saying "I am sorry", relieves us from the responsibility of learning from the mistake, and modifying our behaviour, if required. It works as a shield, or a defence, against any damaging effect of the mistake. As soon as we apologise, for having made a mistake, we seem to have won a right for amnesty! This appears to be a good immediate advantage, but in the long run, it proves to have a strong adverse influence on the development of our personality.

The moment we find ourselves well protected, we see no reason for making any effort for discovering what we did wrong, and what should have been the correct, or appropriate behaviour. Children understand this very well, and play this game all the time. Being more interested in their own activities, and knowing that 'sorry" can relieve them, they say "sorry" almost immediately, often without paying any attention to why they are saying "sorry".

It is normal to make mistakes. But when we do so, there are two courses open to us. We can say, "sorry", and shed off the responsibility of correcting ourselves. Or, we can take the responsibility, strive to dig out the error, think of the lesson that we should learn from that error, and make some conscious effort to modify our behaviour in a similar, future, situation. If we do this, and if we consciously try not to make the same error again, we would soon become a very wise person. But since this requires effort and energy, we shy away from it, by using a simple weapon, "I am sorry".

If we fail to learn from an error, we repeat that error ad infinitum. In fact, we become so used to making the same error that we do not even recognize the existence of error. We think it just customary to say "sorry", whenever we inconvenience someone.

Saying "I am sorry", is like taking an aspirin for curing an illness. You have a vague feeling of something wrong in your system, but instead of making an effort to discover the root of the problem, you may prefer to get away by masquerading the pain by using an aspirin tablet.

When a child does something wrong, most parents commonly ask, "What do you say?" If the child does not say, "sorry", the parents insist that he say so. By repetition the child learns that the appropriate answer to the question, "What do you say?", is "sorry", irrespective of whether he was at fault or not. In the majority of cases, the child finds that he has done "something" wrong, only when he is asked, "What do you say?"

Rather than asking a child, or any person, to say "sorry", I think that you should ask him to explain what he would do differently if he happened to find himself in a similar situation again. This will force him to think about his error. Unless he is able to understand the error, he cannot give you a proper answer. A clear understanding of the error is itself a definite step towards rectifying it.

But just saying what one would do differently the next time, does not guarantee that the same error will not be repeated. Being creatures of habit, it takes us a minimum of twenty-one days to replace one habit with another. Therefore, don't expect instant cure. However, with time, the cure can be effected, provided that the error has been understood, and conscious effort to rectify the error is made.

It has been said that charity begins at home. First we ourselves must practise a new technique before we start preaching it to others. I suggest that starting this very moment, you become aware of your own use of the phrase, "I am sorry", and notice how it influences your personality, especially as it relates to your learning, or failing to learn, from everyday errors.

I strongly believe that "I am sorry" is one of the greatest deterrents to learning. It is simply a cop-out. It provides you with an immediate, and socially acceptable, excuse for getting out of a learning responsibility.

I believe that too much use of "I am sorry" lowers our self image. Therefore, every reduction in its use should enhance our self image. You can easily verify this if you want. Try refraining from using this phrase for just one week, and notice the corresponding change in your own self-image.

"Without self-respect there can be no genuine success. Success won at the cost of self-respect is not success -for what shall it profit a man if he gains the whole world and loses his own self-respect?"

- B. C. Forbes

99

Competition

Can Kill Creativity

Do you enjoy competitions? Do you encourage your children to participate in competitions.

This essay suggests that competitions can be healthy or devastating, depending upon how they are employed.

The essay provides some guidelines to help you check whether a certain competition would be healthy or devastating.

The essay further suggests that a wrong competition generally kills creativity.

Read also essay numbers 16, 24, 38 and 41.

L ife is full of games, and every game involves some degree of competition. We literally live, and breathe some degree of competition almost every moment of our life.

Competition creates challenge which, in turn, stretches us, or helps us to grow. Competitions help us discover, and develop, our dormant abilities.

But is competition always wholesome?

Competition can be healthy, or devastating, depending upon how it is used.

Every competition separates the strong from the weak. It screens out the wheat from the chaff. But, sometimes this screening is simply self-imposed. Some people drop out, because they think that they are too weak to even try. If you are really weak then you need some special regimen to rebuild your strength. Simply sitting by the side of the pool will waste away even those muscle that you have left. And if you jump right away, you risk hurting yourself, and maybe even killing yourself. Competition generally goads you to jump even when your body cannot sustain it.

Another danger of competitions is the halo effect. When a person discovers his weakness in one area, he may assume that he will be weak in other areas as well.

For a competition to be healthy, it must be properly matched. This requires the selection of (1) the right field for the competition, and (2) the right or reasonable stretch for the competitor.

All good trainers know that they must not allow their trainee to fight an opponent who is too strong. The trainee often begs, and feels that he is ready to take on a strong opponent, but the trainer waits, lets him fight some easy ones, and gain confidence, before he allows him to tackle the big one. Hasty moves too often prove to be devastating.

Selection of the right field is crucial, because invariably this makes the difference between a success or a failure.

Every person has some unique strength, and no one can truly beat him in the field of his uniqueness. But outside this unique field, he cannot expect to match everyone. If he chooses to fight in a field in which he is not inherently strong, then he works against the odds.

When Mahatma Gandhi assumed the leadership of the independence movement in India, he realized that the previous leaders had been fighting in the wrong arena. Gandhi pointed out that "guns" were the weapons of the Britishers. The only way to win, he suggested, was to use a weapon, such as "non-violence". With this weapon the Indians were stronger.

Sometime ago, I read a story about one animal school, which adopted a curriculum of activities consisting of running, climbing, swimming and flying. All the animal parents flocked to the new, progressive school, eager to enrol their children, because they wanted the very best for their offsprings.

Mr. and Mrs. Duck enroled their son, Denton Duck, and expected great things from him, because he was an excellent swimmer. In fact, he was better than the instructor. However, Denton had been in school only one week when the administrators discovered that he was quite poor in running. So they made him stay after school and practice running. He also had to drop swimming, in order to work more on his running. Finally, Denton's webbed feet became so badly worn out that he was then only average in swimming. But average was acceptable to the school.

Ronnie Rabbit was at the top of the class in running, but ended up having a nervous breakdown because of having to do so much extra work in swimming.

Sammy Squirrel was excellent in climbing until he developed cramps from over exertion and got a "C" in climbing and a "D" in running.

Ernie Eagle was a problem child and was severely disciplined. In the climbing class, he beat all others, but insisted on using his own way of getting to the top of the trees.

The prairie dogs stayed out of school and fought the tax levy, because the administration would not add digging and burrowing to the curriculum. They apprenticed their child to a badger and later joined the ground hogs and gophers in order to start a successful private school.

Like those animal children, we are also good in certain area and lousy in others. If we try to compete in the areas in which we are lousy, we would meet nothing but frustration.

Creativity, on the other hand, is related to the development of one's skills in the area of one's strength. This can be achieved only if the person is allowed full freedom, free from all competitions, to explore and slowly develop his own uniqueness. Creativity is an unfolding process. Any external pressure, or restraint, such as the ones imposed by competitions, prevents, and may even kill that growth.

During the early stage of its growth, a growing seed needs most protection. Once it develops firm roots and limbs, it is able to sustain many external opposing forces.

In the same way, a young child needs a lot of protection, from external pressures such as competitions. Let a child explore and develop his own uniqueness and then he can stand most of the competitions.

It is good to encourage competition, but first make sure that it is "matched", otherwise it can kill creativity.

"Every year of my life I grow more convinced that it is wisest and best to fix our attention on the beautiful and the good, and to dwell as little as possible on the evil and the false."
- Richard Cecil

100

What Makes A Person Extraordinary?

Why is it that a small handful of people are able to achieve some extraordinary feats while the rest struggle to make their ends meet?

This essay points out that it is only some handicap that enables an ordinary person to turn into an extraordinary one. Although everyone is provided with some handicap, which one could use to spur oneself to extraordinary achievement, the vast majority shies away from the challenge and fails to take advantage of it. We should, therefore, keep looking for our lemon, think how we could convert it into some kind of lemonade and then proceed to work towards doing that.

Read also essay numbers 1, 39, 63 and 92.

$\mathbf{A}$re some persons born "extraordinary"?

Some persons may benefit from unique circumstances, but there is something far beyond these, that make them extraordinary.

John F. Kennedy and Indira Gandhi were definitely born in a family that helped them rise, but we can find dozens, may be even hundreds, of others who were born in similar, or even better, circumstances, who did not rise as high as John Kennedy or Indira Gandhi.

A study of many extraordinary persons reveals that most of them were born as "ordinary" people, like you and me, or in some condition even worse than ours.

Life plays no favourites. It deals approximately the same hand of cards to everyone. Some of us complain about a poor hand and forget that it is not the hand, but how we play it that generally decides the outcome.

At birth, everyone is equally weak and vulnerable. To survive, and to rise above the crowd, one must build strength. This is possible only by working against some opposing forces. Nature provides everyone with ample opposition, in the form of handicaps, or limitations, for combating and thereby building our strengths. But, unfortunately, the vast majority look at the mountain of obstacle, shed few tears, and hope that someone carries them to the top, or at least sympathises with their plight. They sit at the foot of the mountain waiting and living a life of quiet desperation.

But a few persons see the mountain as a challenge, and start climbing to the best of their ability. They soon discover that the more they work at it, the more strength they build and the greater desire they possess to scale it further. Even after reaching the top, they rarely feel satisfied. Having enjoyed the challenge of climbing this mountain, they look for some other mountains to climb. And since they are looking, they invariably find one that appeals to them. In this way, they keep climbing mountains, building their strength and reaching the "extraordinary" status.

I read the other day that our brain has a highly developed "back-up" system. If one area of the brain is damaged, the function of that area is quickly assumed by some other area. Most of us go through our entire life without making any use of our "back-up" facility.

Handicap of any sort forces our brain to activate its back-up system. That is why every handicapped person develops some kind of an extraordinary sensory perception. Psychologists credit this to a process called, "Over-compensation".

Handicaps often help us to unleash our reserve power.

Recently I read the story of Lasse Viren, a boy from Finland, whom nobody expected to even place in the 10,000 meters Olympic race. During the second lap of the race, the man who was expected to win was hit and thrown out in the middle of the field, unconscious. While falling, he also knocked Viren down. But Viren jumped up, rushed back into the race and soon caught up with the rest of the runners. He ended up winning that race and breaking the world's record. Imagine that! Some experts believe that his fall made him more determined to win the race.

Glen Cunningham and his brother were involved in a serious fire explosion. His brother died instantly. Glen's body was so badly burned that doctors suggested amputating his legs. But his father tried to postpone the amputation for a while. The doctors warned that the postponement may prove to be life threatening. But his father decided to take the risk. When the bandages were finally removed, it was discovered that his right leg was almost three inches shorter than the left. The toes on his left foot were almost completely burned off. Though in excruciating pain, Glen forced himself to exercise daily. Slowly he threw away his crutches, began to walk normally, and even started running. With his determination and practice, Glen Cunningham ended up becoming the "World's Fastest Human Being", and was named the athlete of the century at Madison Square Garden!

The story of Wilma Rudolph, Tom Dempsey, Terry Fox and hundreds, maybe thousands of similar men and women is proof of the fact that it was some handicap, some unusual limitation that pushed an otherwise ordinary person to some extraordinary limit. No one has ever become an extraordinary person without struggling with some handicap imposed either externally or internally. The greater the handicap, the greater has been the fire within the person to combat that handicap.

Brooker T. Washington once said, "We measure a man's success in terms of the obstacles he had to overcome along the way." If you do not have some handicap, then how will you measure your success?

Bob Richards, one of the top pole vaulters in history, and the only pole-vaulter to win the gold medal twice in Olympics, once said, "It is impossible to be great in the sports world without being beaten many times. You must be beaten. It is a conditioning factor of the soul and the character, that makes you great."

I think that this applies to every facet of our life. We should not expect to overcome our handicap right away. We must be willing to be defeated by it a few times. We should just remember that each defeat will make us a little bit stronger.

> "The strongest man in the world is he who stands most alone."
> - Henrik Ibsen

"You cannot hope to build a better world without improving the individuals. To that end, each of us must work for his own improvement and, at the same time, share a general responsibility for all humanity, our particular duty being to aid those to whom we think we can be most useful."

- Madame Curie

Index

"Are you disappointed, discouraged and
discontented with your present level of success?
Are you secretly dissatisfied with your present
status? Do you want to become a better and more
beautiful person than you are today? Would you
like to be able to really learn how to be proud of
yourself and still not lose genuine humility?
Then start dreaming! It's possible! You can
become the person you have always wanted to
be!"

- Robert H. Schuller